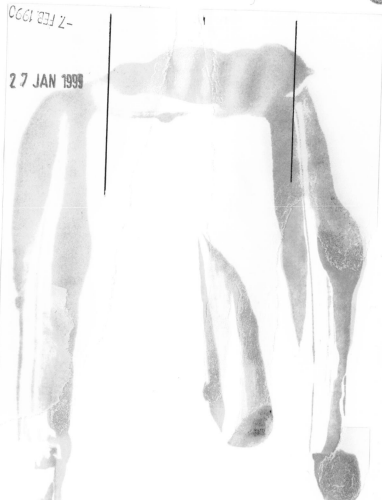

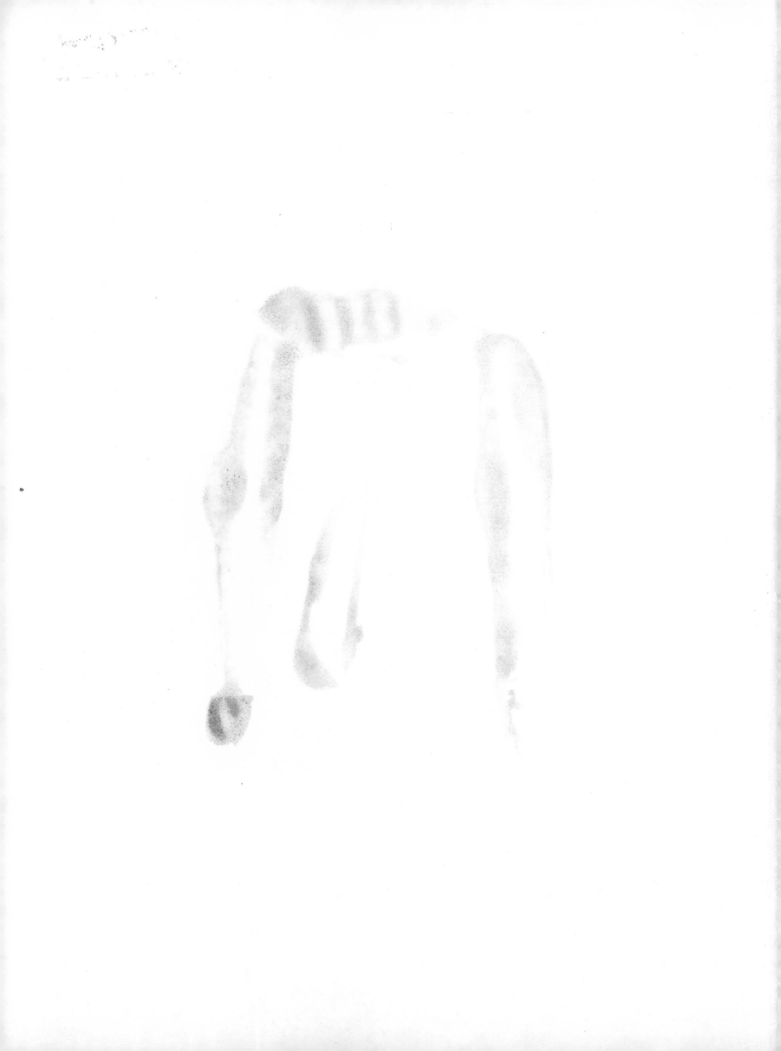

*The Golden Gate
and the Silver Screen*

The Golden Gate
and the Silver Screen

Geoffrey Bell

Rutherford • Madison • Teaneck
Fairleigh Dickinson University Press

New York and London
Cornwall Books

Associated University Presses, Inc.
and Cornwall Books
440 Forsgate Drive
Cranbury, NJ 08512

Associated University Presses Ltd
25 Sicilian Avenue
London WC1A 2QH, England

Associated University Presses
2133 Royal Windsor Drive
Unit 1
Mississauga, Ontario
Canada L5J 1K5

Library of Congress Cataloging in Publication Data

Bell, Geoffrey, 1909–
 The Golden Gate and the silver screen.

 Bibliography: p.
 Includes index.
 1. Moving-picture industry—California—San Francisco
Region—History. I. Title.
 PN19935.U718B44 1984   384′.8′097946   81-71875
 ISBN 0-8453-4750-0 (Cornwall)
 ISBN 0-8386-3231-9 (FDUP)

Printed in the United States of America

For two very special friends
Sally R. Lopez and Robert C. Toll

Contents

Acknowledgments   9

Prologue   13

1 The First Motion Picture Show   17

2 The Adventures of Essanay and
   Broncho Billy   39

3 The California Motion Picture
   Corporation   67

4 The Experimenters: Lights, Camera,
   Distraction   99

Epilogue   135

APPENDIX A: Titles and Production Data of
   Silent Films Produced in Northern
   California, 1897–1930   142

APPENDIX B: Hollywood Silent Films
   about, or Filmed in, Northern
   California   157

APPENDIX C: Personnel of Essanay Film
   Manufacturing Company, Western Unit   163

APPENDIX D: Personnel of California
   Motion Picture Corporation   165

APPENDIX E: Personnel of Various Bay
    Area Independent Companies   166

APPENDIX F: Current Sources of Silent
    Films   168

Notes   169

Bibliography   177

Index   181

Acknowledgments

First of all, I wish to express my profound gratitude to Sally R. Lopez, Robert D. San Souci, and Robert C. Toll for their generous assistance in the preparation of this book. Each brought to the work the challenge of a different viewpoint and the benefits of varied training and experience; their input combined to sustain, encourage, and inspire.

In addition, I am indebted to those who shared with me their professional knowledge of filmmaking and the motion picture industry: Irving C. Ackerman, G. M. Anderson, Hal Angus, Jordan Belson, James Broughton, Karl Brown, Frank Capra, Bert Gould, Wilna Hervey, Sol Lesser, George Middleton, Hal Mohr, Henry Nasser, William Palmer, Mary Pickford, Lela Smith, E. G. Valens, San Warner, and Lois Wilson.

For first-hand information about early San Francisco and about central California people and places, I would like to thank Anne Armstrong, True Boardman, Jr., Cedric Clute, Dorothy Douglass, Letty Etzler, Myrtle Goldman, Aleta Jennings, Lillian Johansen, Ruby Middleton, Tina Pastori, George Skaff, Jack Stauffacher, Philip Tompkins, Steve Totheroh, and Frank and Rolph Winter.

My sincere appreciation goes out also to the librarians, curators, educators, and those in related fields who have gone out of their way to help; Eileen Bowser, Mary Corliss, Joe Coltharp, W. H. Crain, Andrew DeShong, John L. Fell, Robert B. Fisher, Sam Gill, Bunny Gillespie, Ken Gillespie, Jameson C. Goldner, Gene M. Greesley, Gladys Hansen, Russell Hartley, Mandel Herbstman, Ray Hubbard, Jerry Kearns, Audrey Kupferberg, Timothy Lyons, Paul Myers, Kathleen Pabst, Alan Porter, George Pratt, Mildred Simpson, Anthony Slide, Paul C. Spehr, Dorothy Swerdlove, Norwood Teague, and most noteworthy, Val Almendarez. I am especially grateful to Anita V. Mozley for her insights into the history and aesthetics of photography and the significance of the Muybridge years in California.

I also wish to acknowledge the following institutions and organizations in California and elsewhere for the advice and information provided by their members as well as for their courtesy in allowing me to research there:

The Bancroft Library, University of California, Berkeley; California State Library, Sacramento; Fremont Main Library; Jacksonville Public Library, Florida; Los Gatos Memorial Library; Marin County Free Library, San Rafael; Mechanics Institute Library, San Francisco; Metropolitan Toronto Library, Ontario, Canada; Monterey Public Library; Oakland Public Library, The A. K. Smiley Public Library, Redlands; San Francisco Collection, San Francisco Public Library; Stanford University Libraries;

The California Historical Society, San Francisco; Franklin Institute Science Museum, Philadelphia, Pennsylvania; Natural History Museum of Los Angeles County, Los Angeles; Robert H. Lowie

Museum of Anthropology, University of California, Berkeley; Marin County Historical Society, San Rafael; Mission Peak Heritage Foundation, Fremont; The Oakland Museum; San Mateo County Historical Association, San Mateo; Society of California Pioneers, San Francisco; Stanford University Museum of Art; Wells Fargo Bank History Room, San Francisco;

The American Film Institute, Washington, D.C.; American Society of Cinematographers, Hollywood; Archives for the Performing Arts, San Francisco; Art & Music Section, San Francisco Public Library; Billy Rose Theatre Collection, Performing Arts Research Center, New York Public Library at Lincoln Center; Center for Film and Theater Research, University of Wisconsin, Madison; Department of Film, The Museum of Modern Art, New York; Division of Photographic History, Museum of American History, Smithsonian Institution, Washington, D.C.; Hoblitzelle Theatre Arts Library, Humanities Research Center, University of Texas, Austin; International Museum of Photography at George Eastman House, Rochester, New York; Lucasfilm, San Rafael; National Film Information Service, Academy of Motion Picture Arts and Sciences, Beverly Hills; Motion Picture, Broadcasting & Recorded Sound Division and Prints and Photographs Division, The Library of Congress, Washington, D.C.; Pacific Film Archives, Berkeley; Paramount Pictures, Hollywood and New York; Photography Collection, Humanities Research Center, University of Texas, Austin; Photography Collection, Stanford University Museum of Art; Special Collections, University of Wyoming, Laramie; Universal Pictures, Universal City and New York.

In addition, I would like to thank those individuals, institutions and organizations that graciously granted permission to reproduce prints and photographs from their collections. They are credited individually in the illustration captions.

I have exercised all due care in verifying dates, spellings, etc., but if errors have slipped in, I welcome corrections from readers.

Finally, my gratitude to members of Associated University Presses for their assistance, and especially to Thomas Yoseloff, who bore with me until the successful completion of this book.

The Golden Gate
and the Silver Screen

(Photo permission of San Francisco History Room, San Francisco Public Library)

Prologue

Fleeting figures emerge from the shadows of Victorian facades, rushing headlong toward the vehicle waiting for their frantic escape. Tires smoke in instant takeoff as first the pursued, then the pursuers, career up and down San Francisco's spectacular hills. Under the watchful eye of the movie director, racing cars and drivers merge in the fleeting images of prey and predator, now twisting wildly, now braking suddenly, now sliding precariously sideways, now heading toward certain, unavoidable collision. . . .

The famous chase scene from the 1968 smash movie hit *Bullitt?* A good guess, certainly. But the hair-raising episode described above actually predates the *Bullitt* escapade by nearly half a century, having been filmed in the early 1920s by a local San Francisco–based producer for the silent thriller *Going the Limit.*

This and many other cinematic achievements and landmarks were produced in and around the Bay Area throughout the century-long span of motion picture history.

Where, for example, was the world's premiere public exhibition of motion pictures? New York? London? Paris? All logical places. Yet, strangely enough, it was San Francisco, a city not usually associated with the film industry, that hosted the very first movie showing.

Where was the first motion picture studio and the first movie exchange on the Pacific Coast? This model studio was built in San Francisco in the days before the fire and earthquake of 1906.

Where were the origins of the movie Western genre? The trails ridden by the first movie cowboy star lay not by Sunset Boulevard in Hollywood, but along the foothills of San Francisco Bay.

Despite these original contributions, San Francisco is rarely given even fleeting notice in the accepted histories of the movies, which generally concentrate on the glamorous, star-studded achievements of Hollywood, where, to be sure, the bulk of American movie production has taken place. Yet even while Hollywood's star was on the rise, vigorous activities in this new field were taking place all across the United States, from the pines of rock-bound Maine to the palms of Coronado's golden strands.

In the early days of the movies, filmmakers were exploring all geographic and climatic possibilities, seeking the ideal combination of natural locales and mild temperatures. Around 1895, New York City and environs became an initial production center. By 1908 Jacksonville, Florida, with its winter sunshine for outdoor shooting, was active with a number of film companies. Other areas—ranging from Augusta, Maine, with its evergreen forests and lakes, to Colorado with its uplands and mountain grandeur, to Santa Barbara, with its agreeable climate and ocean frontage—were also sites of considerable film activity. The motion picture became far too vigorous an art and communications medium to be limited to one kind of person, mode, or environment. From New England to the Southwest filmmakers were creating a new medium in a variety of settings. Whereas the stories of independent studios and film companies in other parts of the United States remain to be told, the following pages bear witness to the rich and varied range of filmmaking in the Northern California region. Of all possible movie centers, one seemed most likely to become the center of the American motion picture industry: San Francisco.

"By all that is logical, San Francisco should have become the capital of the motion picture world," opined Benjamin B. Hampton in his *History of the Movies*. Hampton argues that "although advantageous conditions were found in the vicinity of both San Francisco and Los Angeles . . . the wealth and prestige now centered in Los Angeles should be in the possession of the City by the Golden Gate."

The Bay Area was indeed where the motion picture itself came into being. That it originated there was neither an accident nor a quirk of fate. Ever since the gold rush days of 1849, San Francisco had been attracting, as it does today, artists and creative personalities identifying with the open, freewheeling spirit of the city. Among those many new arrivals were craftsmen eager to test the possibilities of the newly invented camera. The splendid photographic views of the then unknown land of California produced by these technicians revealed to an astonished world that the reports of earlier travelers had not been exaggerated. The Bay Area and the surrounding central California regions had additional photographic advantages in that the slight moisture in the air both diffused the light, balanced camera exposures, and aided the chemical processes involved. Then, too, a good living could be earned from making camera portraits of other new arrivals, who wished to send back images of their strong, determined faces to loved ones at home. A progressive spirit, a widely varied scenery, a benign climate, and a ready market made the City by the Golden Gate a photographer's paradise.

The lure of the West with its call to adventure and its abundant resources of raw materials, and the nineteenth century ideals of the betterment of mankind through science and industry, were dramatized with the completion of the Transcontinental Railroad in 1869. This momentous engineering feat had enormous and far-reaching effects on its time, just as the space exploration program of the 1960s has had on our own. And photography, as has been the case with the space program, was one of the chief beneficiaries. In each instance, the research engendered led to improved cameras and equipment, and in each, the need to document a new development inspired imaginative uses of the camera. As a result, during the 1870s, under the same California skies which had drawn them westward, men of science and art succeeded in producing the world's first photographic images of living creatures in fast motion. From this remarkable invention it was only a few years to the achievement of the cinematic motion picture, which was first exhibited in San Francisco one spring evening in 1880. Thus began the city's century-long love affair—never quite a marriage—with the movies.

Many advantages for the production of motion pictures were already in San Francisco's possession. Few other cities anywhere could rival the photogenic character of this city, with her many hills reflected in the shining expanse of the bay and her buildings bathed in pearly light. Few other cities were set amid such a wondrous environment, replete with majestic mountains and verdant valleys, mighty rivers and rippling streams, towering forests and open plains, culminating in the magnificient meetings of land and water by the Pacific shores. The balanced climate, varied terrain, and abundant natural resources inevitably made the Bay Area the symbolic fulfillment of the American dream.

In all respects, the new medium of the motion picture could not have found a more natural and fitting environment to nurture it. San Francisco enjoyed a cultural ambience and a zest for the arts and had amply demonstrated its willingness to support these amenities of civilized society. Financial support was available from the many banks and exchanges, which made the city the financial center of the West; scientific and industrial assistance was at hand in the many educational institutions and busy factories; its temperate climate and slightly moist air were conducive to photography; European-trained resident artists were creating visual arts of excellence; writers from Mark Twain to Jack London were publishing stories of proven popular appeal; and a wealth of experienced acting talent and stage technicians was available from local stock companies, such as Morosco's Grand Opera House or the Alcazar Theatre, with their already proven techniques of attracting and pleasing audiences. Here was a city with a flair, whose spirit was typified in such a figure as "Gentleman Jim" Corbett—an Adonis, a Beau Brummell, a connoisseur of vintage wines, a student of Shakespeare, world heavyweight boxing champion, and the signer of the first exclusive motion picture contract. At the very outset, then—because of the benefits of long-established financial, technical, industrial, literary, artistic, and theatrical activities, in addition to superiority in climate and setting—the filmmaker found throughout the Bay Area conditions ideal for the production of motion pictures.

By a strange shifting of fate, the major elements of the motion picture industry ultimately settled in an obscure southern California agricultural town, then little more than a dusty crossroads. Although Hollywood became a movie capital only by chance—and many of its accomplishments have been overlooked by people obsessed with the superstar personality cults—it has produced film art of a quality unrivaled throughout the world. But in the early years of the cinema, Hollywood was only one facet of the epic story of the rise of the American motion picture. Much of the pioneering and innovation in this American art and industry were done in areas other than Southern California—for example, New York, the nation's leading theatrical center—yet no area has had a longer history than the San Francisco Bay region.

This was an era when all of Northern California was alive with intriguing ideas, inventions, and individuals: Luther Burbank was making important contributions to the world's food supply through his creation of new berries, fruits, and vegetables; Mary Austin was awakening America's consciousness to the spiritual values of its Indian subculture; Henry George was initiating an entirely new economic movement with his *Progress and Poverty;* Isadora Duncan was setting forth to revolutionize the world of dance; John Muir was revealing to the world a new understanding of the value, wonder, and majesty of our natural environment.

The Bay Area, then, has always been a matrix, a place of vigorous cross currents regenerating the old, nurturing the new. Its motion picture history likewise is multifaceted and overlapping. For the purposes of discussion and clarity, it can be divided into four major phases: (1) During the 1870s, a visionary Eadweard Muybridge and a pragmatic Leland Stanford transformed the art of photography into the new medium of cinematography. (2) Between 1909 and 1916, he-man "Broncho

Billy" Anderson single-handedly created the role of the movie cowboy hero and established the prototype of the classic movie Western. (3) Between 1913 and 1918, a major studio, the California Motion Picture Corporation, with the beauteous Beatriz Michelena—whether Circe or career woman, or a bit of both—made notable advances in the early quality feature-length photoplays. (4) The fourth phase is less clearly defined, but no less important. Beginning in the 1890s and continuing throughout the silent era, the Bay Area was the home of experimenters of all kinds—from the dashing Miles brothers, who explored new ways to produce, distribute, and exhibit the first flickering photofilms, to the gentlemanly Leon F. Douglass, who crafted some of the first motion pictures in natural color. In the 1920s, when the movies became an established industry centered in Hollywood, a number of independent producers fought to keep feature filmmaking alive in the Bay Area—a fight that demonstrated a great deal about the changing nature of moviemaking and the movie business itself and that also launched many distinguished careers.

The Bay Area was a place, then, that was replete with colorful history and drenched with physical beauty, an area exciting in itself and attracting unusual people imbued with far-reaching dreams. True, many of those involved are now unknown, and many of their efforts are lost. Nevertheless, though young, inexperienced, and very vulnerable, they made notable accomplishments. These were individuals of imagination and idealism, willing to risk their fortunes and their futures on a new frontier of discovery. Yet, however maverick or out of the movie mainstream, they wrote important chapters in the history of the area and the history of film. Impelled by a spirit of dedication to their profession and of freedom of thought, these early film pioneers are linked directly to our filmmakers of today. Their innovative ideas made the area a testing ground for the later achievements of film artists no less original, among the most dynamic of whom is feature-film producer George Lucas. The triumphs and trials of these daring young filmmakers by the Golden Gate celebrate events of far wider than regional interest, for in many ways they epitomize the chronicle of independent cinema everywhere.

Here, then, is the previously untold story of the adventurous world of moviemaking in the robust setting that was, and is, San Francisco.

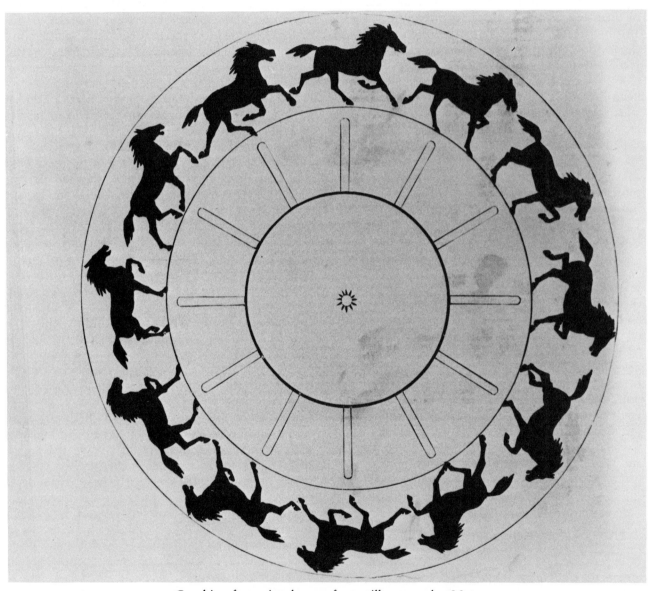

Graphic of running horses from silhouettes by Muybridge as adapted for the Zoetrope. *(Photo permission of Stanford University Museum of Art)*

1

The First Motion Picture Show

Southward from San Francisco on a June morning of 1878, the coast range was already turning the tawny shades that marked the onset of the rainless central California summer. The well-irrigated grass on the Palo Alto estate of Leland Stanford, however, remained lush and green. Nestled comfortably in this rural setting, the commodious villa sprawled in gracious hospitality, betraying a lighter, informal side of its owner, who, though out of office for fifteen years, continued to be honored with the title of "Governor." From the residence a well-kept road wound gracefully among the giant oaks and eucalypti of the parklike estate, passing pastures of grazing cattle and horses, to terminate at a community of imposing carriage houses, stables, and barns. Beyond this working farm area lay Stanford's private race track, on which he exercised his prize horses. These were thoroughbreds that never had known a whip or spur, nor had their delicate ears ever been offended by a harsh word, for Stanford was an owner dedicated to the humane treatment of animals. The steeds were treasured, for this was an age when the horse was far more than a leisure-time pet; indeed, it was a major economic factor in industry and transportation. Here in this spacious setting, horses were being trained as racers, and experiments were being conducted for the improvement of the breed.

Stanford's early interest in livestock had been nourished by his boyhood years on a farm near Albany, New York, and by his recent purchase of a ranch property as a retreat from the myriad social, political, and financial demands that swirled about him at his residence in San Francisco. Stanford's city life was his public life, and was synonymous with the grand movers and the monumental events of the nineteenth-century Western experience.

In the tumultuous years following the gold rush, Stanford's integrity and professional skills as a young lawyer had so impressed businessmen Charles Crocker, Mark Hopkins, and C. P. Huntington that they made him president of their new Central Pacific Railroad. Once in charge of handling its stupendous legal, personal, and engineering problems, he pushed the railroad across the granite ramparts of the Sierra Nevada to the triumphant meeting of the rails at Promontory Point, Utah, in May 1869.

The railroad made Leland Stanford rich—very rich—and with this wealth he was able to purchase vast unbroken acreage at Palo Alto, thirty-five miles south of San Francisco. There, a favorable climate and fertile soil provided ideal conditions for the establishment of a model farm for the benefit of California's agriculture. Botanical specimens were tested to determine their usefulness for the state's farms, orchards, and vineyards. The wealth from the railroad also made it possible for Stanford to extend the operations to include those aimed at im-

17

proving the strength and speed of the horse.[1]

On this already hot morning of 1878, it was apparent that something more than routine animal exercises was to take place. A bustle of activity was underway, and it was being conducted by methods and with equipment more sophisticated than those usually associated with animal husbandry. Leading off the racetrack was a spur straightaway, along one side of which was a long shed. Along the other side of the runway, facing the shed, was a backdrop wall, fifteen feet high, marked off with a numbered grid. Within the shed, a row of cameras occupied the attention of a number of men. Each camera was an equal interval apart, each was equipped with the finest of imported lenses, and each was fitted with specially designed shutters, all linked by the new science of electricity. The plan was to photograph horses passing along the runway, while the backdrop wall and grid gave definition to the subjects and provided numerical reference points on the resulting images.[2]

Today, we take for granted photography of fast action—our news and sport pages are alive with them—but the crude camera of those days could record only static, posed subjects or landscapes, in exposures lasting several minutes. Any motion showed up as a blur. Dismissing these limitations, Stanford sought to use the camera to capture rapid motion and, going beyond this, to record motion too fast for the human eye to see—specifically, images of a horse in motion. This effort was for the advancement of veterinary science, for the resulting stop-motion photographs were to be used to analyze the muscular system of a horse. The immediate usefulness of this object, and all the time and trouble involved, have receded into history; yet the work came to be of a significance undreamed of at the time, for it led directly to the cinematic motion picture.

An atmosphere of mounting excitement was engendered as the corps of technicians readied their preparations. One figure, however, appeared oddly at variance, though definitely in command. In spite of the heat, the man sported a floppy som-

The Industrialist: Leland Stanford. Oil painting by J. L. E. Meissonier, 1881. *(Photo permission of Stanford University Museum of Art)*

The Artist: Eadweard Muybridge, 1882. *(Photo permission of Stanford University Museum of Art)*

The Performer: William Lawton, 1879. *(Photo permission of Stanford University Museum of Art)*

brero and a loosely tied neckerchief. Like some choreographer making final, precise adjustments before a debut performance, this photography impresario darted nervously from camera to camera, occasionally making minute adjustments to the equipment. He snapped impatiently at one of the assistants, who, in a careless moment, had come close to prematurely triggering one of the cameras.

This central figure was Eadweard Muybridge. Born Edward Muggeridge on 9 April 1830 in England, he transformed that plain name into a more romantic one after coming to the United States to seek his fortune. Just as idealistically, he was inspired to become a photographer because he became so transfixed by the scenery of the American West that he was determined to document it. This was attempting a profession of immense challenge. During the 1860s and 1870s no ready goods and services were at hand for the aspiring photographer, who often had to construct his own camera and its accessories, to prepare his own chemicals for coating his negative plate, and to do his own developing and printing as well. In the existing wet-plate process the glass negative was coated with a gluey collodian solution, the exposure was made only when the solution had solidified to the precise degree at which it was most photosensitive, and, finally, the exposed plate was developed on the spot immediately afterward. Because of this demanding procedure, a laboratory and darkroom had to be transported to the site of outdoor scenes. To attain images of high quality under such conditions, a photographer had to have stamina, a working knowledge of chemistry, and a high degree of proficiency in optics.[3]

Muybridge mastered the complex requirements for camera expertise through repeated experimentation and a variety of practical work. In addition to technique, he had both persistence and artistic vision, for the photographic views he produced of California and the American West were as remarkable in execution as they were in artistry. The pictures of the California and Alaskan coasts that he made for the Coast and Geodetic Survey were superior to any other landscape photographs thus far produced. His camera studies of the Yosemite Valley and surrounding regions completed between 1867 and 1873 were of a grandeur and drama that, after more than a century, remains fresh and compelling. A 360-degree panorama of San Francisco produced during 1877 from atop the tower of the Mark Hopkins residence at California and Mason streets was done with such perception that many of the points of interest are still identifiable today.

These achievements, and many other works produced on commission, stamped Muybridge as a camera artist of surpassing excellence (although he was also well-known for his personal eccentricities). He was thus the logical choice when Stanford sought someone to head the advanced project of scientifically analyzing, through camera studies, the gaits of horses.

Both Stanford and Muybridge were men who, although quite opposite in temperament, were similar in having set for themselves standards of uncompromising excellence. Stanford was a towering figure in the state's economic and political life; Muybridge was an influential and dynamic figure in the world of art. The doughty Stanford, trained as an attorney-at-law, was pragmatic to the bone, an organizer, a leader, and every inch the nineteenth-century captain of industry; the mercurial Muybridge, original in thought and appearance, who by his own efforts had mastered a difficult and exacting art, was an individual fired with the creative urge.

It was, then, with considerable daring and innovative spirit that Leland Stanford undertook to finance the experiments and that Eadweard Muybridge undertook to execute them. Originally, it was thought a comparatively simple matter to set up a camera and have a horse trot laterally before it. The attempt was made in 1872, when Stanford lived in Sacramento, but it proved impossible to coordinate the position of the horse with the moment of exposure. The resulting images were found to be mere shadowy streaks on the negative plate. It soon became apparent that single photographs of objects in random motion were inadequate and that the only scientific approach was to arrange a series of coordinated cameras that, collectively, would produce images of all the successive attitudes that the horse assumed while running.

A dozen or more cameras with the finest of matched lenses were obtained from Europe. Yet even though by 1877 advances in photography had reduced the exposure time from minutes to fractions of a second, there still remained the problem of timing each exposure so as to obtain precise images of the fleeting horse. Up to that time the lens simply had been covered or uncovered by hand. Muybridge devised a spring-release shutter (claimed to be the world's first), while an engineer from Stanford's Central Pacific Railroad, John D. Isaacs, designed and installed a system of contacts, in an innovative use of electricity, to link the sequence of shutters. The system was activated by the passing animal itself—the instant its hoof

Stanford's stock farm at Palo Alto. *(Photo permission of Stanford University Museum of Art)*

The experiment track, 1878. *(Photo permission of Stanford University Museum of Art)*

Traditional but erroneous representation of the running horse—the assumption the experiments were to disprove. *(Photo permission of Stanford University Museum of Art)*

An early attempt: Occident, 1877, image heavily re-
touched to improve on the shadowy original and to conform to traditional artist's renderings. *(Photo permission
of Stanford University Museum of Art)*

Twenty-four cameras in alignment. (By a coincidence,
twenty-four images per second is standard in today's
cinematography.) *(Photo permission of Stanford University Museum of Art)*

A camera with back of an electro shutter. *(Photo permission of Stanford University Museum of Art)*

Front of shutter, with positions before, during, and after exposure. *(Photo permission of Stanford University Museum of Art)*

touched an electrical contact, the connection released the shutter opposite to it. Each position of the horse, then, was to be framed precisely in the opposite lens, and each successive image was to depict a slightly advanced phase of one continuous action.

On this early summer day in 1878, the long-sought goal of photographing objects in rapid motion was within reach. As Muybridge, orchestrating the event, moved nervously among the men and equipment aligned along the runway, Leland Stanford stood off to one side in thoughtful silence. A man to whom success and conquest were not new, he instinctively felt the impending triumph of the moment at hand. In this mood of quiet confidence, he reflected on the events of the years leading up to this hour. How often the scene before him had altered during that time—the cameras, their design and numbers, the track itself, the growing number of technicians, and the inclusion of the latest developments in that miraculous new power—electricity. He himself had played a role in the introduction of electricity when, after driving the symbolic final spike on the Transcontinental Rail-

road in 1869, he sparked the telegraph wire signaling the news of that glorious event. Now, nearly a decade later, as he previously had done with the railroad, Stanford forged ahead with an original concept, convinced that by application of scientific principles he would succeed.[4]

Certainly, this tremendous outpouring of energy and capital had not resulted solely from a friendly argument with another horse fancier or from some bravado bet. Stanford long had been skeptical about the traditional renderings of galloping horses depicting the fore and hind legs extended at the same time, rocking-horse style. It also was Stanford's contention that, at one point in its stride, a galloping horse has all four hoofs off the ground—a belief which may have resulted in an amiable wager with a demurring friend.

The exciting possibilities opened up by photography gave Stanford the opportunity both to settle any personal dispute and to produce irrefutable evidence of any and all positions assumed by a horse at the gallop. Furthermore, an instrument produced by his financial backing, which could stop and accurately record movement, would have untold applications in the fields of science and engineering.

Stanford had been warned from the outset about the photographer he had selected for the undertaking. Building a railroad with engineers and scientists was one thing, but to be subjected to the whims of the artist's temperament would be quite another. Stanford had ample reason for any misgivings. After he had commissioned Muybridge, the errant artist became embroiled in a sensational scandal. His young wife, Flora, had become infatuated with "Major" Larkyns, a visiting British rake and possible remittance man (a type later played with a flourish by Errol Flynn). When Flora bore a son who could have been Larkyn's, Muybridge tracked the paramour down and, in a blind rage, shot and killed him. Although acquitted (probably as a result of Stanford's influence) by reason of justifiable homicide, it was felt prudent for the protagonist to absent himself from the local area. Muybridge creatively used the interlude by producing a series of photographs documenting Central America but between 1874 and 1876, work at Palo Alto had to be suspended, which seriously disrupted Stanford's plans and the advancement of photography in general. But now, on this bright summer day, the enormous outlay of cash and energy, the disappointments, the intrigues, the setbacks of the past years—all converged on these few seconds in the life of a horse.[5]

Stanford's reverie was broken by the sight of Muybridge approaching. Neither man spoke as the artist stood beside his patron. Observing the objects near the track—his photographer's eye absorbing the light and dark images with one blink, like a living shutter—Muybridge seemed as though he would capture the action forever. Abruptly, he turned to Stanford and said, "We are ready, Governor." His including Stanford in the final countdown indicated that Muybridge, too, felt the special significance and certain success of this moment.

A score of men had taken their places beside each of the cameras. The easily shattered glass negative plates, each of which had just been coated with an emulsion containing silver particles, were precisely loaded into place. Standing ready in the shed, were temperature-controlled vats of developing fluid and an improvised darkroom for on-the-spot inspection of the negatives. A stable boy led the magnificent thoroughbred Sallie Gardner, the unwitting star in the drama, to a specially marked spot at the beginning of the runway. As the rider mounted, the animal sidestepped nervously, then stood poised and ready, as though a hundred years of breeding had brought it to this special place and time. The rider signaled his readiness to Muybridge, who had returned to the cameramen. The band around his floppy hat had become dark with sweat. "Your positions, gentlemen!" he shouted. "Ready . . . *go!*"

With the downstroke of Muybridge's hand the symphony began—the sure hoofbeats of a horse riding to its place in history: the volley of clicking shutters activated like musketry by the electrical contacts on the track; and the scurrying feet of the disciplined assistants as they rushed to deftly extract the brittle glass negative plates from the cameras with the precision of a perfectly trained corps de ballet. Muybridge, conductor and choreographer of the great performance, moved frantically behind his men, waving his arms, cursing, barking his orders, and finally leading his ensemble, now perspiring profusely, to the laboratory next to the track. Unnoticed, the rider dismounted

Sallie Gardner, 1878. Disproves traditional representations of muscular action. *(Photo permission of Stanford University Museum of Art)*

Image # 2, showing all four feet off ground—the picture that proved the argument. *(Photo permission of Stanford University Museum of Art)*

and led the thoroughbred back to the stable for grooming. The whole event had taken less than a minute.

Moving to the laboratory and darkroom area, the men deposited the containers holding the precious plates as Muybridge checked again to see that all conditions were precisely correct in this final critical stage. The assistants then filed outside to sprawl in the shade and sip cooling lemonade while awaiting the results. Stanford joined Muybridge in the shed as the darkroom technicians carefully drew from the bath the negatives, one by one, in the order in which they had been taken. Scanning each dripping glass plate, the assembly found it increasingly difficult to subdue their mounting ecstasy. As the images resolved themselves, the men saw revealed, with indisputable clarity, all the successive positions the horse assumed during one complete stride. Reviewing the second and third image of the series, Muybridge motioned for Stanford to step closer. As Muybridge held the plate in a viewing position, Stanford looked for a moment,

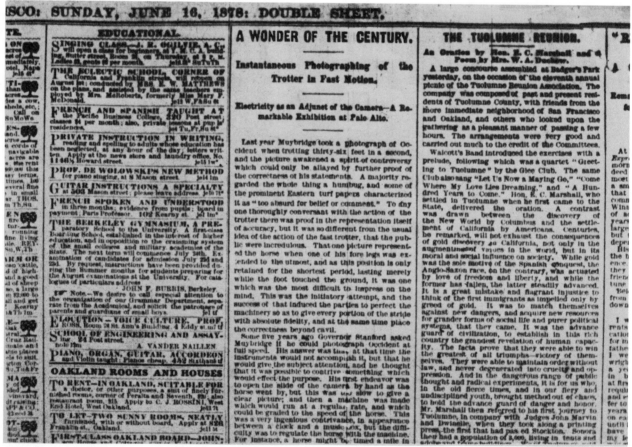

Press report: "A Wonder of the Century." *(Photo permission of Stanford University Museum of Art)*

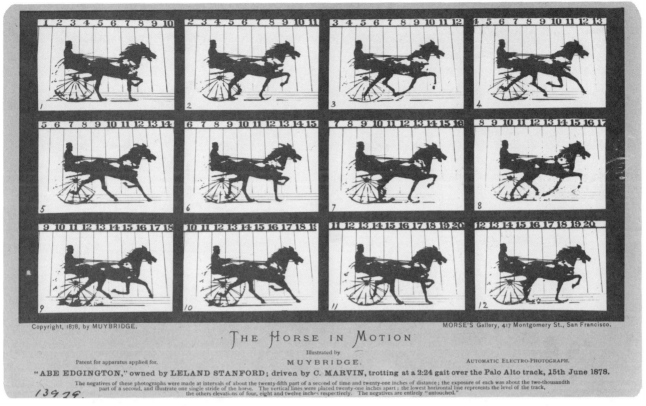

Advertising card by Morse's Gallery. *(Photo permission of Stanford University Museum of Art)*

then smiled broadly, his entire being suffused with the pride of accomplishment. Here at last was the incontestable truth: the horse at full stride had all four hoofs off the ground!

Hailed by the contemporary press as "a wonder of the century," this was a photographic triumph of a significance far beyond its original intent. Insuring both Stanford and Muybridge a place in history, it demonstrated conclusively that living motion can be reproduced realistically by a machine.[6]

The photographic attainment of 1878 was so successful that its range of subjects was extended to include, in addition to horses, oxen, deer, birds—and eventually, man. The resulting illustrations of living motion led to a number of notable after effects. Among these was an unexpected influence on the visual arts. Because of an inherent capacity to capture the unposed, the random and the refreshing quality of the spontaneous, these extraordinary photographs influenced artists to turn from contrived and rigid academic poses to interpretations of the moment. Instead of being seen as frozen in time, life could be considered and represented as an ongoing process. The new photograph reflected

scientific advancement as well. Just as the inquiries of the eighteenth century had led to the inventions of the nineteenth, so now static forms were giving way to the dynamic. In this dawning age of motion, the split-second photograph was its perfect expression.[7]

The immediate response, however, to the appearance of the living-motion photographs was mixed. The world of science and industry expressed keen interest. The *California Rural Press* reported that the photographs show "the gait of the horse exactly, and in a manner before impossible. A long description would be unintelligible, while the photographs show the whole stride at a glance." On the national level, the prestigious *Scientific American* in New York deemed the far-off California experiments to be of such wide interst that it made them the feature story depicted on the front cover.[8]

The reaction to the stop-action photograph from the world of art, on the other hand, was generally unfavorable. When the noted artist Thomas Eakins of Philadelphia, for example, attempted to do an equestrian work based upon the Muybridge photo-

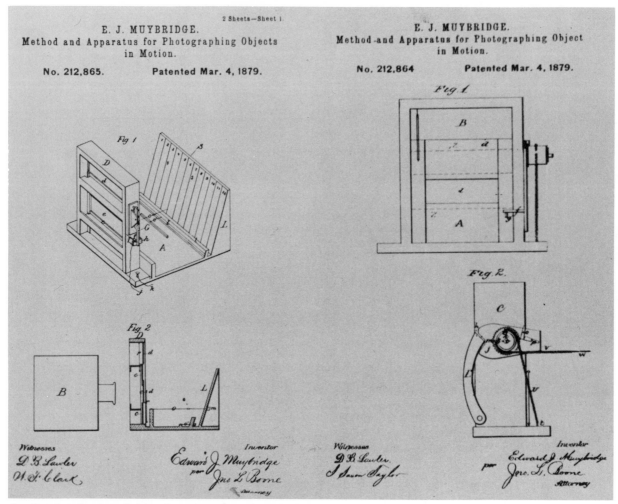

Application by Muybridge for patent on photographic method. *(Photo permission of Stanford University Museum of Art)*

graphs, his efforts were severely condemned by illustrator Joseph Pennell in London. Vehemently denying the value of photography for artists, Pennell stated, "If you photograph an object in motion, all feeling of motion is lost, and the object at once stands still." Although some, such as Frederick Remington, made use of the rapid action photographs, most artists saw them as little more than useful tools. Art experts and aestheticians on both sides of the Atlantic decried the analytical photographs as grotesque. Georges Guéroult in the *Gazette des Beaux-Arts* (Paris), scoffed: "the attitudes are . . . not only ungraceful, but give a false and impossible appearance, and were 'wrong,' visually speaking, because they showed the galloping horse as the human eye can never see it."[9]

Cartoonists had a field day lampooning the effort. The pictorial magazine *American Queen* illustrated a scene of a hunt with riders seated traditionally, while the horses were in the seemingly grotesque positions shown by the living-motion photographs. London's *Punch* ridiculed the photographs in a series of silhouette drawings of "an eminent actor" (presumably Henry Irving) in a series of angular and improbable gestures. The French painter J. L. E. Meissonier, noted for his equestrian scenes, reacted to such photographic analysis with disbelief, accusing the cameras of "seeing wrongly." And the seemingly final blow was delivered by the master anatomist and dean of French artists, Auguste Rodin, who declared, "In reality, time does not stop . . . it is the artist who is truthful, and it is photography which lies."[10]

Thus although the world of technology, concerned with future trends, was in sympathy with this latest development in photography, the world

San Francisco, 1877, by Muybridge. Two panels of a 365° panorama. *(Photo permission of Stanford University Museum of Art)*

of art and culture, steeped in the traditional, was skeptical. To the accusation that the photograph did not conform with established aesthetic norms, Stanford could assert, "The machine cannot lie." But the challenge to the conventional thinkers of the art establishment and the general public was too great. To confound the critics and to convince the public, it was necessary to discover some means by which static images could be presented so as to convey their essence—motion.[11]

With this problem, the second phase of the Stanford-Muybridge association and of their contribution to photography began. In this second phase the setting moved from the rural acres of Stanford's ranch at Palo Alto to the urban environment of the city by the Golden Gate.

The San Francisco of the 1870s and 1880s, even though remote geographically from the world's capitals and barely twenty-five years a metropolitan city, was renowned for its cosmopolitanism, its tolerance, its sophistication, and its receptivity to the new. The busy piers of San Francisco's waterfront were the transshipping point for California's agricultural products and for America's industry up and down the state and across the wide Pacific. The hub of finance was along Sansome and Montgomery streets, as it is today; but the fashionable thoroughfare was Kearny Street, stretching from

Portsmouth Square to the Palace Hotel on Market Street and lined with retail stores of every description. "After the gas is lighted, the stores look more gorgeous than in the light of day," observed contemporary journalist Benjamin E. Lloyd. "The army of promenaders pass and repass, the sound of revelry may break forth from the brilliantly lighted saloons, but there is seldom any boisterous outbreak to grate upon the ear."[12]

From the Kearny Street amenities and the Montgomery Street marts, the California Street cable car ascended to Powell Street, where the Nob Hill residence of Leland Stanford was situated. This town house, with its Italianate design, was one of the handsomest of its day. Within its hushed interior was Stanford's book-lined study. There he had noted the age-old studies by artists such as Leonardo da Vinci depicting humans and animals in motion; there also, he had become fascinated with the illusion of motion when riffling through a series of Muybridge photographs of living motion. In another part of the mansion was the playroom of Leland Stanford, Jr., containing, for the furtherance of the education of the Stanford heir, a number of artifacts, including a magic lantern, a kaleidoscope, and examples of the "scientific toys" that, when whirled, produced the effect of animation.

The picture gallery of Stanford's San Francisco residence—a preoccupation with the visual image. *(Photo permission of Stanford University Museum of Art)*

Study of progressive motion by Leonardo da Vinci. *(Photo permission of Pierpont Morgan Library, New York, N.Y.)*

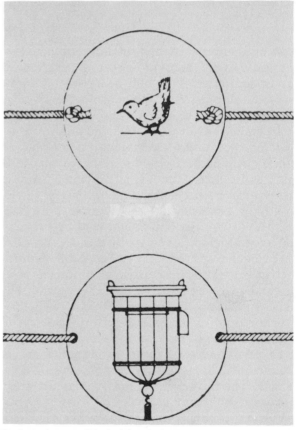

Disk, when twirled, blends images on each side to put bird into cage. *(Photo permission of Stanford University Museum of Art)*

Phenakistiscope disk—its illusion of motion could be seen by only one person. *(Division of Photographic History, Museum of American History, Smithsonian Institution, Washington, D.C.)*

These "scientific toys" dated back to the early nineteenth century, to the time of Dr. Peter Mark Roget (author of the well-known *Thesaurus of English Words and Phrases*). As a physician, Roget had observed the stroboscopic effect when vision is interrupted by moments of darkness, and had come to the conclusion that when the retina of the eye is stimulated by successive images lasting less than one-tenth of a second each and separated from each other by an interval of darkness, the illusion of continuous motion results. Dr. Roget presented his findings about this phenomenon of the persistence of vision to the Royal Society of London in 1824. Roget's intriguing concept stimulated the invention of a number of scientific toys to demonstrate its effect, each emblazoned, in the fashion of the day, with a classically derived name such as "Phenakisticscope." Delightful as they were, however, these inventions could show only line drawings in a very limited cycle of motion, and their effect could be viewed by only one person at a time. A more ad-

vanced version was the Zoetrope, with a sequence of images on a band inside a rotating drum. When the drum was spun rapidly, the images, viewed through slits in the upper half of the drum, appeared to be animated. It was upon these earlier discoveries that Muybridge built. When he replaced the line drawings with a band of his sequential photographs, he found that the horses "galloped" as in real life.

This illusion, however, could be seen by only one or two individuals at a time. What was needed was a motion effect that could be seen by many viewers simultaneously. Groups of people already could observe images, although static, when projected by the "magic lantern." This was a metal box containing a very bright light and reflector aligned with a lens. When the light was focused through the lens, it projected a small image onto a large screen, to be viewed by all. Thus, by 1878, the three elements essential to the motion picture were available: animation, projection, and the serial

Animation: *drawings* rotating in a viewing drum. *(Photo permission of Stanford University Museum of Art)*

Animation: *photographs* revolving in a viewing box. *(Photo permission of Franklin Institute, Philadelphia, Pa.)*

Projection: *drawings* exhibited on a large screen. *(Photo permission of Metropolitan Toronto Library, Ontario, Canada)*

Projection: *photographs* exhibited on a large screen. *(Photo permission of Franklin Institute, Philadelphia, Pa.)*

photograph of fast motion. The next step was to unify all three.[13]

Attempts toward this end had been made in Philadelphia by two members of the Franklin Institute. In 1860 Coleman Sellers combined animation with photographs, and in 1870 Reno R. Heyl combined these two with projection to simulate the movements of a waltzing couple on a screen. But the photographs of both had been posed and, in consequence, could merely suggest what continuous live action is.[14]

At Stanford's suggestion, and backed by Stanford's financing, Muybridge and the technicians constructed an instrument combining the features of the Zoetrope with those of the magic lantern. On a rotating glass disk they mounted a sequence of silhouettes adopted from the living-motion photographs. A counterrotating slotted disk, geared to

The Stanford-Muybridge motion picture projector, 1879–1880, first called the "Zoogyroscope," and later, "Zoopraxiscope." Projected sequential *unposed* photographs of life-motion to be seen by a number of people. *(Photo permission of Stanford University Museum of Art)*

The place where the world's first public motion picture exhibition took place, 1880: the San Francisco Art Association rooms on the second floor. *(Photo permission of San Francisco History Room, San Francisco Public Library)*

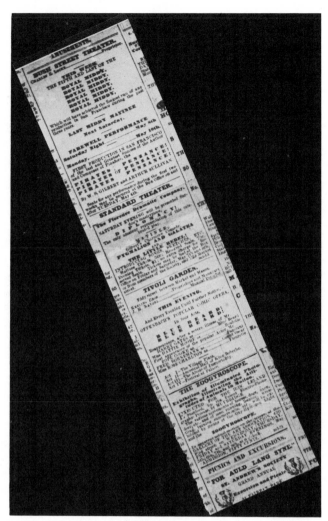

Press: the Zoogyroscope listed with other theatrical events. *(Photo from collection of Geoffrey Bell)*

operate at equal speed, provided the essential effect of intermittent motion in accordance with the theory of the persistence of vision. Uniting the photography of living motion with the techniques of animation and projection, this was the first instrument to successfully project living-motion photographs onto a screen to depict continuous action. The static images initially photographed by Muybridge at Palo Alto could now be synthesized and seen as they should be seen—in action. This was the prototype motion picture projector that made a reality of what man had dreamed of for so many ages: the *picture that moved.*[15]

The public debut of the motion picture took place one spring evening in 1880. The setting for this event was the exhibition hall of the San Fran-

Muybridge and a motion picture exhibition. *(Photo permission of Stanford University Museum of Art)*

Press: "Moving Shadows." *(Photo from collection of Geoffrey Bell)*

cisco Art Association, the leading showroom for the new in visual arts. Sharing quarters with the Bohemian Club on Pine Street between Montgomery and Kearny (now part of the site of Bank of America's world headquarters), the Art Association was then in the center of San Francisco's theatrical district; thus, any exhibition of a performing art faced strong competition. Such theatrical imports from New York and Europe as Offenbach's operetta *Bluebeard,* Sardou's drama *Diplomacy,* and the Pacific Coast premiere of Gilbert and Sullivan's *Pirates of Penzance* were playing on San Francisco's stages. Audiences of the day included such figures as Howard Coit and his vivacious wife, Lillie Hitchcock Coit, eminent merchants Raphael Weil or Solomon Gump, the landscape painter William Keith, or inventor Andrew S. Hallidie of cable car fame. Those who, on 4 May 1880 opted to attend the showing of "Illustrated Photographs in Motion (Admission: fifty cents)," as the Stanford-Muybridge event was advertised in the amusement sections of the local newspapers, were to receive more than full value for their money: they were to witness the dawn of a new era in both entertainment and communications.[16]

The patrons of the Art Association event found that, as in a theater, the seating area was arranged with rows of chairs facing a curtain. But at the rear of the hall was something different. Guarded by an attendant was a projecting magic lantern of unusual size and complexity of design, fitted with a powerful oxyhydrogen lamp. At the appointed hour of 8 P.M., after the audience was seated, the gas illumination was lowered, and a shaft of light was focused on the curtained end of the room. After a moment, Muybridge made his entrance. Addressing the audience, he summarized his work in Palo Alto, illustrating his lecture with slide projections of photographs of the activities and the results. Muybridge went on to trace the efforts of artists through the centuries to depict motion, as illustrated by the Assyrians, Egyptians, Romans, Greeks, and artists of later times. Completing this introduction, Muybridge moved offstage, and the lights were again lowered. The event for which the audience had been waiting was about to begin.

On the screen was projected a luminous life-size image of a horse. A dozen or more static images followed, each depicting yet another attitude the animal assumed in running. Finally, one image was held as if frozen in time. The horse was seen to move one leg, then another, then to begin to gather momentum, and, finally, to run at full speed.

Greyhound running. *(Photo permission of Stanford University Museum of Art)*

Horse running. *(Photo permission of Stanford University Museum of Art)*

William Lawton—gymnast. *(Photo permission of Stanford University Museum of Art)*

Across the illumined screen again and again galloped a delicate-limbed mare. With a clarity exceeding their expectations, the audience saw the superb thoroughbred moving in timeless motion. A reporter from the *San Francisco Call* marveled to see "placed upon the screen apparently the living, moving horse. Nothing was wanting but the clatter of hoofs upon the turf and an occasional breath of steam from the nostrils to make the spectator believe that he had before him genuine flesh-and-blood steeds."[17]

The audience burst into applause, their warm and enthusiastic response guaranteeing the success of the evening. But this was not to be all. In the magic beam of light appeared the figure of a man, aglow with the vitality of youth. This was athlete William Lawton, champion gymnast of San Francisco's Olympic Club. Lawton flexed his muscles, crouched, leaped into a somersault, and finally landed gracefully on his feet, his muscular action admirably shown. This was the first appearance of a human being in action on a screen. However sim-

Lawton executing a high jump. *(Photo permission of Stanford University Museum of Art)*

Lawton executing a back somersault. *(Photo permission of Stanford University Museum of Art)*

Muybridge saluting Lawton. *(Photo permission of Stanford University Museum of Art)*

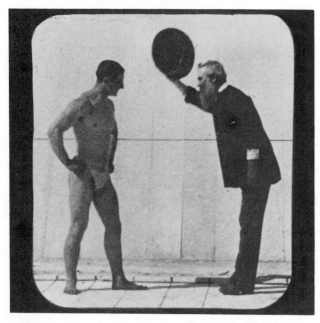

ple its form, it was the initiation of motion picture drama; and however unconscious William Lawton may have been of it, he has the distinction of being the world's first movie "star."[18]

"Other pictures," admiringly observed a reviewer from the *Scientific American Supplement,* "illustrated the actions of the dog, the ox, the deer . . . their shadows traversed the screen, apparently to the eye as if the living animal itself were moving . . . in the graceful, undulating movements we are accustomed to associate with the action of these animals." This immediate response was confirmed by later showings. The prestigious *Illustrated London News* was to remark with awe: "After the horses, dogs, oxen, wild bulls and deer were shown, . . . finally Man appeared (in instantaneous photography) on the scene and walked, ran, leaped, and turned back somersaults to admiration."[19]

With this dazzling conclusion, Muybridge stepped forward to acknowledge the waves of applause. After the house lights went up, he received greetings and congratulations from prominent San Franciscans of the time.

As a result of this San Francisco success, Stanford underwrote a trip for Muybridge to present similar lecture-demonstrations in Europe. Arriving in Paris in August 1881, Muybridge was feted at a reception at the home of scientist Etienne Jules Marey of the College of France, who for some years had been studying and analyzing animal motion and who had been following the work in California with interest. A similar reception was given by painter J. L. E. Meissonier and, according to a lead article in *Figaro,* was attended by "the most eminent artists, scientists and literati of the day."[20] Muybridge gave England's first motion picture show at the Royal Institution, London, in the presence of the Prince and Princess of Wales; the princesses Louise, Victoria, and Maud; and the Duke of Edinburgh. In the wave of enthusiasm that the motion pictures generated, the California phenomenon was acclaimed by the Royal Family and the future King Edward VII. After the performance Muybridge mingled with others of the realm of no less eminence, including statesman and sometime prime minister William Gladstone, scientist Thomas Huxley, poet laureate Alfred, Lord Tennyson, and Sir Frederick Leighton of the Royal Academy. Initially, Stanford's name had been included in the press reports as the enlightened sponsor of Muybridge's work; in time, however, Muybridge accepted full credit and was lionized on his own account.[21]

Meanwhile, since 1880, Stanford had been supervising the preparation of a definitive book on animal locomotion, based on the data obtained from the living-motion photography he had sponsored. Entitled *The Horse in Motion,* the book itself was written by Dr. J. D. B. Stillman, veterinarian and lifelong friend of Stanford, who had worked closely with him since the inception of the animal motion experiments. *The Horse in Motion* appeared in 1882. Muybridge, receiving honors in England, found himself slighted, for the name of Dr. Stillman, not his own, appeared on the title page. To make matters worse, Muybridge found himself described as having been "employed" by Stanford and saw that his own writings had been relegated to the appendix and heavily edited and that his original photography had been reduced to line drawings. His pride stung to the quick, Muybridge sued the publisher, but the suit was later dismissed. He then sued Stanford for $50,000 in damages. Muybridge lost this second case as well. Stanford's reaction to the attacks by his former close associate was expressed in a letter of 1882: "I think the fame we have given him has turned his head."[22]

Fortunately, fate dealt more kindly with the results of the Stanford-Muybridge association than with the partnership itself. The motion picture premiere in San Francisco during 1880 spurred inventors all over the world to transform the original projector into a commercially marketable machine. Meanwhile, by a shift of fate, Stanford's energies were turned in another direction. He and Mrs. Stanford became totally occupied in establishing a university as a memorial to their only son, following the latter's untimely death. Muybridge found another American patron at the University of Pennsylvania, where he continued with the analysis of motion by means of the still camera, and in 1893 repeated his San Francisco exhibition at the World's Columbian Exposition in Chicago. Yet, however swiftly the forces released by Stanford and Muybridge rushed beyond them, it was the ability of the one to organize and subsidize the years of experimentation, and the proficiency in photography of the other to carry the experiments out, that combined to bring into existence, first, the instantaneous rapid-action photographs of life, and, second, the cinematic motion picture. Despite the rift that took place when they were no longer bound by a joint enterprise, their relationship was summed up by Muybridge in these words: "The circumstances must have been exceptionally felicitous that made collaborateurs of the man that no practical impediment could balk, and of the artist, who, to keep pace with the demands of the railroad builder, hurried his art to a marvel of perfection."[23]

This, then, was the origin of the motion picture, the icon and language of our age. A full century has confirmed what was foretold by the wonderstruck reporter from the San Francisco *Alta California,* when he wrote that Stanford and Muybridge "laid the foundation for a new method of entertaining the people, and we predict [that it] will make the round of the civilized world!"[24]

The excitement of the West made perfect movie material. *(Photo permission of Erwin E. Smith Collection of
Range Life Photographs, Library of Congress)*

2

The Adventures of Essanay and Broncho Billy

The peaceful somnolence of Niles, a typical, small agricultural community by the southern shores of San Francisco Bay, was shattered one April afternoon in 1912 by the arrival at the railroad station of a motley company of that exotic calling—actors. Disembarking from the train, the members of the company—character actor Arthur Mackley, juvenile lead Frederick Church, leading lady Edna Fisher, sometime Shakespearian actor Brinsley Shaw, actress and script writer Josephine Rector, comedian and carpenter Ben Turpin—looked around curiously. To these show people, Niles appeared remote from the glittering urban attractions of the theater world only a few miles away in San Francisco and Oakland. On one side of the tracks ranged open cow pastures; on the other side, a straggling row of stores made up the main street of the town, the major industries of which were a nursery, a sand and gravel pit, a tile manufacturing plant, and a poultry research farm. The actors could not have known that this unlikely place was to be their home for the next four years, nor that it was to be the setting for a major advance in motion picture history.[1]

These actors from the stage, now in the new world of the movies, had been preceded by their boss, Gilbert M. Anderson, a film director-producer. On the recommendation of his cameraman, Jesse J. Robbins, Anderson had surveyed the Niles site and had agreed on its advantages for the production of movie Westerns. He had no doubt about the appeal of the scenery but felt uncertain about the temper of the town of Niles itself. This he tested in an unusual way. With all the assurance of youth, this thirty-year-old movie man approached each and every merchant in Niles and informed him that he was Gilbert M. Anderson; that he represented the Essanay Film Manufacturing Company; that he intended to make motion pictures there; that his company would bring considerable business to the community; and that if the proprietor was desirous of Essanay patronage, he should demonstrate commitment by making a contribution on the spot. Anderson really did not need the two dollars here or the five dollars there he collected—a total of about one hundred dollars. His company was well able to finance its activities. This unorthodox introduction was his way of determining who would support his work. And it was a real test, for only contributors received future Essanay business.[2]

If Anderson was unconventional in this approach, it was typical of everything that had gone before. It had been a long way from Little Rock, Arkansas—where he was born Max Aranson in 1883—to the New York of 1900—where he tried to break into show business. It had been a gamble to leave the theater for the outcast "flickers." And

once he was working in the movies, it was still another wrench to leave established studios to form his own company.

Just after the turn of the century, movies were made mostly in New York City, close to the theaters of Broadway. Little, cramped studios in improvised lofts might turn out little novelties, but Anderson felt that the movies should have far greater scope. He had a showman's intuition that the movies were the mass entertainment of the future, that the Western adventure story was an ideal genre for the movies, that they should be filmed in the real West, and that he was the one to do it. Putting theory into practice, he worked to gain experience with the Edison and Vitagraph studios

Gilbert M. Anderson as "Broncho Billy." *(Photo permission of Center for Film and Theater Research, University of Wisconsin, Madison)*

A nickelodeon, early 1900s, when movies were shown in little storefront movie houses to the tune of rinky-tink player pianos. *(Photo from collection of Geoffrey Bell)*

in New York and with Selig's movie studio in Chicago.

On the basis of this practical experience, in February 1907 Anderson teamed with George K. Spoor, a Chicago-based movie distributor and exhibitor, who operated a chain of one hundred and twenty-two nickelodeons in the Midwest. These small movie houses showed programs made up of a number of short, one-reel films—each running fifteen minutes or less—and each program was changed several times a week. Spoor needed a plentiful supply of entertaining short films, and Anderson needed a dependable marketing outlet for the films he was planning. Each needed the other, and from the initials of their last names, *S* and *A,* was formed the name of their new joint company— Essanay.

Spoor, the businessman of the partnership, was in charge of finance and marketing. His interest in the motion picture lay in its money-making potential, its mechanical devices, and in its possibilities for future invention; he was the type who was more at ease with mathematics and machines he could control and master, and less with human unpredictibilities he could not. Anderson, as artistic head of Essanay, was totally dedicated to the movies and, as a producer, knew how to attract talented people and how to get the most out of them. After setting up a production center and studio on Argyle Street in Chicago to fill Essanay's quota of "indoor" pictures, he left its direction in other hands and set forth to produce his quota of "outdoor" pictures—fulfilling his dream of filming Westerns somewhere beyond the wide Missouri.[3]

With a basic technical crew, a motion picture camera, some lights, an electric generator, props, and materials for sets, Anderson roamed through the western states, shooting one-reel pictures where he found suitable scenery, using horsemen and cowboys from nearby ranches and actors from local theatrical stock companies. In time he found that stage-trained, matinee idol types lacked the rough-hewn qualities essential for a Western outdoor-adventure hero, and to maintain his schedule, Anderson stepped in to play the hero. Audience response was favorable. Although he was not conventionally handsome, Anderson's six-foot height, stalwart frame, and large pawlike hands conveyed vigor, determination, resourcefulness, strength, and affinity with the outdoors. Even his lack of acting polish gave him credibility in stories of the primitive West.

Initially, Anderson intended to make his movie Westerns in Colorado, but gusty winds, dark days, and logistic difficulties adversely affected his shooting schedule. After trial location work in New Mexico, the company moved on to Southern California. And by 1910 Anderson was drawn to Northern California, with a climate, though more capricious, differing little from that of the southern part of the state and with greater scenic variety; moreover, it was the site of the California gold rush, where exciting Western history had been made. Early in October the Essanay crew relocated to the coast range between San Francisco and Monterey. There, during the following months, they filmed a series of Westerns among the giant redwoods and in the winding canyons of the Los Gatos–Felton region. In May of the following year the company arrived at San Rafael, Marin County, just north of the Golden Gate. The pictorial beauty of Marin County had long attracted photographers, as it was later to attract the California Motion Picture Corporation and, in our time, the important Lucasfilms of producer-director George Lucas.

During this period, Anderson was thinking, not in terms of a permanent site, but in terms of working where he found the scenery most effective. To augment his mobile camera unit, his technicians outfitted a seventy-foot railroad baggage car with a mobile laboratory that could process motion picture film and production stills on the spot. To enhance his ability to film wherever he found good settings, Anderson assembled a traveling acting company and a large crew of cowboys and horsemen. In time the group was joined by young Max Graf, who was beginning his career as a producer. Among the Westerns that this enthusiastic group made in Marin County were *The Hidden Mine* (June 1911), *The Two-Gun Man* (August 1911), and *The Cowpuncher's Law* (September 1911). Old-time residents still remember the company's filming in the meadows between San Anselmo and Fairfax and in the hill country stagecoach roads between Fairfax and Bolinas. These outdoor-adventure stories, told with vigorous action and enacting strong, simple stories of man against man or man against nature, featured Anderson in the principal role of the miner, sharpshooter, or cowpuncher. As ideal as these conditions of scenery and climate seemed, cameraman Jess Robbins brought in glowing reports of an even greater number of advantages for Essanay in an area centered around the town of Niles, Alameda County.[4]

Lying about halfway between Oakland and San Jose, Niles enjoyed a year-round mild climate— with protection from coastal winds and with de-

Niles and Mission Peak areas, c. 1900. *(Photo permission of Mission Peak Heritage Foundation, Fremont)*

Niles Canyon. *(Photo permission of California Historical Society, San Franciso)*

Niles Main Street, c. 1912. *(Photo permission of Mission Peak Heritage Foundation, Fremont)*

Old Vallejo Mill at Niles. *(Photo from collection of Geoffrey Bell)*

pendable sunshine—in an area ideal for farms, truck gardens, and nurseries. A number of sprawling ranches were sheltered among the hills ranging to the east, through which meandered Niles Canyon with its picturesque stream flowing between rock outcrops, wooded banks, and leafy trails.

At a crossroad for routes east to the Sacramento–San Joaquin Valley, west to San Francisco Bay, and north and south along the coast, Niles had been the site of a flour mill built in 1841 by Jesus de Vallejo, brother of the famous General Vallejo. When the first railroad was run through it in 1869, the settlement of Vallejo Mill was renamed after Judge Addison C. Niles of the state supreme court, an official of the railroad. Niles then became a vital railway junction linking all the major California cities with Chicago and the East. Predominantly rural, Niles still was not far from the financial and cultural center of San Francisco and the important

railroad terminus of Oakland. Under Oakland's progressive Mayor Mott, an impressive city hall and the imposing Hotel Oakland had just been completed, the Oakland Museum was established, and a splendid civic auditorium was under construction. Theaters presenting live attractions included the Orpheum and Pantages vaudeville companies and Ye Liberty Stock Company. At the neighboring university city of Berkeley, the beautiful open-air Greek Theatre made a distinguished setting for many theatrical and musical presentations of international caliber.[5]

Although the name of Niles may now sound unlikely in connection with the movies, in 1912 it was no more unlikely than that of another small California agricultural town called Hollywood, which had far less to offer for moviemaking. Niles had scenery with variety and authenticity, a climate favorable to outdoor photography throughout the year, access to top theatrical talent in San Francisco and Oakland, direct express railroad service to business centers in the East, and proximity to photogenic Niles Canyon, just right for Western movie scenes of gold panning, stagecoach holdups, Indian encampments, and posse riding. Beyond lay the inspiring scenery of Central California with its broad rivers, evergreen forests, and towering mountains.

Anderson's arrival in Niles coincided with his attainment of a worldwide reputation. No longer the outsider in the performing arts as he was in 1902, by 1912 he was one of its pivotal figures. If deceptively genial and rough-hewn, he actually was a very complex individual—creative, yet belittling anything he thought smacked of "art"; married, yet living the life of a bachelor; ingratiating, yet antagonizing; ready with honeyed words to wheedle a farmer out of the use of his ranch, yet quick to accuse an actor of trying to tell him how to run his business.[6]

From his experience in the entertainment world, Anderson knew what audiences liked, and, due to his partnership with a shrewd distributor, Spoor, he could get his pictures into movie houses. In addition, from his five industrious years he knew what it took to make a movie. In producing Westerns, for example, Anderson learned that it was more economical to shoot all the "ride-throughs"—horsemen charging cross-country—at one time for an entire picture, in fact, for several pictures. In directing, he also learned that his adventure stories of action, action, action had little need for the histrionics of "acting" in the theatrical sense, so he needed only a nucleus of one or two skillful character actors. Most other roles could be better filled by physical types. And because movie scenes are rarely shot in the order that they will appear in the finished film, he learned to make sure that an action commenced in one scene was continued in the same direction in a matching scene, that the tempo—slow, normal, or brisk—was consistent in all the scenes of one sequence, and that each scene was filmed so that its action, when edited into the finished film, would never appear to backtrack but would always flow continuously forward. All this may seem obvious *now*, but it was not always so in those pioneering moviemaking days, as many unintentionally funny early movies confirm. Then, too, from a visual point of view, Anderson's testing of different locales throughout the West had given him an understanding of how outdoor scenes can best be photographed—for example, avoiding, whenever possible, shooting long

shots to the east or west, but angling them to the north or south to obtain better natural lighting.

Beyond technique was theme. In selecting the Western genre, Anderson had tapped a theme far, far older than the movies—in fact, far older than the American West itself. The lure of the land beyond the setting sun long had been a symbol of a new and better life. The wilderness also stood for adventure, opportunity, and individualism; the frontier, for stories of courage and heroism—and escape. The background for these legends in America was the majestic and untamed scenery of the great West, a setting that called for men to match its mountains. Myths grew from real-life figures: Daniel Boone came to symbolize the forest hunter; Kit Carson, the plainsman; and Davy Crockett, the soldier-frontiersman. From these elements a body of literature arose during the nineteenth century celebrating the exploration, winning, and settlement of America's frontier. The romance of the West found its first American literary expression in James Fenimore Cooper's *Leatherstocking Tales* (1823–1841). These widely read novels were followed by countless popular variations, ranging from Bret Harte's stories about the California gold rush to the dime novels of the 1880s and the pulp magazines of the 1890s. By 1902 Owen Wister's *Virginian* finally could depict with admiration the Western hero as "a slim young giant, his broad, soft hat pushed back, a loose-knotted handkerchief [at] his throat, one casual thumb hooked in the cartridge belt slanted across his hips," and marvel at "the splendor that radiated from his youth and strength."[7]

Western movies also had precedents in other media. In addition to books and magazines, live presentations capitalized on this growing fascination with the West. During the 1850s lecturers entranced armchair travelers for hours at a time, as did John Wesley Jones with his "Pantoscope of California." Jones, who had been the first to photograph the Rocky Mountains and the Great Plains, had the pictures transferred onto immense reels of canvas, probably ten feet high and hundreds of yards long. As the canvas slowly unrolled with its sequential views "beautifully executed by the best artists from 1,500 daguerreotypes," the audience witnessed a literal moving-picture show. In the 1850s P. T. Barnum brought trappers, buffalos, Indians, and other Western "curiosities" to dazzle Eastern audiences.

The popular theater also was quick to seize on the appeal of the West. The well-known showman

Buffalo Bill Cody appeared on the stage during the early 1870s in a piece called *The Scouts of the Plains*. Cody was no actor, and the play was atrocious, but its success showed that audiences would flock to see dramas set in a romanticized West, built around an engaging central character, and enlivened by plenty of "shoot-'em-up" action. Cody went on in the 1880s to appear in outdoor Wild West shows—arena productions combining elements of the historical pageant, the circus, and the rodeo, with wild-riding cowboys, wagon trains, pitched battles, rampaging Indians, and blazing firearms.[8]

At its very outset, then, the movie Western had a rich store of material from which to draw. The range of characters seemed almost limitless: the heroic outdoorsman as a scout, sharpshooter, or cowboy, whose adventures were set against a colorful medley of characters that included the trapper, trader, miner, prospector, soldier, sheriff, gambler, outlaw, Indian, Mexican, derelict doctor or lawyer, venerable judge, wholesome maiden, dance hall gal, uplifting schoolmarm, or stoic pioneer mother.

The theatrical genre of the melodrama was a particularly useful source for early moviemakers like Anderson. The melodrama's rapid succession of short scenes—augmented by special lighting and scenic effects—adventurous plots, moral dilemmas, and man-to-man conflicts resolved in resounding climaxes, provided perfect material for the movie Western. The moral tone was clear-cut, punishing wickedness and rewarding virtue. And, of special value in the days of silent movies, melodrama depended little on the spoken word—it told its story in visual terms.[9]

Although melodrama offered excellent plot material, its scenic effects necessarily were cramped because of the limitations of the stage. The movies, however, with the realism afforded by photography, could bring to audiences vistas of unlimited space. The impact of actual outdoor scenery was impressively demonstrated in 1903 with the ten-minute movie *The Great Train Robbery*. There was no doubt that its steam engine was made of steel, and there was magic in placing the viewpoint of an important scene at the top of a forward-moving train—something no theater could ever do. This landmark picture was made by director Edwin S. Porter for Edison. As it happened, the Edison company had recently hired the aspiring nineteen-year-old Gilbert M. Anderson. Though Anderson did not star in *The Great Train Robbery*, as some-

times has been said—up to that time his principal preparation for movie Western roles had been posing for cowboy illustrations for the *Saturday Evening Post*—he did, as a bit player, appear in at least three different parts and may have played a bigger off-screen role. Porter was searching for a story idea, and, as Anderson recalled, "I suggested something that had a lot of riding and shooting—plenty of excitement. Why not about a train robbery? Another fellow remembered that there was a play called *The Great Train Robbery* [by Scott Marble, c. 1895] so we stole the title."[10]

Earlier, Porter had made an advertising film that so pleased Lackawanna Railroad executives that they loaned him a train and crew, which he used to film scenes in the autumn of 1903 near Paterson, New Jersey. The riding scenes were shot in Essex County Park, near West Orange, New Jersey. Although by no means "great open spaces," the exteriors brought to the screen vivid images of real trains and real trees, a refreshing change from the usual studio make-believe. While *The Great Train Robbery* was not the first story film, it was the first to capture mass audiences with a story told cinematically. Porter proved that audiences had no difficulty following the continuity of a movie that cut from a railroad office to a train, to a dance hall, to outlaws, and back to the office, without written explanations. Viewers also had no trouble understanding scenes that cut back and forth between different stages of the story, which demonstrated that popular movies could use editing to juxtapose scenes set in different places and times.

The popular and continuing success of *The Great Train Robbery*, which was shown and reshown for years after it first appeared, convinced Anderson that the movies were where his future lay. His timing could not have been more opportune, for after 1903 there was a growing demand for short (ten to twelve minutes), one-reel movies in the many movie houses opening across the country.

Among the people who flocked to these movie houses (often converted stores) were new workers in cities and factory towns, many of whom were immigrants with a language barrier who were away from home and cut off from their traditional amusements. In time, these small movie houses came to be called *nickelodeons* because of their five-cent admission price. Their continuous noon-to-midnight hours made entertainment available whenever working people had a little spare time and a little spare change. Movies also were popular

Old barn, the original headquarters. *(Photo from collection of Geoffrey Bell)*

Open stage rigged beside barn. *(Photo from collection of Geoffrey Bell)*

in suburbs, small towns, and isolated communities without regular live-stage shows, as well as in foreign countries. The movies provided not only cheap, understandable, and available entertainment, but also—in their hypnotic flow of bright images—opportunities for escapes into fantasy worlds. With this broad market the movie company that understood its audience could reap enormous profits. George K. Spoor had taken advantage of this opportunity by distributing and exhibiting films; Gilbert M. Anderson, likewise, by production. Essanay prospered, so that even though initial filming took place under improvised conditions the company soon was operating in a bona fide studio. After the company had arrived in Niles, Anderson established a work center in a wooden barn on a parcel of property on Second Street between G and H. The barn became his ad-

New studio, 1913, as viewed from range just north of Niles. *(Photo from collection of Geoffrey Bell)*

A corner of the studio main building, viewed from the street. *(Photo permission of San Francisco History Room, San Francisco Public Library)*

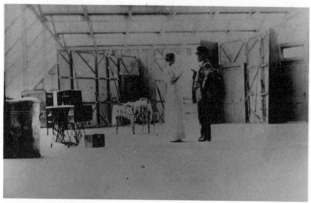

Interior of glass-covered stage. *(Photo from collection of Geoffrey Bell)*

ministration center by day and the crew's storage space for equipment by night, while the railroad car laboratory was shunted over from San Rafael and berthed on a siding on I Street towards the Niles Canyon side of town. The few interior scenes needed for Westerns were shot on an open platform rigged alongside the barn.[11]

The Western movie dramas that came forth from the primitive wooden barn became so phenomenally successful that soon Anderson could spend an estimated $125,000 of Essanay profits for improved technical facilities. By June 1913 the new and fully equipped motion picture studio was ready for operation. From the Niles railroad station the plant was reached by going west on Main Street to the corner of G. The studio administration building was a one-and-one-half story rectangular structure, surmounted by a gable framing a six-foot circle with the Essanay trademark—the profile of an Indian head. Aside from this adornment, the building was singularly unpretentious. In fact, it looked like a factory, as indeed it proclaimed itself to be. Above the line of windows, and running the full 150-foot length of the building, bold black lettering stood forth for all to see: Essanay Film Manufacturing Company.

Inside the entrance was a stark, wooden-benched waiting room, paneled in no-nonsense tongue-and-groove, with a wicket window communicating

Innovative use of arc lighting for interior scenes. *(Photo permission of Mission Peak Heritage Foundation, Fremont)*

Cottages for Essanay personnel. *(Photo permission of Mission Peak Heritage Foundation, Fremont)*

most complete on the West Coast. A separate structure housed the horse stables, all-important for Westerns, and on open land near Alameda Creek stood a permanent exterior set of multipurpose "Western" buildings. Today, the only identifiable portion of the studio complex is a row of cottages along Second Street, which originally were rented to principal players. The cottages are still residences, with later modifications.[12]

A wealth of locations evoking the pioneer West were immediately at hand for the crew of the Essanay company. The town of Niles itself, with its old-time, country-style architecture, was like an extensive three-dimensional movie set. Main Street became the Western Street of a hundred scenes of hard-riding horsemen; its white-painted wooden dwellings with vine-entwined porches became the scene of a hundred romantic trysts; its outlying farms and weathered barns became the scene of a hundred shoot-outs at the corral. Stories reflecting California's Spanish heritage gained authenticity from backgrounds at the Vallejo Mill on Alameda Creek; or at Mission San Jose, close to the foot of

with the clerk's office. A locked door led into a corridor serving the offices of the clerk, Josephine Rector; the company manager, Jack O'Brien; and producer-director Anderson. At the end of the corridor was a row of austere dressing rooms, each for four actors; on a mezzanine above were the costume storerooms. Towards the center of the building were the editing rooms, with benches and equipment for handling the reels of film and for splicing the scenes together. On the far side of the building were the carpentry, paint, and property rooms.

The central portion of the studio building was taken up with the covered stage for shooting interior scenes. Its steel-frame glass roof had a twenty-foot clearance, spanning a floor space of 60 by 120 feet. When not taken up with a set, the stage was a jumble of scenery: doors that opened to nothing, stairways that led nowhere, fireplaces in which no fire was ever lit. A number of arc lights stood about, used for boosting the light on sets and for illuminating special effects, such as "sunlight" through a window. These arc lights, crude though they might have been, were in advance of their time, and the entire studio building, simple though it was, actually was one of the most modern and

Scene from "Broncho Billy's Pal" (Essanay).

Broncho Billy's Pal (1912). Anderson and probably Lee Willard. *(Photo permission of California State Library, Sacramento)*

Mission Peak, the mountain forming a backdrop to the Niles region.

The original misgivings of the people of Niles soon were assuaged by the hard work and dedication of the Essanay company. Although a few were inclined to look down their noses at show people and to consider anything theatrical as sinful, most were well-disposed to helping the intriguing, if unpredictable, arrivals from the world of make-believe. They loaned props, furniture, their houses, horses—even, on occasion, their infants. Many Niles residents appeared as extras for the fun of it.

As the result of this movie activity in Niles and in previous locations in California and Colorado, Gilbert M. Anderson produced over four hundred consecutive film dramas, a record unequalled in motion picture annals. In order to make them, and to make them so that they maintained audience interest, Anderson had to use extraordinary creativ-

ity. By design or by intuition, Anderson composed with excellence in setting, plot, and characterization, so that within twelve to fourteen minutes of running time his films told intense, fast-moving stories.[13]

Characterization was the glue holding the pictures together, for people are primarily interested in people. At the outset of making movie Westerns, Anderson found that something was lacking. "I decided what was needed," Anderson reasoned, "was a central character who would continue from film to film . . . someone the audience would pull for." From the cowboy, a symbol of the West with an enduring hold on the affections of the public, Anderson created his hero—a cowboy with the common touch, a man with human weaknesses, yet who accomplished noble deeds. Anderson also knew that the character had to have a name people would remember, one evoking the cowboy. Since one major test of a real cowboy was to stick on a

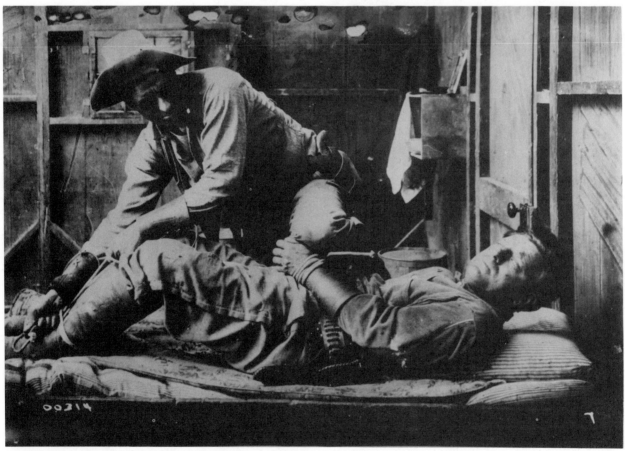

Possibly *The Prospector's Legacy* (1912). Anderson and probably Roy Clement. *(Photo permission of Museum of Modern Art—Film Stills Archive, New York)*

The Naming of the Rawhide Queen (1913). True Board-man, Evelyn Selbie, Roy Clement and Harry Todd. *(Photo from collection of Geoffrey Bell)*

Possibly *The Shotgun Ranchman* (1912). Anderson and Emory Johnson (holding whip, center). *(Photo from collection of Geoffrey Bell)*

bucking broncho and since "Billy" goes with "Broncho," the cowboy would be called "Broncho Billy."[14]

It is frequently stated that Anderson took the name and characterization of Broncho Billy from a story by San Francisco author Peter B. Kyne, and the story often cited is Kyne's "Three Godfathers." In an interview during his later years Anderson confirmed this, stating that when he met Kyne, "Kyne said it was all right." Sometimes, after a half-century, people are apt to weave half-forgotten memories into a good story. "The Three Godfathers" does not contain a character called Broncho Billy, and it was not published until 1913, long after the appearance of Broncho Billy on the screen in *Broncho Billy's Redemption* (July 1910). An examination of the indexes of Kyne's work does not reveal the name of Broncho Billy in a title, although Kyne may well have used the theme of self-sacrifice, characteristic of Broncho Billy, in some now-forgotten story published around the time Anderson was creating his movie characterization. Another possibility: "The Identification of 'Broncho Jim,'" a story by George Ade, appeared in *The Saturday Evening Post* in early 1903 and is

Broncho Billy's Bible (1912). Johnson and Anderson, center. *(Photo permission of California State Library, Sacramento)*

Poster, *The Dance at Silver Gulch* (1913). *(Photo from collection of Geoffrey Bell)*

illustrated with pictures of cowboys. If Anderson had posed for them, he could have half-remembered the "Broncho" from that engagement and confused Ade with Kyne, both popular writers. The name *broncho*—the unmanageable wild horse of the Western plains—has always been associated with the cowboy, the "bronchobuster." It is also noteworthy that the plot of Anderson's *Broncho Billy's Redemption* of 1910 contains many of the elements of the later "Three Godfathers" story. As reported in the contemporary *Moving Picture World:*

> A fascinating story of life on the plains, showing how even a bad man found his heart and developed a strain of goodness he did not know he possessed when he found a girl and her father in need of assistance. He brings them safely to town where they can obtain medicines, but in doing so subjects himself to arrest. With no killing, without even a suspicion of a love story, this film is strangely interesting.[15]

Whatever the source, Anderson knew that the character had to be both likeable and credible. If he were always good, he would seem remote from the common man; if he were always bad, he would lose sympathy. So he became the good-bad man. In one film he might be the upholder of the moral values of his audiences and the defender of the home; in the next, he might be an outsider or an outlaw. But in either case, he always had time to do a good deed. By showing that he cared about others and that others cared about him, Broncho Billy would make audiences care about him. He would be a simple man of the people without much book learning or many worldly possessions—kindly and valiant. As the protector of the weak, he would win back the deed of the ranch for a destitute widow; as the fearless fighter, he would brave bullets to uphold the law; as a compassionate human, he would sell his horse to help a comrade. In *Broncho Billy's Pal* (June 1912), for example, the brave hero sacrifices his own future for his partner. In the final scene "back at the ranchhouse Broncho sits on the doorstep and smiles grimly down the white trail with his pal's confession locked within his stalwart heart." This recurrent theme of self-sacrifice added a vein of unexpected depth to the rough-and-ready antecedent heroes of *Leatherstocking* or *The Virginian* and also brought the warmth of human appeal to the blood-and-thunder plots of melodrama. Broncho Billy was the gallant, if shy, knight who stirred feminine hearts. But he was no lover. This manly cowboy turned into an awkward, shy boy in the presence of the ranchman's pretty daughter or the new schoolteacher, twirling his broad-brimmed hat bashfully in his hands, a business continued by movie cowboys from Anderson's time to John Wayne's. Because of Anderson's winning characterization, moviegoers of all ages returned week after week to follow the fortunes of their hero—and friend—in *Broncho Billy's Adventure* (December 1911), *Why Broncho Billy Left Bear Country* (September 1913), or *Broncho Billy and the Revenue Agent* (January 1916).[16]

After creating and naming his character, Anderson's next step was to put Broncho Billy into exciting plots. With a commitment to themes of the West and to entertaining mass audiences, Anderson chose adventure stories that told of a hero's quest to attain a worthwhile goal, in the course of which he overcomes formidable obstacles in the face of strong opposition. The more courage and determination it took to attain the goal and the more the hero had to remain on guard, the more audiences would be concerned with the story's outcome. The chain of events involving the hero had to build with mounting intensity and be resolved in a satisfying conclusion. After dramatic complications and reverses, when he finally achieved his goal of the restoration of order—the defeat of villainy and the rescue of innocence—Broncho Billy once more won the day. In these plots—and in the many variations, which would keep audiences returning to see Broncho Billy films time after time—one aspect remained constant: justice always triumphed. The villain was always defeated; the hero, no matter what human weaknesses he possessed, always adhered to the right. These were wholesome movies for the entire family, which parents could allow their children to see on their own.

As early as 1939 Professor Lewis Jacobs, in his *Rise of the American Film*, hailed Anderson's formulation of the Western "code":

The cowboy, a fresh and colorful character, was introduced in the Broncho Billy series . . . but with time the frontier became more than a picturesque and exciting locale for movie dramas. By 1909 it was a forceful expression of democratic feeling and moral standards—more forceful, perhaps, than the deliberate morality dramas. Rugged individualism and the triumph of the best man were epitomized in the world of open spaces, where men ruled by democratic community, action, and a sense of honor. . . . Always the Western hero was busy righting wrongs, doing the seemingly impossible through determination and fearlessness, protecting the weak, and thus winning fortune and the girl he loved.[17]

Twenty-five years earlier, contemporary reviewers also had been impressed by the effectiveness of Anderson's plots. For example, a critic wrote:

There's a big, powerful plot in this splendidly dramatic photoplay of life in the West. It is a story that might really be true, for its plot is founded on the early wars of the cattle and shepherd kings of the great Western ranges when these were trackless, fenceless, grazing pastures. It is a story told in a manner which convinces.[18]

Besides characterization and plot, the third element in Anderson's design—setting—was central from the beginning. He had found that the cinematographic eye, hungry for reality, mercilessly revealed painted theatrical vistas as shams. Discarding stage tradition, Anderson trained his cameras on authentic natural settings of pictorial charm so that the actual world, with its breeze-ruffled trees and flashing streams, its rocky canyons and wind-swept plains, its sweating horses and dusty riders, emerged in his films with all the stunning impact of reality.

Anderson's superior locations were enhanced by the artistry of photographer Jess Robbins. The camera and lenses used then would seem primitive today. The film stock also was crude—red photographed as black and men with ruddy complexions had to be photographed carefully so that their faces did not look dark; blue photographed as white and made the sky appear to be an empty, cloudless void. It required constant care to maintain balanced photographic values so that sunlit objects did not appear harsh and glaring, or shadowed places, dark and murky. Robbins's assistant, Roland ("Rollie") Totheroh, of San Anselmo, Marin County, went on to become a cameraman for all the major films of Charles Chaplin. These cameramen often had to work under conditions of real danger, such as filming head-on horse charges, cliff-side rescues, or free-for-all fights under a hail of bottles or bullets. Despite these difficulties, and the limitations of the equipment, Essanay's cinematography often received professional acclaim, as in this review of *Western Hearts* (June 1912):

Taken under the brilliant sunlight of California, the photographic quality of the production is well-nigh perfect, and is a rare treat in clean-cut, clear, snappy values.

Or of *Broncho Billy's Bible* (June 1912):

Unusually beautiful natural scenery abounds

throughout the film, and the scenes in the foothills are particularly fine . . . the audience viewing the characters from far down the canyon, with the plains stretching away to the dim and smoky hills. The photography of all Essanay Western subjects, taken under natural sunlight, is well-nigh perfect, and this film is especially attractive in beautiful tonal values.[19]

In the making of these outdoor-adventure Westerns—after character, story, and setting were established—Anderson let the details of the action arise from the natural surroundings. Free from the burdens of elaborate preplanning and cumbersome technical equipment, Anderson was able to bring forth convincing and apparently spontaneous stories of the actual West. In tune with the environment, he let it speak to him, and it is this that gave his films such absolutely convincing authenticity.

Critic James S. McQuade of the *Moving Picture World* wrote admiringly:

> I was an eager spectator of the wild scenes as they were unfolded, the breakneck speeding of horses along winding roads, the harsh atmosphere in which the men and women of the West moved some forty years ago . . . the punishment of the low-down critter, the rescue of the innocent, and the triumph of the hero . . . are witnessed with increasing interest until the net is drawn tight. . . . In it we have a typical Western story, of the Broncho Billy brand, abounding in thrilling incidents. . . . The production has been carefully made.[20]

That these Essanay Westerns were "carefully made" was due in no small degree to the dedicated work of Anderson's team of artists and technicians. Typical among them was Josephine Rector, the scenario department chief. Early in 1911 Rector submitted some story ideas that showed understanding of the company's need to have available a number of story variations when all stories centered around one central character. She was soon put on the payroll, first at fifteen dollars per week, then at twenty-five dollars per week—a good salary

Two units working simultaneously on Essanay lot. Actor Harry Todd in shirtsleeves, at left; chief carpenter Lorin Abrott in overalls, center; "Spider" Roach, double, wearing white shirt and with cap, by pole; cameraman Jess Robbins wearing hat, at far left. *(Photo from collection of Geoffrey Bell)*

Cameraman Jess Robbins—dedication to duty in a difficult location shot.
(Photo from collection of Geoffrey Bell)

Cameraman Robbins and crew—concentration on setting up a new shot in Niles Canyon. *(Photo from collection of Geoffrey Bell)*

Josephine Rector in *Alkali Ike's Bride* (1912), with Augustus Carney and Johnson. *(Photo from collection of Geoffrey Bell)*

Marguerite Clayton, one of the most popular of Essanay leading ladies. *(Photo from collection of Geoffrey Bell)*

Frederick Church, juvenile lead. *(Photo from collection of Geoffrey Bell)*

Wallace Beery as a director. *(Photo permission of Los Angeles County Museum of Natural History, Los Angeles)*

in days when many families lived on sixty dollars per month. Many of her story ideas were culled from pulp magazines, such as *Argosy;* others, from books in the Oakland Public Library. From these, Essanay evolved basic formula plots for Western movies: the "ranch" story, with ranchers versus rustlers, or cattlemen versus sheepmen; the "revenge" story, with the relentless pursuit of the evil-doer and the redress of a grievance; the "marshall" story, with the dedicated man of the law; the "outlaw" story, with the conflict between good and evil; and various combinations of these basics. A comely young woman, Rector also appeared in films, earning an additional five dollars per day. She played the heroine in *Alkali Ike's Bride* (May 1912). She also functioned as both scriptwriter and actor in *The Dance at Silver Gulch* (November 1912). Billed as "a stirring Western story of the border country," *Dance* ends with a scene in which the hero saves the day with his wild ride to the sheriff's office, and "reaches the office just as the posse is returning from their search, is congratulated, and starts back with the girls as the punchers give him a rousing cheer."[21]

Josephine Rector chose love over a career when she married Hal Angus, an actor with the Essanay company. Mr. Angus later played the lead in the documentary film about the Essanay company, *The Movies Go West* directed by the author. Meanwhile, in the Chicago Essanay office worked Rector's counterpart, an ambitious actress-writer named Louella Parsons, who became one of the first to write about the personalities of the movies.[22]

The scenario department, the camera crew, the players—all working with Gilbert M. Anderson—made up an ensemble whose contributions resulted in an amazing, uninterrupted succession of box-office successes. Such a picture was the Essanay adventure story *Broncho Billy's Surrender* (July 1915), reviewed in the *New York Dramatic Mirror*:

> Owing to the brutality of her husband, a young girl takes her child and runs away to the West, where she obtains a position as a schoolteacher. Later, Broncho Billy, a bandit, is pursued by the sheriff and wounded in the arm. He takes refuge with the school mistress, and she is successful in putting the sheriff off the trail. Later, her dissolute husband appears, and after beating his wife, makes way with the child, boarding the stagecoach for the purpose of leaving the town. But it is at that psychological moment that Broncho Billy decides to hold up the stage. He recognizes the child and takes it back to its mother. He is just in time to run into the sheriff, and is forced to surrender.[23]

With Gilbert M. Anderson in the title role, the girl in the film was played by blond Marguerite Clayton. Other leading ladies in other pictures were likely to be brunette Evelyn Selbie, or the equally pretty Bessie Sankey or Ruth Saville. Sheriffs were portrayed by Arthur Mackley or Lee Willard; "dissolute husbands" or other menaces, by True Boardman or Roy Clement; and Broncho Billy's pals, by juveniles Frederick Church or Emory Johnson.

With the exception of Wallace Beery, then in minor roles, few of the players with the Essanay company are known today. Many were hired, as needed, from local theatrical stock companies; others were called in because they looked the part and could ride a horse. All came and went little noticed, as if they were just other elements of the vast, overarching background of the great out-of-doors. Among the most enduringly popular of the players with names unknown to movie fame were the cowboys. Recruited from rodeos and ranches, they were the real thing. Some substituted for the principals in the many dangerous scenes. Cowboy Bill Cato, for instance, executed the stunt scenes for Anderson; tough hombre "Texas" George was an expert marksman, whose bullet always found its mark; and professional boxer "Spider" Roach doubled in hand-to-hand combat. Anderson was never a cowboy, horseman, or sharpshooter, and in order to make his pictures better he hired experts. In this, he initiated the use of the movie double.

With Essanay's cowboys, marksmen, and athletes, inevitably came high spirits as well. The bars in Niles did a roaring business. "All the movie people were two-fisted drinkers," recalled a local police officer, Leon Solon. There were complaints, as well, that Essanay's wild-riding gang hardly left a building that was not plugged with bullets. With all this excitement, it is a wonder that any films were made at all. But they were—one picture a week was completed by Anderson's Essanay team and sent forth to delight nickelodeon audiences throughout the entire United States, and overseas as well.[24]

Western action melodramas were not the only movie fare produced by Essanay in Niles. If the major unit of the studio was on location making Western dramas, or if Anderson was on a trip to the main office in Chicago, the sets, props, horses, and remaining members of the studio staff were employed in Western comedies. These Essanay one-reelers—actually farces relying heavily on slapstick—were set in a fictional Snakeville, peopled by such characters as "Alkali Ike," played by Augustus Carney, "Mustang Pete," played by

Ben Turpin and Charles Chaplin in *A Night Out* (1915). (*Photo permission of Academy of Motion Picture Arts and Sciences, Beverly Hills*)

"The A.B.C.s of Filmdom, 1914." Essanay actors Anderson, at right; Francis X. Bushman (then a top box-office draw), at left, and Chaplin, center. *(Photo permission of Los Angeles County Museum of Natural History, Los Angeles)*

A Jitney Elopement (1915). Chaplin, Edna Purviance, Leo White. *(Photo permission of Museum of Modern Art—Film Stills Archive, New York)*

The Tramp (1915). Chaplin, Paddy McGuire, Fred Goodwins. *(Photo permission of Museum of Modern Art—Film Stills Archive, New York)*

The Tramp (1915). Chaplin-—and Niles Canyon. *(Photo permission of Museum of Modern Art—Film Stills Archive, New York)*

Brinsley Shaw, or "Slippery Slim," played by slender Victor Potel. The Snakeville series began at San Rafael with *Alkali Ike's Auto* (May 1911) and continued with such shenanigans as *How Slippery Slim Went for the Eggs* (January 1915) and *What Others Started Sophie Finished* (July 1915).

One Essanay comedian, who went on to fame in Mack Sennett comedies, was Ben Turpin. Turpin turned a serious handicap, crossed eyes, into an asset when appearing in vaudeville as the comic-strip character "Happy Hooligan." Joining Anderson shortly after Essanay was formed, Turpin continued to practice comedy routines at Niles—doing double somersaults into bars, falling into horse troughs, appearing as "September Morn" in local parades—endearing himself to the everyday people of Niles.[25]

Another Essanay comedian of a quite different disposition was Charles Chaplin. Anderson first saw Chaplin at San Francisco's Empress (now the St. Francis theater), where Chaplin was performing in *A Night in an English Music Hall.* Though he

had heard favorable reports about the comedian's pantomime and timing, Anderson was still not prepared for Chaplin's deftness. Knowing, through his showman's intuition, that Chaplin would make superb movie material, Anderson immediately went backstage and introduced himself. After the show, and over supper at the Hotel St. Francis—where Anderson relished being deferred to as "the millionaire cowboy"—Anderson asked Chaplin if he would like to try the new medium of the movies and make comedies with his Essanay company. Any contract would have to be approved by Spoor in Chicago, and while Spoor was deliberating, Chaplin was snapped up by Mack Sennett in Los Angeles. After a short time, however, Chaplin realized that his finesse was lost in the frenetic Sennett comedy mayhem. Anderson then reopened negotiations with the added lure of promising Chaplin a free hand with his material.[26]

Initially, Chaplin was to work at the Essanay studio in Chicago. Spoor, however, proved to be less than accomodating, and after completing *His New Job* in the Windy City, Chaplin begged to return to California. Grudgingly, Spoor agreed to let Chaplin go to Essanay's West Coast studio. After shooting *A Night Out* with Ben Turpin however, Chaplin was still dissatisfied—the casual atmosphere of the Niles studio, he felt, did not provide the seclusion he needed for his work. Anderson's attempts to make his new star comfortable—including Anderson's making a guest appearance in Chaplin's boxing comedy, *The Champion*—failed. Chaplin remained unhappy, not only with his working conditions, but also with Niles, the cows and chickens and other rustic elements of which were alien to the London-bred comedian.[27]

These trials for Chaplin were offset by a delicious diversion—the selection of a leading lady. Anderson had offered him the company's best, but Chaplin, more attuned to San Francisco's attractions, found his ideal in Edna Purviance, who, originally from Nevada, was one of the blond lovelies at Tait's Cabaret on O'Farrell Street, near Powell. The poise of the statuesque Purviance made her a perfect foil for Chaplin's high-keyed antics. Always reacting to him with just the right note of amused surprise, she remained Chaplin's leading lady in many comedies to come.

At the Essanay studio near San Francisco Bay, Chaplin completed five films. The exteriors for *A Night Out* (February 1915) and *The Champion* (March 1915) were shot in and around Niles and Oakland; and those for *A Jitney Elopement* (April

1915) and *In the Park* (March 1915), in and around San Francisco and Golden Gate Park. Through his work in these light-hearted exercises, Chaplin was evolving many of his screen techniques. In his final comedy of the series, *The Tramp* (April 1915), he arrived at his inimitable cinematic style. In this brilliant film Chaplin created a screen comedy that, more than a succession of slapstick incidents, told a real story with a beginning, development, and ending—a story told innovatively, with laughter underscored by pathos.

Just as Anderson's stories of the frontier West grew out of their environment, so Chaplin's story of the tramp grew out of the country setting of Niles, giving an authenticity to the film that no studio settings could. The germ of the story was sparked by the actor's chance meeting with a real tramp in San Francisco. The man told Chaplin about the joys and sorrows of a hobo's life—unburdened, he carried his few possessions tied in a bandana; if hungry, he could always eat grass; if troubled, he could always move on.

Chaplin's *Tramp* opens on a country road. A tramp enters, sporting a cane—indicating that he has ideals of elegance—and carrying a little bundle of worldly goods—which establishes him as an individual, one as real as the country road itself. Later, the tramp dines fastidiously on a handful of grass, transformed into a gourmet delicacy by a dash of salt. In time, after a series of incidents, he finds a haven on a farm, where he begins working, and a heaven in the imagined love of the farmer's beautiful daughter. Discovering, however, that the girl is already engaged, the tramp knows he must leave the idyllic spot, in which he has no place. "He goes off, once more alone," writes Roger Manvell, "a small figure isolated in the straight, relentless perspective of the empty road stretching to the horizon." *The Tramp* established Chaplin's world-famous tramp characterization and also defined his classic closing scene—the final fade-out, in which the little figure, valiant though dejected, walks hopefully down a road and into a better tomorrow. When Chaplin walked down that road in Niles Canyon, he walked into history.[28]

While Chaplin's star was ascending, Anderson's was passing its zenith. The very financial success that rewarded the Essanay chief so lavishly (his annual income by 1915 was an estimated $125,000) and those traits of self-confidence and originality, which had propelled him to ascendancy, became the factors that hastened his downfall. Humanly enough, Anderson had enjoyed to the fullest his

Unsung heroes who gave the Western visual dynamism: the cameramen. *(Photo from collection of Geoffrey Bell)*

youth, fame, and wealth. The wine, women, and song of San Francisco's night life drew him like a magnet. He was besieged by alluring beauties who would do anything to get into the movies. With these temptations, he decided to expand his theatrical reach by producing musical reviews and building a theater to showcase them. Anderson's Gaiety Theatre—named after the London show house, famed for its pretty girls—opened in 1913 on O'Farrell Street (near Powell, next to Tait's Cabaret, and across from that temple of vaudeville, the original Orpheum Theatre). Among the other artists engaged for the musicals was the rotund comedienne Marie Dressler. Anderson soon found, however, that producing musicals was a business very different from producing movie Westerns. His Gaiety live-show business drained all the profits he made from his movies, while also stealing time from his work at the studio. As a result, the important Broncho Billy series suffered.[29]

There were other, subtler factors hastening the end of Anderson's career and of the Essanay company. Anderson's musical comedy venture was an

Other heroes not known by name: the cowboys. *(Photo from collection of Geoffrey Bell)*

antidote for his growing anxiety about his movie work. Underneath his apparent movie success was the corrosive realization that others were taking his Western genre and making it better. Since early 1915, the William S. Hart feature-length Westerns, produced by Thomas H. Ince, were blazing the future trail. In the face of this threat, Anderson

Still another essential for the Western: the stagecoach.
(Photo permission of Society of California Pioneers, San Francisco)

The cowboy camaraderie as celebrated by Gilbert. M. Anderson in his movie Westerns. *(Photo permission of Erwin E. Smith Collection of Range Life Photographs, Library of Congress)*

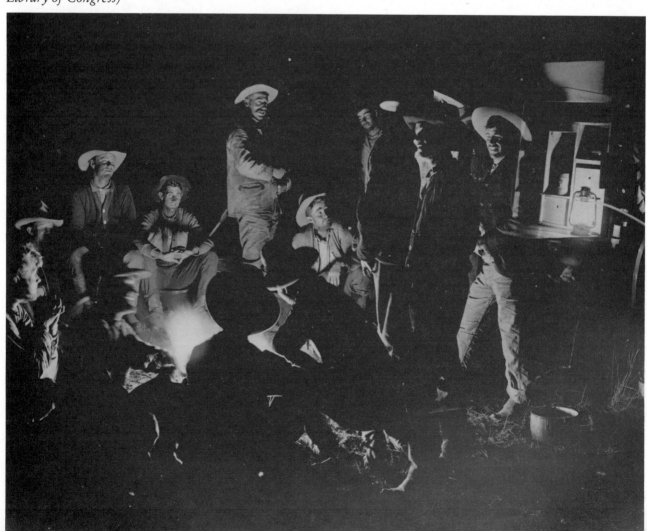

The Essanay gang: Top row: the cowboys; Middle row: Johnson, unidentified actor in top hat, Victor Potel, True Boardman, Margaret Todd, Willard, Todd, Clement; Lower row: unidentified actor with bandana, Evelyn Selbie, Anderson and Clayton. *(Photo permission of Mission Peak Heritage Foundation, Fremont)*

Broncho Billy and the Vigilante (1915). Anderson, at left; Willard, center with rope; Todd, white vest. *(Photo permission of Museum of Modern Art—Film Stills Archive, New York)*

became anxious to progress from short nickelodeon fare to feature films. Spoor, however, who controlled the business, was content to limit the company to the sure profits of the one-reel films. He estimated that the feature film was a far greater risk, both initially in production costs and in the uncertainty of audience acceptance. A one-reel film could be brought in for one thousand dollars, but a feature easily could cost from twenty-five to a hundred times more; further, audiences could forgive the producer for a dud if it was just one of a dozen offerings, but not if it was all they got for their admission fee. Other producers, like Adolph Zukor and William Fox, more attuned to the future, went on to make feature films, and their companies prospered. Spoor did not, and his decision spelled the end of Essanay.

At the same time, George K. Spoor was going through his own career reevaluation. Looking upon motion pictures as a business proposition, he was impatient with the creative aspects of production. Essanay had been useful, but now he was ready to sell out while he was still ahead. He also wanted to get away from the burden of administration in order to pursue his ambitions as an inventor. Furthermore, Spoor was becoming increas-

Broncho Billy and the Claim Jumper (1915). Clayton and Anderson. (Photo permission of Museum of Modern Art—Film Stills Archive, New York)

Broncho Billy Well Repaid (1915) (also known as Broncho Billy's Kindness Repaid). Anderson, Clayton, Willard. (Photo permission of Museum of Modern Art—Film Stills Archive, New York)

Broncho Billy's Teaching (1915). Anderson, unknown actress, Clement. (Photo permission of Museum of Modern Art—Film Stills Archive, New York)

ingly antagonistic toward partner Anderson, whose drinking bouts and absences from the studio while engaging in such injudicious activities as producing girlie shows and promoting prize fighters were hurting Essanay's profits. And this was the man with whom Spoor would have to divide the estimated million-dollar profit from the Chaplin comedies.

The tension between Spoor and Anderson mounted—Spoor furious at Anderson's carousing; Anderson impatient with Spoor's niggling. In one final incident—recalled by Bill Cato, Anderson's hard-riding double—Spoor ordered a time clock installed at the Niles studio, and Anderson, raging at the affront to his dignity, smashed the instrument with an axe and had it returned personally to "Mr." Spoor. Nothing further was heard for awhile. The company continued its usual pattern of making one Western a week. Spoor was biding his time. When Chaplin's contract ran out, Spoor did not offer to match the $670,000 per year that Chaplin was offered by another movie company, Mutual, and, as soon as Chaplin signed with Mutual, Spoor acted.[30]

On 16 April 1916, a telegram from Chicago arrived at the Niles studio. The personnel were to be dismissed; the equipment was to be sent back to headquarters; and the Niles studio building was to be boarded up and padlocked. With the final editing of *The Man in Him*—for which Anderson was scriptwriter, director, and leading actor—all production at the Essanay studio in Niles ceased. The players and technicians, who had arrived so hopefully one spring day in 1912, were scattered to the winds.[31]

While the immediate reason for the closure of the Western studio was the clash between two strong-willed men—between business and creative personalities—the closure also reflected a much broader, national trend. During its early years Essanay had enjoyed a protected position as a member of the Motion Picture Patents Company, a mo-

Broncho Billy—Guardian (1914). Potel, Anderson. *(Photo permission of Museum of Modern Art—Film Stills Archive, New York)*

Portrait signed by Anderson as "Broncho Billy." *(Photo from collection of Geoffrey Bell)*

nopoly of a few top companies that controlled the patents on movie equipment and that could thus demand that theaters show only their wares. This monopoly was bitterly contested, and in October 1915 the Supreme Court ruled that the patents company was in unlawful restraint of trade. Essanay was then placed in direct competition with energetic movie companies that had been improving their position with new feature-length films, made with increasingly lavish production values and with exciting new stars. At the same time, audiences were demanding more luxurious and comfortable theaters with improved projection facilities. The small nickelodeon movie houses no longer could compete—and nickelodeon fare had been Essanay's stock in trade.

Moreover, Anderson's specialty, the Western, was evolving. Audiences were flocking to see the new feature-length Westerns made by William S. Hart and Tom Mix. "Strong silent man" Hart, who had grown up among Indians and knew their ways, enhanced his Westerns with authentic Indian lore and background locations. Formerly a real U.S. marshal and cowhand as well, the magnetic Mix enlivened his films with athletic stunts, sharpshooting expertise, and dazzling horsemanship. Thus, both Hart and Mix could attain far more scope in the longer format than Anderson. Ironically, their initial success, to a great extent, was built on what Anderson had originated, for both used the cowboy's character traits of dauntlessness and honesty, as well as Essanay's plot patterns and moral tone. Anderson had taken the Western theme from indoor melodrama to the outdoors; now Hart and Mix were able to carry this refreshing, strong, ex-

Anderson as the Western hero. *(Photo permission of Museum of Modern Art—Film Stills Archive, New York)*

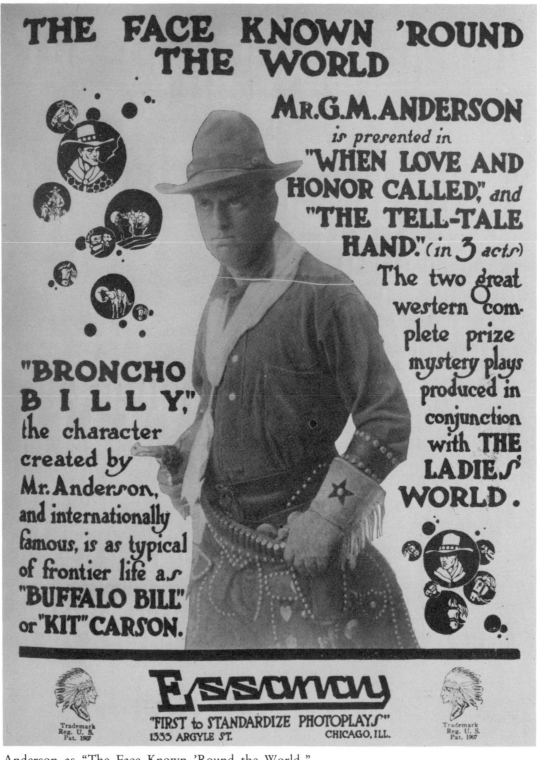

Anderson as "The Face Known 'Round the World."
(Photo from collection of Geoffrey Bell)

citing dramatic success into the full-length theatrical feature form.

Still, the Broncho Billy figure remains today as much a part of American film tradition as any characterization ever developed. It is no mean accomplishment to have created the prototype of the movie cowboy hero and to have established, artistically, the format of the classic movie Western. Even though Anderson paid the price for too sudden a success, the value of his overall achievements cannot be taken from him. Today, whenever we see a Western hero riding across a screen horizon, we can salute Gilbert M. Anderson.

CMPC logo. *(Photo from collection of Geoffrey Bell)*

3

The California Motion Picture Corporation

"A Winner!" headlined a glowing review in the authoritive *New York Dramatic Mirror,* hailing *Salomy Jane,* the first feature film produced by the San Francisco–based California Motion Picture Corporation (CMPC). Billed as "America's greatest picture play," the 1914 release was greeted by accolades from coast to coast. San Francisco critic Walter Anthony wrote, "I will not hesitate to say that in theme, dramatic treatment, and in cumulative, growing and finally thrilling interest, 'Salomy Jane' is a masterpiece of dramatic construction." The *New York Dramatic Mirror* praised its "reel after reel of gorgeous scenes . . . towering mountains threaded with winding roads, rivers breaking their way through primal forests," going on to say that "this is creating an environment in the best sense, for it does on the screen what an author aims to accomplish in his descriptive passages; it gives the characters a true background, a great, free, seemingly limitless background—the most inspiring of its kind that we recall."[1]

Salomy Jane's excellent settings reflected a growing awareness of the importance of natural locations to establish environment and to enrich dramatic value. The earlier Broncho Billy movie Westerns of Gilbert M. Anderson had made good use of authentic scenery for stories of the outdoors, but their running time was only about ten or fifteen minutes. The feature-length *Salomy Jane,* on the other hand, running seventy minutes or more, had spaciousness of time for far wider scenic effects.

"Photographically, the whole production is of the highest order; no more artistic backgrounds could possibly have been found," declared Peter Milne of the New York *Motion Picture News,* going on to praise the picture as being "so far above the average that it will stand out like a bright star."[2]

The superiority of *Salomy Jane* resulted not only from its location shooting, but also from its story source. Its author, Bret Harte, was America's foremost writer of early California mining days, and the picture was a version of his "Salomy Jane's Kiss," adapted into dramatic form by Paul Armstrong. It is a story, as described in the program for the picture's premiere at the Alcazar Theatre in San Francisco, that "harken[s] back . . . to that romantic epoch in California history known as the 'Days of '49' . . . the time of the great gold rush, of a lawless abandon redeemed by an almost paradoxical generosity and love." It tells of the romance of a prospector's fair daughter, Salomy Jane. The remote mining community in which they live is aroused by the arrival of a stranger, known only as "The Man." The stranger has come to the area to avenge the betrayal of his sister by a gambler, Baldwin. Shortly after his arrival, The Man comes upon Baldwin, who is making unwelcome advances to Salomy Jane. He then challenges Baldwin and, in the ensuing struggle, kills him. The crime occasions a meeting of the town vigilantes, who begin to search the countryside for the offender. In the midst of this excitement, Salomy Jane unex-

Star Beatriz Michelena hailed in New York. *(Photo from collection of Geoffrey Bell)*

Poster, *Salomy Jane* (1914). House Peters and Michelena. *(Photo from collection of Geoffrey Bell)*

CMPC location setting in authentic Big Trees of old West. *(Photo from collection of Geoffrey Bell and by courtesy of Cedric Clute, Letty Etzler, and Lillian Johansen)*

pectedly discovers the hiding place of the outlawed Man. In gratitude for his protecting her—and with dawning love—she brings him provisions. In time, the vigilantes, rifles in hand, discover the outlaw and bring him to trial. They decide that Baldwin's assailant is to hang, and when they ask if anyone would offer the stranger a good-bye, Salomy Jane comes forward and embraces and kisses him. That night, The Man escapes, and Salomy Jane joins him. When their flight becomes known, the vigilantes, armed and on horseback, pursue the fugitives. The vigilantes converge on the fleeing pair by the bank of a river, but the two outwit their pursuers by submerging themselves and, clinging to a log, floating down the river past their unsuspecting pursuers. Setting forth for a new life, Salomy Jane finally asks the man with whom she has eloped, "What's y'r name?"[3]

This was the first appearance on the screen of the Latin-American beauty Beatriz Michelena, who performed the title role so winsomely that she went on to star in all of the California Motion Picture Corporation's notable feature films. Though not well-known today, in 1915 she was extolled nationally as the "greatest and most beautiful artist appearing in motion pictures."[4]

Despite its record of quality feature films from 1914 to 1918, its wide and enthusiastic contemporary reviews, and its exciting female star, the California Motion Picture Corporation (CMPC) is virtually unknown today and unrecognized in movie annals. Theirs is the story of what happened to an early film company that in its time was able to compete successfully with the giants of the indus-

SAN FRANCISCO CHRONICLE, TUESDAY, JANUARY 6, 1914.

Modern Manufacturers of Motion Pictures

THE up-to-date business man and manufacturer knowing the effectiveness of judicious direct advertising is rapidly taking advantage of the Motion Picture as a medium to place his goods, labels and trade marks directly before the thousands who daily visit the movies.

The firm of Rice & Einstein, with their laboratory at 1932 Center street, Berkeley, Cal., ranks among the leaders on the Pacific Coast as producers of industrial and educational motion pictures.

The senior member of the firm, Mr. A. W. Rice, has been actively identified with the art of photography for over eighteen years. Mr. E. M. Einstein is a graduate of the University of California class of 1912, and has a finished training in the technical knowledge essential to the making of good motion pictures.

Among the many achievements of this firm in the motion picture field may be mentioned the producing of 26,000 feet of pictures for the California Viticultural Exhibition Association, for exhibition at the Panama-Pacific International Exposition in 1915, as the feature of the California wine exhibit. These pictures show the various stages

Motion Picture Concern Is Backed by Millions

California Motion Picture Corporation Has Developed in a Few Months

THE California Motion Picture Corporation, organized and incorporated during the fall just past, has developed in a few months from an idea brought home from the East by Herbert Payne, the young millionaire clubman of Menlo Park, into the strongest and most widely known moving picture concern of its age in this country. At its very beginning the advent of this company was heralded as an event of momentous importance in the motion picture activities of the Far West. It was deemed particularly significant of the place that this State is coming to hold in the production of moving pictures and the well founded anxiety of California capital to take advantage of the opportunities offered. The personnel of the new corporation represents an aggregation of many millions of dollars. Nearly every name on the board of directors

able then that a campaign directed with conscious intent to boost her scenery, climate and resources, should be conducive of greater results. It was some such idea as this that Mr. Payne gave purpose for organizing the California Motion Picture Corporation.

One of the earliest enterprises undertaken by the new company to place California prominently before the world was the "Golden Gate Weekly," a topical reel of California events. So successful has this weekly been in its attempt to mirror happenings in this State that it now has a regular booking in hundreds of photoplay houses throughout the country. Something of the esteem in which it is held may be gathered from the fact that it is the first film ever produced by a local concern which either the Orpheum or Pantages theaters accepted for their circuits. The "Golden Gate Weekly,"

Press announcement of establishment of the company.
(Photo from collection of Geoffrey Bell)

Producer-director George E. Middleton. *(Photo from collection of Geoffrey Bell and by courtesy of Cedric Clute, Letty Etzler, and Lillian Johansen)*

try. The history of the CMPC—its successful and creative years, its problems, and its ultimate demise—is a microcosm of the far wider history of the emergence of the full-length American theatrical feature film; it is set against the same tossing winds of uncertainty and human frailty that have challenged all aspiring moviemakers from that day forward.

The California Motion Picture Corporation was one of the many independent movie studios established in the formative years of the silent movies. Although many were launched by promises, IOUs, fast talk, and smooth salesmanship, the CMPC, backed by solid Nevada silver dollars, could announce that it was incorporated for one million dollars![5]

The newly organized CMPC made as its presi-

dent, Comstock mining heir Herbert Payne. More dilettante than businessman, Payne (who gave as his occupation "clubman" and sometimes "capitalist") moved among the pleasure-seekers of San Francisco's gilded society. The Payne family mansion, situated on an estate of over three hundred acres and copied after a European palace, was one of the showplaces of the Peninsula residential area south of San Francisco (it is now in use as the administration building of the Menlo Park School for Boys).[6]

The business manager of the CMPC was Alex Beyfuss. Not backed by inherited wealth, Beyfuss had worked himself up to become an advertising executive. With this background, he was able to bring to the CMPC his experience in promotion and publicity, his knowledge of accounting, and

Marin County, Mt. Tamalpais in background, studio in middle distance. *(Photo from collection of Geoffrey Bell and by courtesy of Cedric Clute, Letty Etzler, and Lillian Johansen)*

View of studio under construction. *(Photo from collection of Geoffrey Bell and by courtesy of Cedric Clute, Letty Etzler, and Lillian Johansen)*

Studio complex. Glass-enclosed stage at right; laboratory and editing rooms, foreground; housing for rolling stock, left background. *(Photo from collection of Geoffrey Bell and by courtesy of Cedric Clute, Letty Etzler, and Lillian Johansen)*

his mastery of the mysteries of double-entry bookkeeping.[7] The executive producer of the CMPC, George E. Middleton, came from a clan long prominent in the Bay Area. One of the Middleton interests was the Ocean Shore Railroad, running south through the big tree country near Boulder Creek and Felton to Santa Cruz. Another was the Middleton Motor Car Co., of San Francisco's automobile row on Van Ness Avenue. After graduating from Lowell High School and gaining experience with the automobile agency, Middleton was active with various San Francisco fairs, exposi-

tions, and automobile shows and in arranging visual displays and producing entertainment attractions.[8]

Given the fact that both the Payne and Middleton families were connected with the history and development of California and that Beyfuss was a part of the business world of San Francisco, it was natural that California, with its beauty and colorful history, should provide the setting for their new company, which the buoyant Middleton named the "California Motion Picture Corporation."

At first, the CMPC made short films advertising the Middleton automobile for showings at the 1912 San Francisco Automobile Show. Beyfuss interested other clients, and on commission the company made a number of short industrial films, among them *Winning a Peach*, hand-tinted in luscious colors, as a promotional film for the California Packing Corporation. Then, encouraged by their reception and excited by reports of quick profits from hit movies, Beyfuss persuaded Payne to finance the production of theatrical feature films.[9]

At that time, the surefire box office success was the short, one-reel movie of the nickelodeon trade. These "flickers"—ten to fifteen minutes in running time—were, for the most part, ground out with an eye for quick profit, hurriedly patched together, and rushed into small store-front movie houses for showings on a rapid-turnover, daily-change basis. But a few of these moviemakers had far higher standards. Gilbert M. Anderson of Essanay, for example, made the short film format a vehicle for taut, exciting Westerns played against the authentic

Interior of glass-enclosed stage. *(Photo from collection of Geoffrey Bell and by courtesy of Cedric Clute, Letty Etzler, and Lillian Johansen)*

scenery of the Old West. Sidney Olcott, of the Kalem Company, transcended current limitations in running time by means of imaginative location work, filming Dion Boucicault plays in Ireland and a story of the Christ in Egypt and Palestine. And D. W. Griffith, of American Biograph, directed short-story gems with increasing mastery—a typical example of which is *The New York Hat,* based on a story by Anita Loos, starring Mary Pickford and Lionel Barrymore.

Intimations, then, were in the air that the story film was ready to advance from the one-reel format to the full-length format of five to six reels. These pictures—to be presented, not in cheap movie houses one step away from the penny arcade, but in quality theaters on a parity with the dramas of the legitimate stage—were to confer prestige on the previously outcast movies. Even though the feature film was far more expensive and difficult to produce, ambitious moviemakers all across the continent, full of wide-eyed enthusiasm, were making plans in 1913 to advance into the new field. In New York a group of hopeful unknowns—Jesse Lasky, Cecil B. De Mille, and Samuel Goldfish (later Goldwyn)—were attempting, with difficulty, to raise enough money to get started in the business. Their company, known as the Lasky Feature Play Company (later to become the West Coast unit of Paramount Pictures), shakily got under way with a bare $26,500 in capital—quite in contrast to the million-dollar backing of the CMPC.

Financing was an important element in organizing a motion picture studio, but even more essential was experience. While the prime movers of the CMPC had only the energy of their idea, both Lasky and De Mille had considerable on-the-spot working knowledge of theatrical production methods—Lasky, as a performer and as a producer of vaudeville acts; and De Mille, as a dramatist and actor on the legitimate stage under David Belasco. The officials of the CMPC, despite their total inexperience in show business, rushed to compete with professionals like Lasky and De Mille. Other new companies, equally ambitious to achieve dominance and permanency, included such proud names as Biograph, Bosworth, Lubin, Majestic, Morosco, Mutual, Pallas, Reliance, Rex, Selig, Solax, Thanhouser, and Vitagraph. Joining their ranks, the CMPC, with all the exuberance of youth (president Payne was only twenty-seven) proudly emblazoned on its logo—a California bear rampant on an outline map of the state—"Our Trademark, we have determined, shall, whenever flashed on the screen, immediately connote the ultimate achievement in picture producing art."[10]

Inspired by this ideal, the CMPC set out to find the "perfect" location for its studio. The movie business was by no means yet concentrated in Hollywood, though southern California municipalities were offering such inducements as utility and tax benefits to lure new businesses and industries to develop its miles of open land, and its realtors were enticing movie companies with assertions of year-round sunshine—a prime consideration when moviemaking was frequently at the mercy of the weather. The semiarid southern California areas provided a fairly dependable, if harsh and glaring, sunlight in those days, before its present smog problem.

Even so, weather conditions in Hollywood itself were not always ideal as Jesse Lasky, the executive producer of the Lasky Feature Play Company, wrote in his autobiography, *I Blow My Own Horn:*

> Work stopped on the open stage as soon as the sun went behind a cloud [and] . . . on a very cloudy day the cast didn't even show up, knowing there would be no shooting. If it looked like rain, the set was quickly covered with huge tarpaulins to protect the props. Cold weather brought a special plague of problems. It caused tiny flashes of static electricity inside the cameras . . .[and this] ruined the film. On chilly days a group of drawing-room sophisticates in cutaways and low evening gowns might feature goose pimples, chattering teeth, and congealed breath.[11]

Another first-hand observer, Charles Ray, a popular star who also produced his own pictures, bemoaned:

> In my first picture I was suddenly and fearfully thrust up against stern reality with a loss in the making of ninety thousand dollars. This was caused mainly by rain, which washed one of my sets down and rendered the dirt roads in such a condition as to not match up with previously shot scenes in the same sequence.[12]

Meanwhile, on the basis of extensive training in Europe, photographer Arthur Caldwell declared that the Bay Area had ideal atmosphere and lighting conditions for motion picture work. In actuality—and this could be confirmed by the official U.S. Weather Bureau statistics—there was slight difference in the number of sunny days per year between the Bay Area and the Los Angeles coastal region.

After evaluating photographic conditions throughout California, the San Francisco–based CMPC chose Marin County, across the Golden Gate from San Francisco. With nature at its most prodigal, Marin County provided an unrivaled variety of sites for motion pictures. From the county's Mount Tamalpais and other peaks of the coast range, numberless valleys ran down among meadows and woodlands to the many islands, sheltered coves, and inlets of San Francisco Bay to the east and to the rocky headlands and sweeping beaches of the Pacific Ocean to the west. Nearby, in and around the great Sacramento–San Joaquin Valley, were scenic locations on a vast scale, with plains, rivers, and lakes, and, beyond, the evergreen forests and peaks of the titanic Sierra Nevada.

In view of these rich scenic resources, the CMPC built its studio and production plant on open ranch lands near San Rafael, in northern Marin. Its white-painted wooden buildings were purely utilitarian in design, the most conspicuous feature of which was a covered stage—30 feet high, 100 feet long, and 60 feet deep—with walls of large panes of glass. This glass stage, like an extraordinarily large photography studio, was designed for filming interior scenes by natural light. One of the great advantages of California was its year-round photographic conditions. Movie studios in the East often had to make use of artificial illumination, particularly during long, dark winter months but the lamps available at the time were cumbersome fire hazards, producing only crude effects and, at best, illuminating only a small playing area. California sunlight, tempered by overhead muslin diffusers, produced more even lighting for interior scenes. The glass stage of the CMPC studio adjoined a two-story office and dressing-room building and an extension housing the carpentry and plaster shops of the set construction crew. A separate building contained the laboratory, projection rooms, and film editing areas. Other structures included a commissary–dining room and a commodious barn for rolling stock. On the lot was ample space for exterior sets.[13]

In addition the CMPC maintained a ranch for large-scale exterior scenes in the Big Tree Country near Boulder Creek, Santa Cruz County. Undoubtedly, a factor in the selection of a site in another county was the Middleton family's considerable interests in and around Boulder Creek, which stood to benefit from movie business. Nepotism or no, CMPC technicians constructed on the site, with its background of evergreen forests, an authentically designed exterior set representing a gold rush village. This was one of the first movie "Western streets," and it was so convincing that it was later leased to a number of Hollywood movie companies. Among the pictures later shot there were Cecil B. De Mille's *Romance of the Redwoods,* starring Mary Pickford; Marshall Neilan's *M'Liss,* also starring Mary Pickford; and such Thomas H. Ince productions as *The Primal Lure* and *The Aryan,* starring William S. Hart, and *The Half Breed,* starring Douglas Fairbanks.[14]

To further equip the studio for the production of California themes of the Old West, the CMPC staff assembled a large collection of historical furniture and props. Some of these they obtained as loans or donations from early Marin County settler families and interested citizens; some were obtained from curio and second-hand stores. Other historical acquisitions included such rolling stock as ox carts, Spanish *carettas,* and prairie schooners. Nor did the studio overlook that vehicle which was to become classic in the movie Western—the Wells Fargo stagecoach. A veteran Wells Fargo driver, Dan Bart, was hired to handle the reins, while equestrian events were supervised by Don Nicholas Covarrubias, a bona fide descendant of the Spanish conquistadores who, in his earlier days, had served as a U. S. marshall.[15]

The CMPC's earlier industrial films had been made under improvised conditions; but as soon as the plant was completed in San Rafael, everything was ready for full-scale production. The new studio's organization and equipment were tested in a newsreel series, *The Golden Gate Weekly,* under the direction of Earl Emlay, a former actor with the Alcazar Theatre stock company in San Francisco. *The Golden Gate Weekly* was aimed for vaudeville houses, such as the Orpheum, as a novel nonverbal opening act. Typical subjects included scenes of hunting wild geese on the lower Sacramento River or a production of *Robin Hood* at the Greek Theatre in Berkeley. Though pleasant enough, they lacked immediacy—the equipment and personnel available could film predictable events but were not mobile enough to film on-the-spot coverage of exciting unplanned happenings such as fires, street accidents, or athletic triumphs. One of its pictures, even so, was of unusual anthropological interest—a film record of the indigenous California Indian, Ishi, the last of his tribe, who had lived in nature completely apart from the white man. After he was discovered in Northern California, Ishi was under the protection of Al-

fred L. Kroeber, the distinguished authority on Indian lore. A reel of the CMPC movie of Ishi was
given to the anthropology department of the University of California, but like so many films of its
day, it deteriorated with time, and apparently no
copy has survived—only a series of still photographs remain.[16]

The CMPC's *Golden Gate Weekly* was useful as
an exercise, but the important task ahead was to
channel the company's entire energies into the
making of the theatrical feature film. In addition to
Earl Emlay of *The Golden Gate Weekly,* the CMPC
engaged William Nigh as a director. Nigh's original
name was Emil Kruschke—he had adopted an
Anglican name for a career as an actor on the legitimate stage. Nigh later continued as a director for
Universal and other studios. To assist these directors were scriptwriters Charles Kenyon—news-
paperman and aspiring dramatist—and Leslie T.
Peacocke, whose movie scripts included the box-
office hit *Neptune's Daughter.*

Visual effects were under the direction of Edwin B. Willis, later of MGM, whose background in
theater arts gave him the professional expertise to
design and to dress sets with striking effectiveness.
His work probably was seen to best advantage in
the CMPC feature film *The Woman Who Dared,* a
drama, which, set in Rome, won high praise for its
convincing Italian atmosphere. The combined
knowledge and understanding of camera artists
Frank Padilla, Robert Carson, and Arthur Powelson enabled the CMPC to achieve the highest quality of photographic image. Like Nigh and Willis,
Carson and Powelson later continued their movie
careers in Hollywood. Padilla, who was from a
California Spanish-American family, remained in
San Francisco as a high-caliber still photographer.

Superior photography was an important factor in
the production of the feature film. In the earlier
nickelodeon pictures, eyestrain was a common
complaint of patrons in their efforts to follow a
hodgepodge of murky shadows, glaring light
flares, and flickering and out-of-focus scenes. Such
crudities would be intolerable in a feature film of an
hour or more, and so in time the function of the
cameraman was advanced from that of merely recording a scene on film to that of furthering the
mood, atmosphere, and dramatic effectiveness of
movies. He became a cinematographer with highly
developed technical and artistic photographic
skills.

The immediate task of the CMPC technicians
was to expand what they knew about making the

short film to enable them to make a film six or
more times longer. But the feature film could not
be made by merely extending a short film; the technique had to be vastly different. Financially, advance funding was required, and money would be
tied up far longer until the returns came from the
box office. Logistically, a far larger technical crew
was required to keep track of all the complex elements of the work, which extended over a month
or more. The actors, for instance, had to be scheduled to work at different times during the weeks of
shooting. Even the weather was a far greater problem—exteriors for a short film usually could be
completed in one or two days, but it required careful planning to match exterior scenes taken weeks
apart. Organizationally, a feature-length film was
far more exacting. A short film, often shot in a day
or so, had its own momentum, but when scenes
were filmed at different places and times (sometimes extending over a month or more), meticulous
care was required to ensure that the mosaic of individual scenes coalesced into a seamless, unified
whole. The mood and tempo of the successive
scenes had to be consistent in matching scenes and
to build with intensity to the climax. Scenes that,
when shot, seemed lively and significant might,
when edited, appear static, dull, empty, or confus-
ing. The director had to make clear the passage of
time, to introduce several sets of characters and
situations convincingly, and to control the various
plot lines so that the audience would understand
what was happening at all times.

At the Biograph studio in New York, D. W.
Griffith was finding ways to solve these problems
in cinematic terms, but his films were still in the
short one- or two-reel form. The few feature films
that might have served as patterns were imports,
such as the Italian *Cabiria,* slow-moving pageants
lacking convincing characters or dynamic plots. In
the absence of movie models to guide them, it was
inevitable that aspiring moviemakers would look to
the successful dramatic forms of the theater.

A valuable theater resource already existed in San
Francisco and in surrounding cities. The region's
many dramatic, musical, and vaudeville playhouses
had available a wealth of trained actors and stage
technicians. Then, too, the theater had evolved
techniques from which the new movies could
draw—how to construct compelling plots, establish convincing characterizations, and achieve eye-
appealing spectacle. These three attributes were
combined in ways particularly adaptable to the
movies in the genre of melodrama. Although the

word *melodrama* suggests a form of musical theater, musical accompaniments, which originally played a prominent part in its presentations, had long since been minimized. Melodrama was an ideal model for silent moviemakers to follow because it depended on action-filled plots, clear-cut characterizations, and realistic spectacle.

The plots of melodrama unfolded in a quick succession of scenes toward a sensational climax. The aim of melodrama was suspense and thrills, and to achieve this end, one of its most effective devices was parallel action, in which two or more story lines progressed concurrently through many changes of scene, until they converged and were simultaneously resolved in the plot's denouement. A classic example of parallel action is Augustin Daly's melodrama *Under the Gaslight* (1867). In its climactic scene, the protagonist is tied to the railroad tracks by the villain, and the heroine, trapped in a shed and hearing the train approaching, struggles to break free so that she can rescue him. In a background of mounting excitement, one line of action involves peril; the other, rescue. Audiences caught up in the reality of the scene would holler out the location of the concealed axe, which the harried heroine could use to escape and to save her man at the very last minute from the onrushing steam locomotive.

Simplicity of characterization was another advantage of melodrama. While traditional drama depended heavily on dialogue to reveal character, melodrama relied heavily on visual means, which proved particularly useful to silent films. Stock types included the valiant, upright, manly hero; the virtuous, and often golden-haired, heroine; the detestable, oily villain; the kindly and wise uncle, grey-haired and bespectacled; the comic female servant with hair knotted atop her head, standing with feet apart, hands on hips; and the scheming lawyer, dressed in funereal black, rubbing his hands together. Although the situations in which these characters were embroiled varied from play to play, the basic theme remained constant—after hours of anguish and spine-tingling threats to life and virtue, the wicked were punished; the virtuous, rewarded; and hard work, justice, and morality prevailed.

Besides its gratifying affirmation of traditional values, the great forte of melodrama was its ability to present realistic spectacle. Its stage effects often included such marvels as waterfalls, produced by piping water onto the stage to tumble into a trough pool; live dogs or chickens in farmyard scenes;

Exterior set on lot. *(Photo from collection of Geoffrey Bell and by courtesy of Letty Etzler)*

"Western Street" set. *(Photo from collection of Geoffrey Bell and by courtesy of Cedric Clute, Letty Etzler, and Lillian Johansen)*

horse races, with horses running on treadmills; boat races, executed in miniature with silhouettes of boats running on grooves; ocean scenes, with waves of rounded painted cut-outs and spray of rock salt; fires, with flames made of jagged red and yellow silk streamers, agitated from below by forced air and illuminated by flickering lights; and the excitement of that symbol of power and energy, the steam engine. Clever as these effects were, however, they were always necessarily limited onstage. *Under the Gaslight*, for example, had to crowd an interior of a shed with a working door and window, an exterior of a railroad track in perspective, and a three-dimensional steam locomo-

Battery of cameramen (cinematographers), Frank Padilla at left. *(Photo from collection of Geoffrey Bell and by courtesy of Cedric Clute, Letty Etzler, and Lillian Johansen)*

A consultation during filming of *Pageant of San Francisco* (1914). *(Photo from collection of Geoffrey Bell and by courtesy of Cedric Clute, Letty Etzler, and Lillian Johansen)*

editing. The movies could put the spectator into the best possible viewpoint for each part of each scene, so that, like the day-dreamer, he is always front-and-center in every situation. After the establishing shot of the entire scene by the railroad tracks, for instance, the next shot might be a close view of the agonized man tied to the tracks. His foremost thought was rescue, so the next shot pictured his thought of the rescuer, the girl in the cabin, attempting to reach him. Since the rescuer's foremost thought was reaching the victim, the next shot pictured her worries about the increasingly dire plight of the victim, perhaps a close-up of his hands tightly bound by rope to the tracks. Each alternating shot intensified the viewer's involvement in the emotionally-charged progression of events by projecting him into the minds and feelings of the protagonists. After this barrage of alternating staccato shots, hammering at the consciousness of the spectator, the final rescue, resolving the suspense and reuniting the principals, attains its maximum cumulative effect.[18]

The visual thrills; the swift, rousing plots; and the vivid characterizations of melodrama became far more convincing through the realism of photography. In motion pictures, the audience knew that the force of the steam locomotive was *real.* Many of melodrama's other special stage effects also gained in effectiveness in the movies. In order to link two scenes, the theater might mount two sets onstage and effect a scene change by dimming the lights on one set while simultaneously brightening them on the other. The movies, however, could

tive—all within the confines of the stage area, which in theaters of smaller towns might be no more than thirty feet wide and twenty feet deep.

The movies, however, could use the limitless space of the outdoors and, with the realism of photography, could show a man tied to an actual railroad track in the path of an entire steam train. This exterior scene, spliced with the matching interior scene of the beleaguered heroine in the shed (filmed at some other convenient time and place), attained a smashing intensity through the new art of film

Pageant of San Francisco, exterior set on lot. *(Photo from collection of Geoffrey Bell and by courtesy of Cedric Clute, Letty Etzler, and Lillian Johansen)*

easily blend two successive scenes by a lap dissolve on film, so that the first scene appeared to flow into the second. On the stage, actors or animals could be made to appear to be progressing by mounting them on treadmills before unrolling backgrounds; the movies could carry the spectator along with the actors by photographing the scene with a camera mounted on wheels in a tracking shot. In the theater, attention might be drawn to an actor's expressions or gestures by a spotlight; but the movies could rivet the audience's attention with a close-up.

In time, more and more of these cinematic possibilities were used by the CMPC as it gained experience in feature-film production. For example, *The Unwritten Law* (1915) revealed an imaginative use of the close-up in making an inanimate object a dramatic agent. In the drama's courtroom scene, the jury's verdict was emphasized by close-ups of the verdict slips as they were successively passed to the foreman. "The audience is thus held in a double suspense," admiringly commented a contemporary critic. "He is forced to wonder, first, at the appearance of the slip, what the writing on the next will be; and, secondly, since a minority of opinions only is conveyed, he is left for the moment wondering what the final verdict will be. The effects are pyramided."[19]

According to contemporary reviews, however, the CMPC's first feature film, *The Pageant of San Francisco* (1914), still relied largely on outdoor spectacle. Doubtless planned to capitalize on the Panama Pacific International Exposition, scheduled to open in San Francisco in 1915, *Pageant* also was an expression of the CMPC's original intent to make movies that drew from the history of California. This picture of the early West was enlivened with cavalcades of caballeros, led by Don Nicholas Covarrubias, bands of Indians, Yankees in broad-brimmed hats, senoritas in mantillas, and monks in long robes and sandals—contrasting the simple pastoral life of the missions with the wild abandon of the gold rush bonanza days, with a realism and scope possible only on film. Adroitly combining the appeal of patriotism, religion, and nostalgia, the piece was to pave the way for an even grander production, *Gold!*, based on the momentous discovery of gold in California. Yet, despite this ambitious ideal and the widespread appeal of stories based on the colorful history of the Far West, this plan was abandoned in favor of producing films depending on a different type of attraction.[20]

By 1914 it was clear that a surefire source of immediate box-office returns lay in the star system.

In New York shrewd producers were already building their movies around popular personalities like Mary Pickford. So the CMPC wanted to bank on its own star. A constellation of talent was available to them from the many theaters, vaudeville houses, and cabarets operating in San Francisco, Oakland, San Jose, Sacramento, and other cities. San Francisco's Alcazar Theatre alone could boast a galaxy of stars of international renown, including such favorites as Theodore Roberts, Marjory Rambeau, Bert Lytell, Bessie Barriscale, Forrest Stanley, Laurette Taylor, Edmund Lowe, Alice Brady, Mary Boland, and Lon Chaney, all of whom went on to notable careers in motion pictures. Others in the area, yet to be "discovered," included Ruth Roland, Jean Hersholt, Lois Wilson, John Gilbert, Irene Rich, David Butler, Aileen Pringle, Frank Fay, and Eric Von Stroheim.[21]

Out of all these stellar personalities, the one making the biggest impression on the CMPC management was Beatriz Michelena, "the California Prima Donna." This Latin-American artiste had been successful primarily in musical comedy. Her mentor and drama coach, Fernando Michelena,

A Star is created—Beatriz Michelena! *(Photo from collection of Geoffrey Bell and by courtesy of Cedric Clute, Letty Etzler, and Lillian Johansen)*

had been a leading tenor with San Francisco's Tivoli Opera Company. Although spoken of as her "father" (it was whispered that Beatriz was not really his daughter but his "protégée"), Fernando proved to be the ideal Pygmalion to the Galatea Beatriz. He was kindly, humanitarian, gentle, and solid, whereas Beatriz was volatile, vivacious, and flighty. Like a young hummingbird, Beatriz needed a secure nest and attentive nurturing to flourish. Fernando supplied this; he played the role of protector, companion, and, it was rumored, lover. It was a safe relationship, and though Beatriz was to be known by many men, Fernando remained her only true love.

Michelena could depend on Fernando for sound advice and guidance in her theatrical career. His life-long experience on the opera stage had given him a command of techniques for playing many different roles. In one performance he might be the swordsman Manrico in the tragedy *Il Trovatore* ("The Troubador"); in the next he might be the suave Almaviva in the comedy *The Barber of Seville*. From this wealth of knowledge, Fernando trained Beatriz in theater crafts, teaching her how to make gestures with simplicity and authority, to establish a characterization, and to build intensity. By the time she had reached early womanhood, she was well prepared as an actress. Her body was lithe and well-formed, and she had learned to use it as an instrument. She could move across a room in varying ways to express different moods and use her hands expressively and gracefully to convey emotion. Above all, she could make her eyes light up so as to appear to be wells of emotion, in a rippling spectrum from livid anger to warm caresses. Alive, vibrant, compelling, Michelena was a magnificent actress who used her craft just as well in her private life to convince others that she was interested in them when she was actually working for her own ends. Perhaps she was not so much a bird as a glittering, jeweled dragonfly.

Michelena's seductive beauty, vivacious style, and Spanish-American background made the raven-haired enchantress an ideal California *favorita* type, while her proficiency in horsemanship and with the lariat lent conviction to her portrayals of a woman of the frontier West. In addition, her appearances on the stage in such musical comedies as *Princess Chic*, *Peggy from Paris*, and *Girl from Dixie*, gave her the assurance of an accomplished professional. When, in time, she was featured artist at the San Francisco Automobile Show of 1913, exhibit manager George Middleton was captivated

by her abilities and joi de vivre. Both were possessed by the same ambitions—to soar in the world of entertainment. While Middleton was working on *Pageant*, the two were married. On Middleton's not impartial urging to the CMPC's Payne and Beyfuss, Michelena was given a screen test, which proved her to be in all ways photogenic and which revealed—in addition to her evident Latin beauty and grace—that she was that rara avis, an emotional actress of magnetism, intensity, and passion. In other words, a star.[22]

Charmed by Michelena and aware of the enormous profits earned by Mary Pickford's pictures, the CMPC management regularly cast her in film romances featuring an alluring young woman rather than the more expensive, more risky historical epics. Scrapping the plans for *Gold!* was the first step in this concentration on stories of romance. Projects originally designed to advertise the attractions of the state of California were redesigned to advertise the attractions of Michelena. Historical artifacts of museum quality were turned into background props for love stories. In place of dramas bursting with the power and energy of

Bret Harte, late 1860s. *(Photo permission of Bancroft Library, University of California, Berkeley)*

California's lumbering, mining, shipping, or harvesting industries, the CMPC's themes of the pioneer West were turned into idylls of the wooing of a wistful maiden by a gallant suitor amid the flowers and sunlight of an idealized Golden West.

Granted that the decision of the CMPC to channel its studio operations into the production of love stories was logical in view of the enduring appeal of romance in literature, stage, and screen, the choice had to be justified by the selection of certified story sources that would take full advantage of the company's regional resources. The CMPC could have drawn from any number of California writers, including such internationally known favorites as Robert Louis Stevenson, Mark Twain, Jack London, Gertrude Atherton, or Peter B. Kyne. One particularly promising source was Kathleen Norris, a native of Marin County, whose best-selling romances were to prove their strong box-office value repeatedly in such popular movies as *Change of Heart* or *Second-Hand Wife*. The Kathleen Norris stories—with their appropriateness for audi-

ences of the day, warm, human appeal, and delightful heroines—could have made unusually attractive vehicles for the company and for an actress like Michelena.[23]

There still remained, however, the commitment by the CMPC to motion pictures about California history, a genre in which the company had heavily invested. Given Bret Harte's renown for his stories drawn from California's history and given the success of his *Salomy Jane*, the CMPC negotiated exclusive rights to all of Harte's literary work. To ensure authenticity, the CMPC engaged Harte's daughter, Jessamy, as historical consultant. With confidence that its scripts would supply that attribute known in the trade as "class"—that is to say, something that adds an atmosphere of certified quality to the still artistically questionable medium of the movies—and that its star, Michelena, would supply that dimension, later known as "sex appeal," the company embarked on the production of theatrical feature films. After acquiring basic techniques from the stage-trained Emlay and Nigh,

Middleton, Bret Harte's daughter, Michelena. *(Photo from collection of Geoffrey Bell and by courtesy of Cedric Clute, Letty Etzler, and Lillian Johansen)*

Peters and Michelena in a scene from *Salomy Jane*. *(Photo from collection of Geoffrey Bell and by courtesy of Cedric Clute, Letty Etzler, and Lillian Johansen)*

George Middleton served as the director.

Eyewitnesses recall the filming of *Salomy Jane*, the first of these Westerns, along the Russian River, near Monte Rio in Sonoma County. Townspeople and vacationers at that popular summer resort town were intrigued by the appearance of the CMPC crew—with their cameras and light reflectors, bands of horses and riders, brightly costumed and theatrically made-up actors and actresses, and pretty heroine and stalwart hero. Onlookers became even more excited when, during the filming of a cliff-side scene, fearless equestrian Jack Holt jumped his horse off the cliff, and both rider and horse fell fifty feet into the river without the benefit of a double or of trick special-effects photography![24]

Michelena's masculine counterpart in *Salomy Jane* was House Peters. This actor had come to motion pictures from leading roles on the London, New York, and Canadian stages and was well-known for his screen appearances with Famous Players–Lasky studios. Both Michelena and Peters went on to appear in other CMPC photoplays, yet the daring horseman of *Salomy Jane*, Jack Holt, whose capabilities and appearance were so ideally

suited for the role of the Western movie hero and who had so much potential for success at the box office, went totally unnoticed by the management. But then, the CMPC was not looking for a rip-roaring adventure hero, but rather a romantic type to pair with Michelena.

The Michelena-Peters team, despite the fact that both had much to gain from their association, failed to prosper. Peters, already a recognized star, assumed that his position was more important than that of newcomer Michelena and felt slighted because he was billed after Michelena and because his dressing room was merely adequate while hers was spacious. Michelena, despite her special relationship with the CMPC management, felt upstaged by Peters on the set because of his take-charge style of acting. During *Salomy Jane* things went well enough but rapidly deteriorated during the production of the folksy drama *Mrs. Wiggs of the Cabbage Patch*. Manager Beyfuss had bought the rights to this popular play before the company signed Michelena. Michelena hated the picture and resented the fact that she did not have the title role— she felt that her part of simpering Lovey Mary was

Jack Holt—a box-office bet the CMPC overlooked. *(Photo from collection of Geoffrey Bell)*

Just Squaw (1919). Michelena as an Indian maid. *(Photo from collection of Geoffrey Bell and by courtesy of Letty Etzler)*

The Lily of Poverty Flat poster (1915)—a genteel approach to the Western that withered at the box office. *(Photo from collection of Geoffrey Bell)*

too small and too unglamorous. Likewise, Peters was not happy with his role of Handsome Bob, protesting that he got too little footage and that the animals in the farm and circus scenes got too much. A long-simmering feud came to a head during the filming of one of the final scenes. Peters was to greet Michelena, and the two were to exit together. After director Middleton's call for action, Peters, with all the experienced actor's craft, moved stealthily to the best position before the camera and deliberately edged Michelena out of camera center. After a third take, Michelena's volatile Latin temper exploded, and the fiery actress delivered a smart slap across Peters's cheeks. Valuing his face as his fortune, Peters strode from the set, swearing angrily and yelling "Foul play!", vowing never to return. Although director Middleton tried to patch up the continuity in the editing process, the gaps in missing scenes were noticeable, and the picture was never a success.[25]

A new leading man, William Pike, replaced Peters. Pike, whose good looks caused many a feminine heart around the CMPC studio to flutter, had been playing second leads. Pike had come to the studio through his friend Andrew Robson, the company's dependable character actor, and, with the benefit of coaching by Robson, continued to give accomplished performances in both indoor and outdoor pictures. The classically featured Pike had both the smoothness of style for dramas and the manliness and strength of character to appear as an effective foil for Michelena in Westerns. All of the CMPC-romanticized pictures of the Old West, as their feminine titles indicated, were stories with outcomes that hinged on the matrimonial fate of the heroine: *The Lily of Poverty Flat, The Rose of the Misty Pool, A Phyllis of the Sierra, The Heart of Juanita* (filmed as *The Passion Flower*), *Just Squaw,* and *The Flame of Hellgate*—all drawn from the works of Bret Harte.[26]

The CMPC found a bonanza of story ideas in the writings of Bret Harte. His tales seemed ideal as a source of material because of his skill in evoking the atmosphere of California's "Days of '49" and in creating picturesque characters. Yet he wrote short stories, and this genre rarely had the breadth of vision, the texture, or the complex plot development of the full-length novel or drama. Harte, in fact, attempted to write plays, but only one of his works written expressly for the stage, *Sue,* was ever produced. Even this failed to hold the public and had to be withdrawn after a few performances. His *Salomy Jane* owed its success on

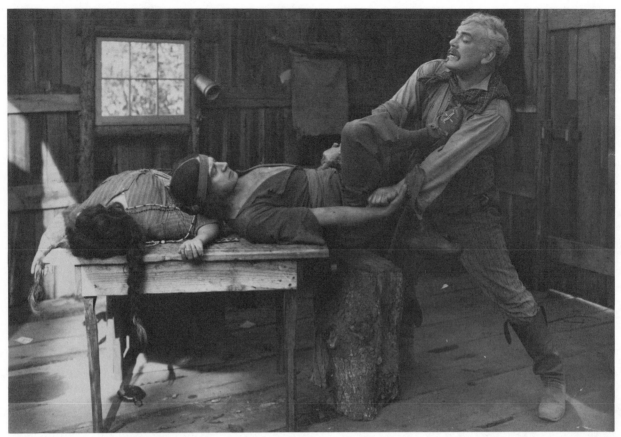

In *Just Squaw*, Andrew Robson battles a redskin. *(Photo from collection of Geoffrey Bell and by courtesy of Letty Etzler)*

Minty's Triumph (1917) (working title, *A Phyllis of the Sierra*). Robson and Michelena. *(Photo from collection of Geoffrey Bell and by courtesy of Cedric Clute, Letty Etzler, and Lillian Johansen)*

The Heart of Juanita (1919) (working title, *The Passion Flower*). Michelena and William Pike. *(Photo from collection of Geoffrey Bell and by courtesy of Cedric Clute, Letty Etzler, and Lillian Johansen)*

Michelena as a demure ingenue. *(Photo from collection of Geoffrey Bell and by courtesy of Cedric Clute, Letty Etzler, and Lillian Johansen)*

Michelena as an outcast of the underworld. *(Photo from collection of Geoffrey Bell and by courtesy of Cedric Clute, Letty Etzler, and Lillian Johansen)*

on the draw and triumphant over all opponents, such yarns were the stuff from which the classic, feature-length movie Western emerged.

But whether in Westerns or in dramas, Michelena remained the prime asset of the CMPC. The expressive, even tragic, quality of her acting justified the studio's original expectation that Beatriz Michelena would become "the Bernhardt of the screen." Critics were at one with their praise, judging her performances as the equals of the greats of the New York stage. The *New York Dramatic Mirror* critic felt her portrayal of "Salvation Nell" gave the character "the force it had in Mrs. Fiske's remarkable portrayal. That it has such force is our compliment to Miss Michelena." The same journal, reviewing *Mignon*, found it "hard to imagine a person more estimably fitted to portray the difficult character of this wild child of nature and to do it in such a manner as to subtly suggest the heritage of noble lineage than Beatriz Michelena . . . for Miss Michelena *is* Mignon."[28]

Similar emotional roles also were the forte of Nazimova of Metro and of Pauline Frederick of Famous Players, yet even with the competition of

Michelena playing an unblemished maid of classical romance. *(Photo from collection of Geoffrey Bell and by courtesy of Cedric Clute, Letty Etzler, and Lillian Johansen)*

Broadway to the craft of playwright Paul Armstrong, who revised the dialogue from literary to spoken form and strengthened the story line by changing it from the discursive to the dramatic.[27]

The Harte material provided adequate vehicles for Michelena; however, as movie Westerns, they tended to lack dynamism and to appear as drawing-room romances set in sylvan surroundings. For all their technical superiority, they never attained the box-office appeal of the movie Westerns made by the neighboring Essanay studio in Niles. Essanay's cowboy thrillers—no sentimental romances, they—were told in terms of action, action, action. Centering on the two-fisted masculine hero, quick

Michelena as a Continental sophisticate. *(Photo from collection of Geoffrey Bell and by courtesy of Cedric Clute, Letty Etzler, and Lillian Johansen)*

An American wife and mother as portrayed by Michelena. *(Photo from collection of Geoffrey Bell and by courtesy of Cedric Clute, Letty Etzler, and Lillian Johansen)*

Michelena as an independent woman on a parity with men. *(Photo from collection of Geoffrey Bell and by courtesy of Cedric Clute, Letty Etzler, and Lillian Johansen)*

their expensively advertised films, such a CMPC picture as Michelena's *Unwritten Law* more than held its own in the affections of its audiences by virtue of the star's tour de force performance. "Miss Michelena's work on the witness stand . . . is the most real and convincing emotion I have ever seen in pictures," wrote playwright Edwin Milton Royle, author of the stage and screen success *The Squaw Man*, "so free from exaggeration that it approaches artistic perfection. It is a very great triumph." A London reviewer acclaimed Michelena's acting as "marked by extraordinary 'grip' and a full appreciation of the dramatic possibilities of her part. She plays with all the Southern fire and intensity." Because of her Latin qualities, Michelena was immensely popular south of the border, where her box-office success often sustained those CMPC productions, which were less than successful financially in the U. S.[29]

Michelena's childhood tutelage under Fernando Michelena also had given her an understanding of theater management, which impelled her to become an executive producer, in fact if not in name. Like Bernhardt before her and Mary Pickford after

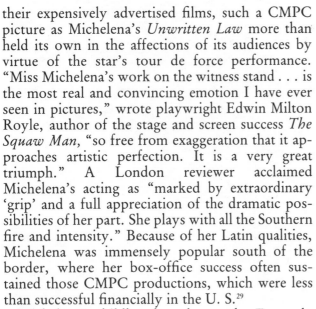

Salvation Nell (1915). Myrtle Newman, left with dark hat; Michelena, Pike. *(Photo from collection of Geoffrey Bell and by courtesy of Cedric Clute, Letty Etzler, and Lillian Johansen)*

Pike, Earle Emlay, Michelena in *Salvation Nell*. *(Photo from collection of Geoffrey Bell and by courtesy of Cedric Clute, Letty Etzler, and Lillian Johansen)*

Salvation Nell. Michelena and Pike. *(Photo from collection of Geoffrey Bell and by courtesy of Cedric Clute, Letty Etzler, and Lillian Johansen)*

Michelena in *Salvation Nell.* *(Photo from collection of Geoffrey Bell and by courtesy of Cedric Clute, Letty Etzler, and Lillian Johansen)*

her, Michelena saw to it that she had final decision in choice of stories and casts, as well as of the allocation of funds for sets, wardrobe, location junkets, and other extra production values to enhance her work. Like Bernhardt and Pickford, she shaped her career, instead of having her career shaped by others or by destiny. In the virtually all-male business world of her day, this was a remarkable accomplishment.

Michelena's performances and productions were enhanced by the CMPC's company of actors,

Mignon (1915). Exterior on studio lot. Emil Krushe (later, William Nigh), Michelena, and acting company. *(Photo from collection of Geoffrey Bell and by courtesy of Cedric Clute, Letty Etzler, and Lillian Johansen)*

Clara Byers and Michelena in *Mignon*. *(Photo from collection of Geoffrey Bell and by courtesy of Cedric Clute, Letty Etzler, and Lillian Johansen)*

trained in the repertory pattern of San Francisco's long-successful Alcazar Theatre, which, since 1880, had been the home of many of America's best stock companies. With one or two stars and a nucleus of seasoned character actors, the repertory company could successfully present its performers in a succession of different plays and in a wide variety of roles, providing opportunities for ensemble playing and unified acting styles. In company with the similar CMPC acting ensemble, Michelena was able to balance her portrayal of the wholesome, guileless, straightforward Western heroine with other, more complex types—such as a youthful central European street dancer, a dedicated New York evangelist, a maiden of feudal Germany, a flirtatious Italian diva, and a typical American housewife. In *Mignon* (autumn 1914)—a film based on a poem by Goethe—Michelena played an eighteenth-century teenage waif who fell in love with a nobleman. In *Salvation Nell* (summer 1915), she appeared as a battered woman of the Bowery. This emotional drama of sin and suffering, created by the noted playwright Edward Sheldon, set forth an outcast's struggle from the depths

A scene from *Mignon*. Ernest Joy, Byers, Michelena, Belle Bennett, Peters, Pike. *(Photo from collection of Geoffrey Bell and by courtesy of Cedric Clute, Letty Etzler, and Lillian Johansen)*

Robson, Michelena, Bennett, Joy, Peters, Byers, Pike in *Mignon*. *(Photo from collection of Geoffrey Bell and by courtesy of Cedric Clute, Letty Etzler, and Lillian Johansen)*

of degradation to the heights of religious redemption. The adaptation of another Goethe classic, *Faust* (early 1916), represented another big change in style, for Michelena played Marguerite—a symbol of virginal purity. In *The Woman Who Dared* (spring 1916)—a spy thriller of international intrigue—the actress switched to playing an Italian princess and coquette. At the premiere of this CMPC feature film in London, a drama critic observed: "The story is laid chiefly in Rome, and it is paying the director and his associated artists no mean compliment to say that the picture is so perfectly acted and set that it might quite easily be mistaken for one of Italian origin."[30]

In contrast to the sophisticate of *Dared*, in *Mrs. Wiggs of the Cabbage Patch* (December 1914) Michelena appeared as a demure ingenue. On the other hand, in *The Unwritten Law* (Autumn 1915) the star played a young American married woman torn between love and duty in a story of family heartache. The acting performances of Michelena thus brought to the screen some of the rich acting tradition of the repertory theater.[31]

The high caliber of Michelena's acting in these CMPC dramas was matched no less by the excellence of Middleton's direction. For example, critic Patrick Kearney of the *New York Evening Mail* praised *The Women Who Dared* noting, "interest never lags. It is a strong, sympathetically constructed piece of work—a marvel of expert craftsmanship." "F.R.B." of the *Motion Picture Mail* extolled *The Unwritten Law* as "a picture in

Mignon. Robson and Michelena. *(Photo from collection of Geoffrey Bell and by courtesy of Cedric Clute, Letty Etzler, and Lillian Johansen)*

The Unwritten Law (1916). Michelena. *(Photo from collection of Geoffrey Bell and by courtesy of Cedric Clute, Letty Etzler, and Lillian Johansen)*

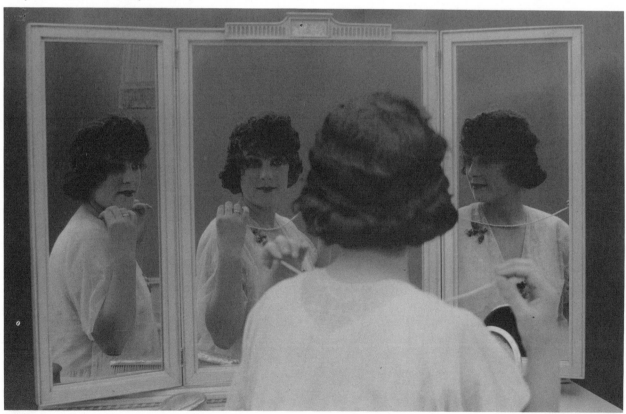

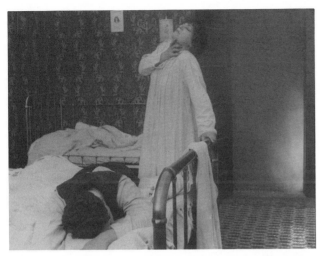

Pike (face down on bed) and Michelena in *The Unwritten Law*. *(Photo from collection of Geoffrey Bell and by courtesy of Cedric Clute, Letty Etzler, and Lillian Johansen)*

Faust (1916). Exterior location in California vineyard (Korbel, Sonoma County). *(Photo from collection of Geoffrey Bell and by courtesy of Letty Etzler)*

Musical score for *The Unwritten Law*. On cover are pictured Michelena, Felice Rix, Pike. *(Photo from collection of Geoffrey Bell)*

MUSICAL SETTING
For the presentation of
Beatriz Michelena
in
"THE UNWRITTEN LAW"
By EDWIN MILTON ROYLE
A Seven Reel Film Dramatization
produced by
California Motion Picture Corporation

which there are no flaws. It is wonderful. It goes into the exclusive class which we can recommend to any exhibitor, anywhere, as an absolutely certain success." Yet Michelena's versatile acting talent was the stuff of which *stage*, not movie, careers are made. Mary Pickford played essentially the same role of the blond Little Girl in movie after movie and became "America's Sweetheart." Theda Bara won renown portraying the brunette femme fatale in a number of pictures so popular that they consolidated the financial structure of Fox Films. Michelena, however, working essentially in the theatrical repertory format, never created the predictable, bigger-than-life image, which in itself lured movie fans again and again into movie houses.[32]

Cut off from the business centers of moviemaking and using stage models, the CMPC management proceeded on the assumption that if their films excelled in acting quality, artistic mise en scène, and photographic excellence, they would make as much money as their competitors. Yet, while the CMPC photoplays were extensively—and expensively—advertised in the leading trade journals, they were exhibited less and less at the showcase movie palaces, which now were almost entirely owned and operated by major production companies. The studio also faced growing competition from the new movie capital to the south and the new kinds of movie fare that Hollywood found most profitable.

These changes were marked in signal fashion by D. W. Griffith's *Birth of a Nation* (1915), with its

Pike and Michelena in *Faust*. *(Photo from collection of Geoffrey Bell and by courtesy of Cedric Clute, Letty Etzler, and Lillian Johansen)*

Because the CMPC, in its deference to the theater, tended to rely too much on traditional dramatic pieces, even its contemporary stories were several seasons old. *The Woman Who Dared* (1916), a story of pre–World War I days in Europe, was already dated by the time it was released during the war, when audiences were lining up to see rabble-rousing fare like *To Hell With the Kaiser*, which capitalized on current newspaper headlines. *The Unwritten Law* (1915), a contemporary story of domestic conflict, made a good profit but lacked the smashing box-office appeal of such artistically inferior films as Cecil B. De Mille's *Don't Change Your Husband* or *Why Change Your Wife?*, concoctions that bordered on the salacious and, as film historian John L. Fell wittily observed, "combined social comedy with scanty costume." So, while Hollywood was learning to crank out sensationalized money-making movies about war, divorce, infidelity, and other previously forbidden subjects, the CMPC expended precious funds on such esoteric adaptations from the classics as *Mignon* (1915) and *Faust* (1916), both written by a German and with German themes at a time of anti-German hysteria. Besides, although both *Mignon* and *Faust* were popular in opera form, their greatest attraction, music, was lost in a silent movie medium. Unmarketable, *Faust* finally had to be shelved.[33]

Although lacking in Hollywood-style stories and stars, the CMPC had the will and the energy to survive. But those in artistic control had plunged enthusiastically into production without real awareness of the all-important next step. Intoxicated with the creative aspects of cinema, they neglected to see far enough ahead to secure a dependable means of getting their product before the public. They lacked the strong ties with major national distribution combines like those enjoyed by rival Bay Area producer Gilbert M. Anderson for his Broncho Billy Westerns.

The CMPC's Middleton, Beyfuss, and Payne expected to enjoy artistic autonomy as independent producers, and gambled that superior pictures would automatically result in wide audiences. They failed to see that the structure of the movie business was changing. In their innocence, they allowed Lewis J. Selznick, general manager of World Film Corporation in New York, to convince them that he could distribute their pictures so that they would be playing in the best show houses from coast to coast. This was no idle boast, for World was on the verge of a merger with the mighty

stirring story, appealing characterizations, and sweeping spectacle. For a number of years Griffith had been making a succession of short story-telling movies, testing many possibilities, so that when he came to the feature film, he had at his command a vast accumulation of experience and knowledge. Among other things, he found that accelerating the cutting intensified the drama. His climaxes were often a hail of short shots in rhythm with the heartbeat of the spectator. Minimizing the use of subtitles, he let pictures tell the story, often linking scenes with a fade rather than with a title card. He photographed settings and props in ways that enriched the emotional content of a scene. For example, in *The Lonedale Operator* (1911), the heroine telegraph operator falls in love with a train engineer. As the train bearing him swings by her window at an angle, it carries him further and further away; with each shot, he becomes more faint and distant, graphically emphasizing their forced separation. Later, while menaced by holdup men, she desperately telegraphs for help as a window curtain billows behind her, its agitation expressive of her anxiety.

Faust stars Pike and Michelena. *(Photo from collection of Geoffrey Bell and by courtesy of Cedric Clute, Letty Etzler, and Lillian Johansen)*

Michelena as the vision of Helen. *(Photo from collection of Geoffrey Bell and by courtesy of Cedric Clute, Letty Etzler, and Lillian Johansen)*

Shubert theater chain, controlling the best theaters along Broadway and in the majority of major cities; furthermore, it also operated the Shubert Film Corporation with the aim of totally dominating motion picture production. Unknown to Beyfuss and the management of the CMPC, however, Selznick's position with World Films was by no means as important or as secure as he made it out to be. Selznick may have been a supersalesman, but he was no match for far more experienced movie distributors. Movie tycoons Adolph Zukor, William Fox, or Carl Laemmle, for example, began in the business not by making films, but by showing them. They learned their trade from the ground up, working in penny arcades, nickelodeons, and storefront movie houses, which taught them the importance of effective distribution. Through this actual day-by-day contact with the public, they gained a keen sense of what audiences would pay to see. In contrast, Selznick had little show business experience, and his promises of widespread and lucrative distribution far exceeded his ability to deliver. The aspiring CMPC could not have foreseen that Zukor's, Fox's, and Laemmle's small-time operations would prosper mightily and grow into the powerful Paramount Pictures, Twentieth-Century Fox, and Universal Studios, respectively; or that Selznick's vaunted World Film Corporation, the exclusive distributor for the CMPC pictures, would be forced out of business within a few years.[34]

In February 1916, World Films was reorganized under theater magnate William A. Brady, long an associate of the Shuberts, and in the shuffle, World dropped its option with the California Motion Picture Corporation. Ignorant of this fact, the CMPC studio was in full production with a lavish feature, *The Woman Who Dared.* For her role as a European princess, Michelena ordered from French couturier houses exhibiting at the San Francisco Exposition of 1915 her most elaborate wardrobe yet; and for her coiffure, a favorite hairdresser from I. Magnin's came from San Francisco to San Rafael each morning. For a scene in a Roman palace, Edwin B. Willis had designed a handsome classical ballroom and adjoining winter garden, set in Louis XVI style. Turning from luxuries and a fantasy world, star Michelena and director Middleton were jolted to receive the harsh report from Beyfuss: he had been outmaneuvered at the market place, and the CMPC had lost its distribution outlet in New York.

Desperately, *The Woman Who Dared* was

In the role of Marguerite from the opera "Faust," the prima donna princess (Miss Michelena) accepts the wooing of Prince Maximille (Mr. Morrison) with evasive coquetry.

The noted prima donna, Princess Beatriz de Rohan, portrayed by Beatriz Michelena, star of "The Woman Who Dared."

The Woman Who Dared (1916). Publicity flyer, gravure. *(Photo from collection of Geoffrey Bell)*

rushed to completion in hope of quick income from exhibition. Then—on the basis of the assumed popular acceptance of *Faust* as the most esteemed opera of that day and on the momentum of Michelena's publicity as "prima donna"—the beleagured company, financed shakily by promises, began on a production of this classic. Yet, hardly had the initial scenes been shot than Middleton and Michelena were struck yet another blow. In a devastating admission, company President Payne had to report that his checks were being returned stamped "Insufficient Funds." He had overextended his bank balance in underwriting the CMPC.[35]

Payne, whose principal business experience had been cashing remittances from his mother, was ill-equipped to deal with the buffetings of the marketplace. Beyfuss, who formerly could rely on his skills at bluffing, was not able to talk his way out of the relentless facts before them. Director Middle-

ton, however, knew how to meet challenge head-on. Having solved problems in mounting automobile shows and producing films, he felt confident he could negotiate new financial backing from his many connections in the Bay Area. Michelena, temperamental though she was, knew she could rely on her intuition and her strong sense of self-preservation. She felt that she could produce her own pictures—with Middleton handling the practical details—and that through sheer personality she could promote her pictures with distributors and exhibitors on trips to New York; with her reputation as a star, she thought her pictures would continue to be popular with the public.

Middleton and Michelena made a deal with Payne and Beyfuss: in return for the back salaries that the company owed them, the two would accept the deed for the studio property—its land, buildings, furnishings, and equipment. Beyfuss

Exterior set on CMPC lot representing a continental railroad. *(Photo from collection of Geoffrey Bell and by courtesy of Cedric Clute, Letty Etzler, and Lillian Johansen)*

threw up a cloud of words—like a trapped squid sending out a cloud of ink to cover its escape while scuttling to a more advantageous position—but the force of economics was inexorable. After a token argument—a concession here, a minor point there—Beyfuss conceded defeat. With only airy assurances about future speculative projects and with Payne in tow, Beyfuss made his exit—although he was not too grandiose to attempt to borrow a fiver from the studio gateman.[36]

Middleton and Michelena now had to contend with the stubborn problems of management, the most important problem of which was a means of getting their pictures marketed. While former outsiders Jesse Lasky and Cecil B. De Mille, who had started with only $26,500, now enjoyed the assurance of having their pictures booked from coast to coast under the aegis of Paramount Pictures Corporation, CMPC's original million-dollar backing had evaporated, and its survivors were without a firm distribution outlet. Without distribution, there could be no dependable income, but the distribution outlets were by then controlled almost exclusively by the New York–Hollywood studio cartels; their closed, interlocking systems of production, distribution, and exhibition were each under one strong management, blocking all competition. The movie business had become big business—no less than the great American coal, steel, or oil industries had become earlier. Even the great Griffith was in trouble. He had created a screen spectacle that exceeded anything yet attempted—*Intolerance*. But even this great work suffered because of distribution problems. His original back-

Ballroom staircase on the set of *The Woman Who Dared*. Michelena and Pike, center. *(Photo from collection of Geoffrey Bell and by courtesy of Cedric Clute, Letty Etzler, and Lillian Johansen)*

Albert Morrison, Michelena, Pike in *The Woman Who Dared*. *(Photo from collection of Geoffrey Bell and by courtesy of Cedric Clute, Letty Etzler, and Lillian Johansen)*

ers, who had made a fortune from his *Birth of a Nation*, were aghast at the complexity of *Intolerance*. Griffith attempted to distribute the opus himself, but because he was not commercially minded, the operation saddled him with debts for the rest of his movie career.

It is ironic that the individual who had been a major factor in the formation of the high and mighty Paramount Pictures, W. W. Hodkinson, had also been active in motion pictures in San Francisco at the time of the formation of the CMPC.

Hodkinson was the operator of a large chain of movie houses between Salt Lake City and San Francisco, which, in advance of their time, were not only fireproof, but also so well-cleaned and well-patrolled that they were suitable for women to attend alone. Hodkinson, then, was a successful movie distributor and exhibitor, and he was also active in the financing and production of the important 1913 movie version of Jack London's *Sea Wolf*, one of the earliest of feature-film successes. Such strong capabilities in the business aspects of the movies were just what the CMPC should have had at the time it was originally organized, and what it desperately needed later when its distribution system crumbled. Hodkinson shared the CMPC's ideals for motion pictures but was at the same time a highly practical man of business, who looked for high-caliber family entertainment films to keep the turnstiles clicking at his many neatly managed, wholesome, and well-paying movie houses. He endeavored to exhibit films that he was proud to link with his name—films very much indeed like those made by the CMPC.[37]

Manager Beyfuss, however, had linked CMPC's distribution with Louis J. Selznick—someone much of his own ilk.

By 1916, in the wake of the havoc the CMPC management had wrought, Middleton and Michelena attempted to market each release separately, using the system called "states rights," which meant that the state or area distributors acquired for a flat fee the exclusive right to show the picture in their territory. Under this arrangement, however, if the picture was popular, the distributor, not the producer, reaped the profits. The states rights system was thus undependable, but it was still better than no system at all. The Middleton-Michelena company had to take the enormous risk of making pictures on speculation, pinned only on tenuous hopes of their being distributed. With costs a primary consideration, the two concentrated on making outdoor pictures of early California days, for which they already had the props, costumes, and rolling stock. *The Heart of Juanita* (1916) set forth the story of a Spanish-American girl torn by love for a Yankee trapper. *Just Squaw* (1917) depicted an Indian maid upholding the honor of her tribe and protecting the Indian brave she loved. In both of these last-ditch efforts to avert disaster, star, director, cast, and crew had to work with a sense that their entire artistic endeavor was threatened. The company assembled for what was to be the last time with the production of *The*

THE NEW YORK DRAMATIC MIRROR

MAY 13, 1916   PRICE TEN CENTS

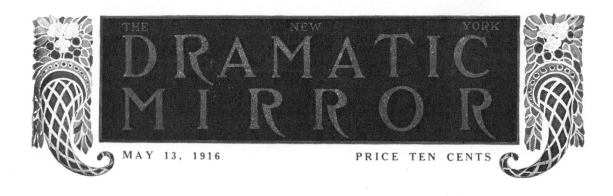

BEATRIZ MICHELENA
in ''The Woman Who Dared''

All the News of the Play World

Cover page, *New York Dramatic Mirror. (Photo from collection of Geoffrey Bell)*

Flame of Hellgate (1917), starring Michelena as a dance-hall gal of many loves. Despite all the hopes and care that went into its making, the returns from the distribution of the other outstanding pictures were found to be insufficient to continue the company's enormous overhead. When director Middleton called "Cut!" on *The Flame of Hellgate*'s final fade, the whirring cameras of the CMPC were silenced forever.[38]

The ultimate concession to fate came only later when a devastating vault fire destroyed the CMPC's master prints and the negatives of all their work. The nitrate film of the day was highly volatile and flammable and easily affected by air temperature and moisture levels. The explosive potential of nitrate film was not fully understood, and one hot summer day the entire collection burst into flames and was utterly destroyed, thus depriving

future generations of that superior body of work, which distribution problems cut off from the public of its time. Long search, however, has brought to light some all-too-brief footage from *The Flame of Hellgate*, which was incorporated into the documentary film *Those Daring Young Film Makers by the Golden Gate*, directed by the author. The film clip depicts a parallel action sequence. In one progression of events, forty-niners organize a posse to apprehend the villain, while, simultaneously, hero William Pike battles menacing Andrew Robson in a cabin as heroine Michelena escapes from the fray. These bits of live action are all that remain today to bring, across the years, glimpses of how those movie people of the silent days realized their concepts on film through the direction of George Middleton, the cinematography of Frank Padilla, and the performances of the CMPC acting ensemble.[39]

The story of the CMPC reveals what it meant to make a film at a time when the many small, inde-

Final fade-out, *Salomy Jane*, Peters and Michelena. *(Photo from collection of Geoffrey Bell and by courtesy of Cedric Clute, Letty Etzler, and Lillian Johansen)*

pendent studios, often in areas other than Hollywood, were striving for expression—studios that were little different from those that later came into prominence under the astute guidance of a Zukor, a Fox, or a Laemmle. The events surrounding the rise and fall of the CMPC also reveal some intimation of the commitment and professionalism required to sustain a performing arts career. Those in the company who viewed the CMPC as a commercial enterprise found that the motion picture business is a stern taskmaster, demanding more than a lust for quick profits. Both clubman Payne and opportunist Beyfuss found themselves cut out of any glittering financial spoil; both, in time, were reported suicides. Middleton resiliently bounced back, utilizing his talents and inventiveness to further an expanding and less chancy automobile business. Beatriz Michelena, forsaking anything less than movie stardom, returned to the live stage, touring with particular success in Latin America, her programs made up of scenes from her various pictures, enlivened by an ensemble of Spanish dancers, and centering around herself as soloist, warbling such favorites as "La Golondrina." With no further need for George Middleton, she divorced him and, having shrewdly invested her American earnings, retired to Spain. There Michelena spent her final years, sustained in the land of Fernando's birth by that love of which she could not speak but which was in her heart forever.[40]

Those, on the other hand, who had come into the CMPC with an awareness of, and a concern for, the limitless possibilities of the new medium—technicians Edwin B. Willis, Robert Carson, and William Nigh; or actors House Peters, Belle Bennett, William Pike, Marin Sais, Lois Wilson, and Jack Holt—all went on to dedicated careers on the screen.

While the death of the CMPC may have been typical of its times, its life certainly was not. However flawed, the company had a sense of destiny. Its initial work contributed significantly to the format of the full-length feature film (only later brought to full acceptance with D. W. Griffith's *Birth of a Nation*). Its Westerns brought to the screen, as had rarely been realized before, the freshness, space, and authentic beauty of the great West. And its production values placed it high among those pioneers whose work elevated the movies from a mere nickelodeon pastime to the status of a new and lively art.

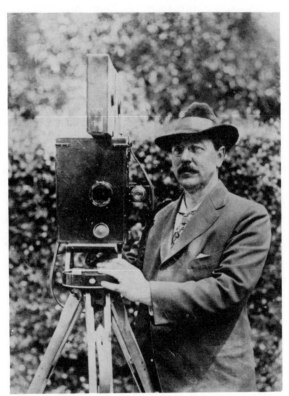

Leon F. Douglass, a pioneer of color films. *(Photo permission of California State Library, Sacramento)*

4

The Experimenters: Lights, Camera, Distraction

By the alchemy of the movies, the famed Monte Carlo casino, the villas that look over the blue Mediterranean, and the terraces which are the playground of a luxurious world, were brought into physical reality yesterday along the most picturesque acre of seacoast in California. Those who preened proudly and tramped the terraces with fastidious toes were made up of San Francisco and Del Monte society—fully three hundred of the smartest and richest people on this side of the continent taking part in several scenes of Eric Von Stroheim's *Foolish Wives.* Through the long hot hours this billion-dollar cast paraded and played in the sunlight for a battery of moving picture cameras, against the loveliest background ever reflected in a lens—the green sweet hills of Monterey on one side, the blue water of Monterey Bay breaking into silver over the rocks on the other.[1]

These were some of the phrases used by a contemporary witness, writing of the filming during November 1920 of Universal Studio's feature film, *Foolish Wives,* on the coast south of San Francisco. Director Eric Von Stroheim had always considered San Francisco, with Vienna and Paris, as his favorite of the world's cities, and filmed scenes there for two of his greatest successes. Other directors, equally enchanted, strove to do more than location shooting, and to produce their pictures entirely in the Bay Area. In the afterglow of the work of the California Motion Picture Corporation they continued to experiment with the medium as they had

done through the years when the Essanay and the CMPC studios were the brightest lights in Bay Area filmmaking.

These experimenters had the example of the runaway box-office success of the San Francisco-made documentary *The Barbary Coast* (1913) and found ways to please audiences of the silent movie era with such locally produced theatrical feature films as *Her Accidental Husband* (1923) and *The Awful Truth* (1925). The former was praised by the *Moving Picture World* for its "luxurious settings and splendid photography" and for a story "told so smoothly and with such care in construction that it cannot but register as a hit at the box office." Of the latter the *New York Times* wrote: "This is one of those pictures that is consistently amusing. After it had begun to unfold only a little way you sit back in your seat confident that you are in the hands of intelligent direction and acting."[2]

These non-Hollywood movies, even without the advantages of presold distribution, star-studded casts, or scintillating publicity, were striking examples of what the independent filmmaker could accomplish with dedication, enthusiasm, and knowledge of motion picture production. And, if such producer names as Harry, Herbert, and Earl C. Miles; Thomas Kimmwood Peters and Leon Douglass; Hobart Bosworth and Max Graf; Elmer Harris and Frank E. Woods; Edward Belasco,

Harry Revier, or Paul Gerson are not enshrined in any movie pantheon of today, it is because they chose to work as individuals. Even though they knew that motion picture financing was centered in New York—and the industry, in Hollywood—they felt that in producing apart from the movie establishment, they could be free to express themselves in a wider variety of ways.

What sustained these producers was the feeling that this was the place of all places to be. They found in the Bay Area, with its alertness to new ideas, its cosmopolitanism, and its affinity for the arts, a sustaining environment different from any other. These filmmakers welcomed taking their stand in a place with a style and flavor of its own, and one so full of tradition. San Francisco had a cinematic history longer than that of any other community in the world—a history of innovation that stretched back into the nineteenth century to the very origins of the motion picture and that continued throughout the years of its establishment as an art form and entertainment medium.

The activities and work of these independent filmmakers comprise the fourth major phase of the motion picture in San Francisco. The wide spectrum of their kaleidoscope of activity extends from the mid-1890s to the late 1920s. This fourth phase began in 1896, when the first motion picture films were shown as novelty acts in such variety houses as Koster and Bial's Music Hall in New York or the Orpheum Vaudeville Theater in San Francisco. These brief films, running for scarcely more than a minute and depicting such nonstory incidents as *Sea Waves, A Boxing Bout, A Butterfly Dance*, and *A Train Arriving at a Station*, were not true cinema, yet their exhibition in theaters symbolized the birth of the movies as popular entertainment. And, while their subjects had been innocuous enough, they had shocked people who had never seen anything like them before in a theater. Audiences had shrunk from the photographic reality of waves curling over and breaking on the beach and at an apparently real steam engine churning down the tracks right at them.[3]

Filmed oddments were one thing, but the movie's true potential was not established until it was presented to the public as an attraction in its own right. San Francisco's Cineograph Theatre, opening in 1897 on Market Street, was one of America's first show houses to exhibit motion picture films exclusively. This prototype movie theater pioneered both in use of the word *cine* and the five-cent admission charge. Soon the five-cent movie house, eventually labeled the "nickelodeon," spread throughout California, attracting widespread audiences with its modest ticket fee and bright, ever-changing entertainment.[4]

Sensing the vast potential of the movies, San Francisco's Miles brothers—Harry, Herbert, and Earl C.—established in the city the first motion picture exchange in the United States. Previously, the brothers had been exhibiting movies in Alaska, during the gold rush of 1898, and, following 1900, in San Francisco and environs. Up to that time, they and other exhibitors had to purchase movies directly from their manufacturers. Each film quickly exhausted its entertainment value, and, as each short film cost in the neighborhood of one hundred dollars, an assemblage of films necessary to make up a complete movie program imposed a heavy burden of expense on the exhibitor. But in 1902, Harry Miles, the most imaginative of the brothers, conceived the plan of *renting* films. The Miles brothers would rent to exhibitors the films they already owned and, in turn, would buy back the films that exhibitors were holding as dead assets. With this innovation, movie house operators obtained a variety of movies for their programs at a fraction of the former cost, while the Miles brothers made a double profit on each transaction. "It seemed an interesting but unimportant venture then," commented film historian Terry Ramsaye in *A Million and One Nights*, "but it was the most important development in the motion picture since the invention of the projection machine."[5]

Of the three brothers, Harry was the most aggressive, even flashy. Driven by a strong ego, he was the nattily dressed playboy with a gregariousness that engendered valuable business contacts. His brother Herbert, more serious and methodical, did not always approve of Harry's extroverted, often extravagant, behavior, but realized that floridness in style was part of show business. In the daily business of the exchange, Herbert preferred to remain in the background and let Harry deal with the public. The youngest, Earl C., at first felt outclassed by his apparently cleverer brothers; in time, however, he was able to overcome his inhibitions, assume executive roles, express genuinely original and creative ideas, and advance from a peripheral participation to become president of the Miles Brothers Motion Picture Company. Harry's flamboyant style, Herbert's solid business competence and stability, and Earl's steadily improving business know-how produced a partnership in which each complemented the others. Their unity and support for each other, at a time when the movie business was weak, fragmented, and without status, gave the trio strength, cohesiveness, and dominance.

The Miles Brothers film exchange prospered after 1902, but the pictures available for them to exchange were limited both in variety and in quality. Some of the pictures were the already hack-

---

July 15, 1916   THE MOVING PICTURE WORLD   399

San Francisco, Cal., Dates Back to the Year 1894

Peter Bacigalupi was First Dealer--Greatest Development Has Come Since the Earthquake and Fire of 1906

ONE of the pioneers in the moving picture business on the Pacific Coast is Peter Bacigalupi, of the firm of Peter Bacigalupi & Sons, 908 Market street, San Francisco, now handling phonographs and automatic musical instruments. Mr. Bacigalupi was interested in the moving picture industry from 1894, when the first machines were brought here, until the great fire of 1906, when he turned his attention to other lines. His memory is clear on the early days of the industry and he has some interesting relics to show of the pioneer days. Among these are business cards he had made shortly after the first films were brought to the Coast. Whenever a film became torn or badly worn it would be cut up and a section pasted over a hole cut in a business card, making a souvenir that was in much demand in those days. One of the most interesting relics in his possession, however, is a card establishing the date when moving pictures were first shown here. This reads as follows:

> San Francisco, June first, 1894.
> This is to certify that Captain John F. Ryan, United States Government Diver (a Christian), was the first man who paid to see the Edison Kinetoscope west of Chicago.
> (Signed) HOLLAND BROS.

This was written in the back of a business card bearing the following wording:

> Edison Kinetoscope,
> Holland Bros.,
> Ottawa, Canada.
> Foreign Agents.
> Represented by A. Holland.

"When Holland Bros. brought the Edison Kinetoscope to the Pacific Coast," said Mr. Bacigalupi, "I closed a deal at once for the five machines they had, paying $2,500 for them. These were set up in a store in the Chronicle Building at Market and Kearney streets and people stood in line to see the pictures, paying a fee of 10 cents. This was before a screen was used, one person monopolizing a machine during the run of the film, which was, of course, very short. Backed by himself and others E. H. Amet of Waukegan, Ill., commenced the manufacture of a machine called the Magniscope, but only a few were made.

"Walter Furst was the first man to have a five-cent show here, his house being located on Market street about where the Odeon theater now is, this being known as the Cinegraph. At first vaudeville was given upstairs and when the performance here was over the audience would go to a room below where moving pictures were shown, everyone standing to see them, there being no seats. At first ten cents was charged, but later the vaudeville was eliminated and straight pictures were shown at five cents.

"One of the first attempts to use a screen in connection with moving pictures was made by a man named Wright who came here from Portland and worked for the late Charles L. Ackerman, the attorney. He took one of the coin-in-the-slot machines, turned it on its side and with but a few changes threw a picture on a screen. He later opened a theater on Market street, near Ffith, where the Lincoln

Peter Bacigalupi, San Francisco, Cal.

Market now stands, and this house, with the one conducted by Walter Furst were among those destroyed by the fire of 1906.

About 1898 D. J. Grauman entered the field, after working for Walter Furst for a time, opening the Unique theater on Market street, near Mason. He made a big success of the business and bought a large part of the films I was importing at that time. In 1900 I made a visit to Paris and bought a large quantity of Pathe, Gaumont and other foreign films and sold most of these to Mr. Grauman upon my return. Most of these films came in lengths of from fifty to one hundred and fifty feet and sold at about $25 for the shorter lengths. Some of these early subjects would be very interesting now. For instance, among the first films shown here were some featuring Ruth St. Denis, the dancer, Sandow and Anna Belle Moore.

"Among the first Biographs brought here was one showing Pope Leo XIII. I brought this to the Orpheum and at the

Unique Theater, Seattle, Wash., First Picture House of Miles Bros., Herbert Miles in Lobby.

same time brought John Brandlein, an operator, to the city, and he is still to be found here. The pictures of Pope Leo were also shown in Metropolitan Hall on Fifth street, but although they were excellent, about the best that had been shown here up to that time, the attendance was very light. Mrs. McEnerney, wife of the well known attorney, was an enthusiast over this picture, and saw it many times.

"At the time of the fire of 1906 my headquarters were at 786 Mission street, up to then, and I was doing a big business in moving pictures, Edison machines and penny arcade goods. I operated two of the latter, one being on Market street, at Stockton, and the other in the historic old Bella Union theater on Kearny street. When I lost the Edison agency it was taken over by George Breck, the supply man."

Miles Brothers Made Early Start.

ALMOST every one who has been connected with the moving picture business in any way at San Francisco during the past fifteen years knows of Miles Bros., now located at 1145-47 Mission street, and of James A. Sciaroni,

---

Article appearing in *The Moving Picture World.* (Photo from collection of Geoffrey Bell)

Cineograph Parlor program cover. *(Photo permission of California Historical Society, San Francisco)*

neyed filmed vaudeville acts with the addition of such stars as strong man Eugene Sandow, sharpshooter Annie Oakley, or "Buffalo Bill" Cody; others repeated the same old scenes of motion for motion's sake—the repetitious parades, waves breaking on a beach, trains entering stations, or fire engines racing to conflagrations. To improve their stock of offerings, the Miles brothers began to film scenes of San Francisco's cable cars with muscular gripmen and moustached conductors, the Easter parade on fashionable Van Ness Avenue, visiting admirals with the Japanese fleet, or, further afield, the State Fair at Sacramento. With this adjustment to the law of supply and demand, they entered motion picture production.[6]

Up to that time, the standard approach to moviemaking was to film each scene with a static camera as if from the distance of a seventh-row center orchestra seat in a theater. But to make their travel pictures come alive, the Miles team began to use the camera lens as the eye of a moving spectator. One of the films in which they put this concept into practice, *A Trip Down Mt. Tamalpais,* is still in existence. The setting, Mt. Tamalpais, a peak of unusual beauty across the Golden Gate from San Francisco, was then served by the diminutive "Crookedest Railroad in the World." With pictures shot from a camera mounted on the front of a train going down the winding track in its descent from the mountain top to the towering evergreens of Mill Valley, the unfolding panoramas of Marin County valleys, the bay, and the ocean thrilled and astonished moviegoers.[7]

Despite the visual attractiveness of *Tamalpais,* such documentations of the outdoors lacked real stories. In 1902 drama was added to realistic footage by Edwin S. Porter, a cameraman with the newly formed Edison studio in New York. In his film *The Life of an American Fireman* Porter took the often photographed scene of a fire engine with its horses galloping to a fire, and added two protagonists and an exciting story of the rescue of a baby in a burning building.

Inspired by Porter's example, the Miles brothers envisioned surpassing their travel films by introducing narrative into their films. In a burst of creative energy, the brothers commenced construction in San Francisco of a complete motion picture plant, the equipment of which, when evaluated by the technical standards of a decade later, was still deemed to be unsurpassed. In a 1915 article headlined "Miles Brothers: Pioneers. The Firm Which Built the First Motion Picture Studio on the

Herbert E. Miles. *(Photo permission of California State Library, Sacramento)*

Leon Douglass working on one of his inventions. *(Photo permission of California State Library, Sacramento)*

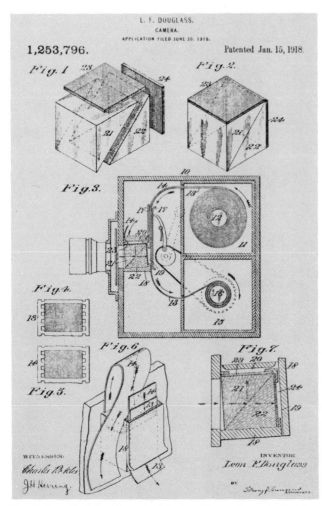

Patent application by Douglass. *(Photo from collection of Geoffrey Bell)*

journal in the industry, however, was close enough in time to have been based on firsthand interviews and observations.

Far more was lost in the fire of 1906, however, than the fortunes of the Miles brothers. The entire financial, business, and transportation facilities of the key city of America's Pacific Coast were crippled. Virtually all of San Francisco's manpower, industry, and creative energy during the ensuing years had to be directed into the colossal task of reconstructing an entire city. Ironically, these were the years of the great growth in the motion picture industry. The 1906 disaster, *Moving Picture World* concluded, "was responsible for keeping San Francisco off the film manufacturing map for a number of years, perhaps of depriving the coast city of eminence in the industry." While San Francisco was prostrate, its rival city to the south, Los Angeles, was waging a vigorous campaign for ascendency. Its chamber of commerce offered strong inducements to businessmen to locate their companies within its extensive boundaries. Of all the companies wooed, among the most prominent were those in the burgeoning movie business.[9]

Despite the increasing, and eventually dominant, concentration of movie studios in the Los Angeles

Ruth Roland, star of *Cupid Angling* (1918). *(Photo from collection of Geoffrey Bell)*

Coast," *Moving Picture World* called the company the "largest and finest studio in the country . . . unique in many respects and possess[ing] equipment that has not yet been equalled." The *World* singled out Harry Miles as a man whose "inventive turn of mind . . . had designed a system of electric control that operated the entire factory and studio." Before this incredible motion picture complex produced even one film, however, fate dealt it a death blow with the earthquake and fire of 1906.[8]

Intriguing as it is to speculate about the details of the Miles Brothers Motion Picture Studio and tantalizing as it is to read of "equipment not yet equalled" or of "systems of electric control," all plans, specifications, and photographs of the plant—as far as is known—were destroyed on that disastrous April 18. Documentation in the *Moving Picture World* of 1915, the most authorative trade

The Finger of Justice (1918). *(Photo permission of Sunset Magazine, Menlo Park, California, and California State Library, Sacramento)*

area, a number of film companies were active throughout the entire silent era in Northern California. North of the Golden Gate in Marin County were the California Motion Picture Corporation, the Keanograph studio, and the Leon Douglass Natural Color studio; across the bay to the east in Alameda County, were the Essanay and Vim studios; to the south were the Exactus Photo-Film Corporation in Palo Alto and the Liberty, Banner, and Pacific studios in San Mateo; and in San Francisco itself a studio was in operation on Page Street near Golden Gate Park. Some of the studios were engaged in producing theatrical feature films; others, comedy shorts; and still others, nontheatrical films.

The possibilities of using films for education, not only for entertainment, was an exciting new concept that attracted, among others, Thomas Kimmwood Peters and Jack Hawks. Peters was not new

to filmmaking, having worked at the turn of the century on animation and special effects for Pathe Films and later as a technical advisor for D. W. Griffith's *Birth of a Nation. The American Cinematographer* would much later describe Peters as "the last survivor of an age that saw the birth of the medium of film and the development of the art of film making . . . the first to see the historical significance of every step." Peters designed and built a patented motion picture camera with a time-lapse mechanism that captured on film such amazing phenomena as the unfolding of growing plants and flowers. With time-lapse cinematography, a subject changing form is filmed, frame-by-frame, over a long period of time, so that an event that takes place during hours or days appears on the screen to take place in minutes or seconds. A time-lapse film of a leaf unfolding or of a building being constructed could, for instance, be used in classes in botany or architecture. Peters planned to use his special camera for a series of educational films. In 1914 he became one of the organizers of the Exactus Photo-Film Corporation. Among its products was a film about the California wine industry, which, shot at fifty-four wineries, depicted every aspect of the wine industry, from vine to table. The documentary won a gold medal at the 1915 exposition.[10]

High-quality educational films were also the goal of Jack Hawks of the Vim Motion Picture Company, located in a former streetcar barn in Alameda. Later a director with Essanay, Goldwyn, and Universal, Hawks produced a feature-length educational film, *The Realm of Children* (August 1916), which explained the Montessori method of teaching children and demonstrated how this foreign educational method could be introduced into American schools.[11]

Neither Peters nor Hawks succeeded financially, perhaps because they lacked the salesmanship necessary to market their industrial films or the contacts with school boards that would have helped sell their educational offerings. But more than that, the educational film itself was in advance of its time. The medium still depended on the expensive and difficult-to-operate thirty-five millimeter equipment, which was too cumbersome and flammable for school use. It was not until 1923 that Eastman Kodak was able to manufacture nonflammable acetate film and reasonably portable and simple-to-operate projectors in the less costly sixteen-millimeter gauge, and it was still another decade before this gauge was agreed upon as the international standard for the educational film. The

FEW people would associate a sensational moving picture production with the Methodist church, yet the Reverend Paul Smith, a San Francisco pastor, endorsed by his Bishop, his congregation and his friends, has filmed a smashing eight reel melodrama which he confidently hopes will daily preach silently and forcibly the sermons which now fall from the preacher's lips.

It was Miss Grace Marbury Sanderson, successful scenario and short-story writer, who first suggested the idea of screen sermons to Mr. Smith. His comments were very favorable and he would gladly endorse it, but no, that was not what she wanted—*she wanted the church and Paul Smith to produce it!*

It was rather a staggering proposition, but its possibilities at once appealed to the minister eager to get his message into a broader sphere. It was a radical step for a conservative Methodist church, but the traditions which had so long bound the church no longer applied to clean theatricals, particularly if they contained a moral. The longer he pondered the more convinced he became that here was a great opportunity. He sought out some of his congregation and financed it; then he engaged the company to stage it and in less than a week active work had begun.

The sermon the "Finger of Justice" preaches contains two lessons. The first deals with the men of the underworld, the "ring" of exploiters who recruit the borderline girl to fill the places of those who pay the price and whom the hand of time relentlessly crushes, the political boss, the "dive" keeper, the property owner, the money lender, the liquor interests and the male parasite. The second moral is the tragedy of ignorance, of allowing young

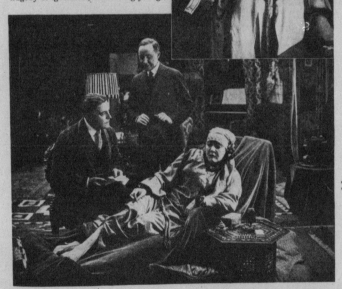

While "Flip," the underworld rat, wires his boss of a new victim, Edith sees with dismay that the train is pulling out of the way-station

girls to go abroad unwarned of the hazards of pick-up companionships.

All types of the underworld are represented, but the leading figure is the fighting parson, portrayed by Crane Wilbur, the ideal type of 20th century preacher. A spirited football scene—really done, by the way, at the University of California—serves to introduce this modern preacher, who is a human two-fisted man of his time.

Through the theme and closely connected runs an allegorical story, the settings of which are elaborate and beautiful and give to the production a touch of dignity and refinement which otherwise might be lacking.

The spectacular visit of the women of the underworld to the church of the Reverend Paul Smith several months ago is also in this production, and the pictures taken in and around the California street Methodist church. But there has been no attempt to associate San Francisco with this picture any more than New Orleans or New York. It is aimed at conditions, not localities.

And now that the Methodist church has broken the crust of traditional conservatism to present its preachments on the screen, the future may be looked into without foreboding but rather with the assurance that if the gospel message has been haltingly impressive in the past, it will, in the future, spread its wings of healing over untouched areas and turn the hearts of thousands who normally dislike and chafe under religious restrictions toward the goal of salvation. It is a unique experiment likely to provoke a good deal of criticism at first but in the end calculated to give religion a fresh hold, something it needs if the empty pew is the serious problem which churches and preachers declare it to be.   MAUDE C. PILKINGTON.

Henry Barrows, as the vice boss, and Jane O'Roark, as the woman of the abyss, the allied powers of darkness whom the minister is fighting. Center: Mae Gaston, as "Mary," who goes into the depths and comes back

The Finger of Justice (1918). *(Photo permission of Sunset Magazine, Menlo Park, California, and California State Library, Sacramento)*

problem, then, was inherent in the medium and not in the geographical location of the filmmaker—the problem would have existed in Hollywood or in any part of the country for those seeking to use the motion picture as an educational tool. Pushing beyond the limits of the day, Peters and Hawks had little chance for economic success. In their ventures, they were typical of the imaginative filmmakers who worked in the Bay Area.

No less innovative in production was Leon F. Douglass, who produced in the San Francisco area some of the earliest American-made motion pictures in color. Douglass had previously been active in the Victor Talking Machine Company's promotion of the disk phonograph record (superseding Edison's less convenient cylinder records) with its recordings of Enrico Caruso and other artists of the Metropolitan Opera Company. Following this technical, artistic, and financial triumph, Douglass turned to another medium that could bring art to the masses—the motion picture. Attracted by the climate and beauty of the Bay region, Douglass chose as his residence San Rafael in Marin County. There, he established the Douglass Natural Color Motion Picture Company, which perfected a system of filming, in the camera, color motion pictures (heretofore, "color" movies had been hand-tinted, frame by frame). The Douglass travelogues of California included scenes of golden blossoms against azure skies and flaming sunsets so vivid that audiences gasped in astonishment. Verifying the high caliber of this work, the *New York Times* observed, "[Douglass's] device reproduces every shade and tint of the colors of nature . . . the range being apparently unlimited, depicting all of the delicate shades and hues." With the advice of George E. Middleton of the California Motion Picture Corporation, Douglass also produced what may well have been the first American feature-length color film exhibited before paying theater audiences—*Cupid Angling* (June 1918). The film starred titian-haired Ruth Roland and included guest appearances by Mary Pickford and Douglas Fairbanks, who were then considering using the Douglass color system in their forthcoming costume pictures. The *San Francisco Chronicle* described *Cupid Angling* as "a springtime romance which gives full opportunity for the introduction of a wealth of colors. It is like viewing nature at its grandest through an open window to disclose the colorful glories of Yosemite Valley . . . the poppy-splattered fields of Marin County." Despite favorable response critically and artistically, exhibitors

balked at booking the Douglass color films because additional equipment and specially trained operators were required to project them. Once again, a Bay Area innovator was far ahead of the industry; in time, however, the Douglass process became one of the many factors in the formation of Technicolor.[12]

During this same era the San Rafael studio was the production center for a feature film that dealt, not with romance, but with another aspect of Cupid's work—commercialized vice. Envisioning a broader educational role for film, the Reverend Paul Smith of the Temple Methodist Church of San Francisco believed movies could be used to fight evil. A leader in the Vice Crusade, which aimed at making San Francisco a wholesome place to visit during the 1915 exposition, Smith felt that he could use films to gain national exposure for this moral message. With the concurrence of his bishop, he obtained funding from his congregation to produce a picture that would do the work of the church by telling a story which would "turn the hearts of thousands . . . toward the goal of salvation." The resulting feature film, *The Finger of Justice* (July 1918), had the dual purpose of awakening the public to the evils of commercial prostitution and of warning young women of the "hazards of pickup companionships." To attract conventional moviegoers, who might otherwise stay away because of its daring theme, the film featured matinee idol Crane Wilbur, following his triumph in the now classic movie serial *The Perils of Pauline.* Cast in the role of the "Fighting Parson," Wilbur sought to destroy a ring of vice operators whose aim was to exploit girls and drag them into the depths. Because of these efforts, the parson was framed by the vice boss, but, ironically, it was the vice boss's sequestered daughter who became the victim of his evil machine. The parson's zeal in exposing this vice ring was finally crowned by his marriage to a wealthy social worker, who had joined him in his cause.[13]

The picture generated nationwide controversy. Although the word *whore* was not explicitly mentioned in the publicity, the subject so horrified the commissioner of licenses in New York City that he forbade the booking of the picture into the Lyric Theatre on Times Square. Other reactions were less self-righteous. In Washington, D.C., for instance, the President of the National Police Chief's Association stated, "I cannot understand why anyone would oppose this picture unless he has an interest in commercialized vice," while the mayor of Seattle, Washington, declared, "I am willing that the country at large should know that we of the great Northwest do not fear the exposure of vice and political conditions." Protesting the New York ban and other such censorship, producer Paul Smith vowed that "the fight has not yet begun." Nonetheless, the many months of legal harassment, which kept *The Finger of Justice* off the screen, seriously damaged its commercial potential.[14]

Irrespective of subject, movies made by San Francisco–based companies and by other independent, nonestablishment companies faced formidable opposition from the giant Hollywood studios, which, with New York financing, had won the war for the dominance of American motion pictures and which, between 1915 and 1920, had established an empire centered in Southern California. With little or no competition from a war-devastated Europe, Hollywood had consolidated its interests so that it now dominated the entire world market. Its major studios—such as Paramount, Fox, and Universal; and later, First National, United Artists, and Metro-Goldwyn-Mayer—controlled all three major aspects of the industry by making their own pictures, channeling them from coast to coast through their own distribution systems, and showing them exclusively in their own movie palaces. The profits from their own box offices flowed back to provide a continuous source of interest-free funding for new productions.

In the face of such overwhelming competition, the small, independent moviemaker had to exercise the greatest ingenuity to continue production. Each movie was extremely costly to make, yet investors saw the futility of fighting the major combines, which had under contract the popular movie stars and which controlled the popular movie houses, drawing huge crowds on a daily basis. Those few gutsy moviemakers who decided to fight, despite the odds, had to do it on terms set by Hollywood. Those who chose to make feature-length entertainment films had the best hope of surviving in the business if they produced formula-plot pictures which, if made with skill, could provide a pleasant evening's entertainment and show a predictable profit at the box office. By necessity, then, these later producers could not be the pioneers that Essanay's Anderson or CMPC's Middleton and Michelena had been—artists whose innovative work had real impact on the motion picture business. Thus, the story of movie production in the Bay Area during the final decade of the silent era is the story of a valiant stand by a few small producers against the formidable organizations of the giant producers. It is also the story of a number of individuals whose work, however unheralded, swelled that swift, strong international current that kept motion pictures diversified and personal.

High hopes were generated for the future of Bay Area filmmaking in the new era following World War I with announcements of a six-million-dollar local production company headed by the prominent figures of W. W. Hodkinson, Dudley Field

Panoramic views of Pacific Studios, later Peninsula Studios. *(Photo permission of California Historical Society, San Francisco)*

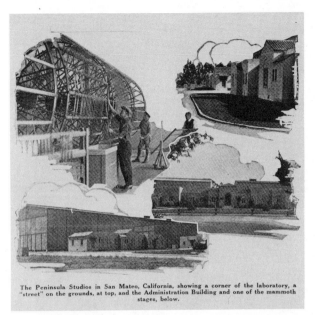

The Peninsula Studios in San Mateo, California, showing a corner of the laboratory, a "street" on the grounds, at top, and the Administration Building and one of the mammoth stages, below.

Activities at Pacific Studios. *(Photo permission of California State Library, Sacramento)*

Jack London. *(Photo permission of San Francisco History Room, San Francisco Public Library)*

Hobart Bosworth. *(Photo permission of California State Library, Sacramento)*

Malone, and Thomas Dixon. Hodkinson, the much-respected national distributor of independently produced films, was a man of superior cast and total commitment to excellence. "I propose to establish a reign of quality," he declared. "I want the quality of my pictures to lead all other pictures aspiring to high quality." Dudley Field Malone was a former Attorney of the City of New York and a noted trial lawyer. Thomas Dixon was author of the novel *The Clansmen*, on which D. W. Griffith based his landmark motion picture achievement, *The Birth of a Nation*.[15]

At a luncheon held at the Palace Hotel in June 1919, the San Francisco Industry League was apprised of the "mutual advantages to San Francisco, the Bay section, and the moving picture industry that would result from establishing a film industry in the area." Joseph A. Eliason, motion picture expert, pointed out that "the diffusion of light here is more uniform than in the southern part of the state and, on account of the absence of glare, is better suited to the purposes of the business," and also that "Marin and Lake counties, the Peninsula, and the eastern side of the bay [are] all virgin terri-

White Hands (1921), starring Bosworth and Robert McKim. *(Photo permission of Museum of Modern Art—Film Stills Archive, New York)*

Freeman Wood, McKim, Elinor Fair, Bosworth in *White Hands*. *(Photo permission of Museum of Modern Art—Film Stills Archive, New York)*

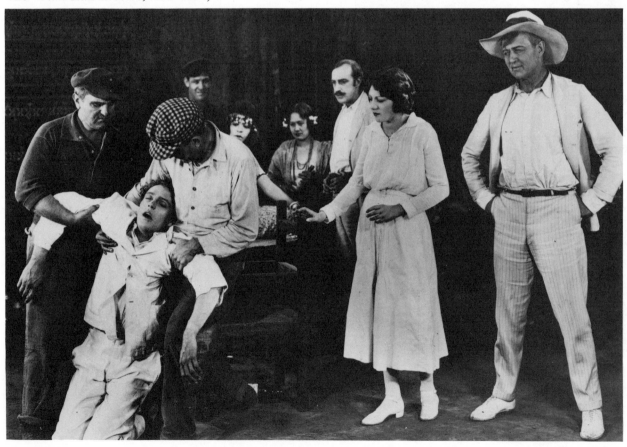

George O'Brien, who began his starring career with a bit part as a sailor in *White Hands. (Photo from collection of Geoffrey Bell)*

tory as far as the movies are concerned." On 8 April 1920, the executive committee of the San Francisco Civic League recommended to the Board of Supervisors "a special committee to induce and encourage motion picture makers to locate in this city." On 26 August the *San Francisco Chronicle* reported the establishment of a new motion picture plant, endorsed by the San Francisco Chamber of Commerce, the San Francisco Civic League, and the Motion Picture Committee of the Board of Supervisors. The *Chronicle*'s banner headline proclaimed, "Motion Picture Plant to Go Up in San Mateo."[16]

San Mateo was a thriving city on the Peninsula, an area some seventeen miles south of San Francisco, that is bordered on the east by the southern

The Great Alone (1922). Monroe Salisbury, Maria Draga, Walter Long. *(Photo permission of Museum of Modern Art—Film Stills Archive, New York)*

Salisbury and Draga in *The Great Alone. (Photo permission of Museum of Modern Art—Film Stills Archive, New York)*

shores of San Francisco Bay and sheltered on the west by the coast range. In its foothills nestled the luxurious communities of Woodside and Burlingame, renowned for their magnificent country estates surrounded by landscaped gardens. The San Mateo area not only had more open land than was available within San Francisco's confined limits, but also could boast thirty-two more days of sunshine per year than Los Angeles—and had statistics to prove it. At the same time it was cooler for work under the sizzlingly hot arc lights then required for shooting interiors.

Cinematography expert John Jasper, manager of the Hollywood studios in the Los Angeles area, designed a motion picture studio that was to be the major production center for San Francisco and northern California filmmakers. It also was planned to be a facility for Hollywood units on location in the Bay Area. These units then could have their film processed overnight and screen it before the next day's shooting; in addition they could shoot matching interior scenes in between shooting exterior scenes. The site chosen for the studio was a 103-acre tract of land on Peninsula Avenue, which bordered both San Mateo and Burlingame and ran east from the railroad tracks toward Coyote Point on San Francisco Bay. Along the south side of the avenue lay the lot of Pacific Studios. The street facades of the studio buildings were in the so-called Spanish style, in vogue during the early 1920s—tan stucco walls, arched doors and windows, terra-cotta tile roofing—designed to suggest a street in some Mediterranean town. Inside

the lot a studio street ran behind the entrance administration buildings. Opposite these were the dressing rooms—those for stars with private baths; all others, with adjoining showers.

The further side of the dressing rooms, opening onto another parallel studio street, provided access to the studio's two mammoth stages, each built with a steel frame over 40 feet high, 120 feet long and 60 feet wide. In contrast to the crudely built sheds that did duty as stages on most movie lots of the day, each stage was so carefully constructed that the walls and roof were separate from the floor so that no vibration could shake the cameras while they were running. Electrical equipment for filming interior scenes included over fifty banks of twin-arc lights for general illumination and over twenty-five arc spotlights for key lights and backlighting.

Across the west end of the lot, paralleling the Southern Pacific Railroad tracks, was a laboratory with dust-proof facilities capable of developing and printing fourteen thousand feet of thirty-five millimeter film per hour. Adjoining this were film storage vaults and film-editing rooms. Another service building contained the carpentry and plaster shops; and still another, a garage. On the east side of the lot was extensive open land for construction of exterior sets. All-in-all, this movie studio plant left little to be desired for the production of high-quality theatrical and industrial films. But the question of marketing its product still had to be addressed.[17]

When this cinema city, known as Pacific Studios, was ready for operation in late 1920, the names of Hodkinson, Malone, and Dixon no longer appeared in connection with the new plant. Realizing that financing to sustain long-term production was not clearly established, Hodkinson wisely withdrew, taking with him Malone and Dixon. The new officers of Pacific Studios had no known experience with motion picture production, distribution, or exhibition, although one director of the corporation, Frank Burt, had been the director of concessions and admissions for the Panama Pacific International Exposition of 1915.

In spite of the lip service paid to encourage local film companies and in spite of the building of Pacific Studios, there was no real financial support that could rival that of the Hollywood–New York conglomerates—or that could even make it possible to offer the industry something distinctive and innovative. Even the astute A. P. Giannini, president of the Bank of Italy (later the Bank of America), who resided near Pacific Studios in the San Mateo–

Burlingame area and who was involved financially with various motion picture enterprises in Hollywood, apparently did nothing significant to aid his hometown motion picture industry.

Any producer who leased space at the Pacific Studios had to be keenly aware, whether the studio management was or not, that his medium was one of enormous risks. Each feature-length production cost approximately the same amount as a five-story, steel-frame luxury apartment or office building, which had an assured rental income. He had to gamble that an equal amount spent on the production of a movie would earn comparable profits. No moviemaker could afford the luxury of an artistic triumph that was a commercial failure. Because cost was such an overriding factor, pictures had to be made with the box office in mind and aimed for the widest possible mass audience. Movie men, however, had before them the example of surefire success—film adaptations of the nineteenth-century popular theater, which had pleased audiences for years on end with their cheerful plots avoiding the obscure, the challenging, or the depressing while affirming the cherished middle-class values of the mass audience. Such escapist fare, made with predictable plots and conventional themes in accordance with audience responses, tabulated by showmen of both the stage and screen, had a reasonable expectation of earning a return on its very costly investment. It aimed at that large percentage of moviegoers who regularly paid to see the outdoor-adventure drama, the crook-melodrama, the society or domestic drama, the comedy romance, or such combination genres as the small-town–domestic drama, or the society-comedy romance.

Despite their obvious artistic limitations, formula pictures cannot be dismissed as crassly unimaginative. Their standardized plot—the "iron clad script"—was not necessarily inferior or limiting, as Shakespeare or Shaw well knew. Many a modest picture with adroit direction and accomplished acting was lifted above the ordinary to become something refreshingly different in movie fare. Among them was even an occasional "sleeper"—a modestly produced film that has the good fortune to attain extraordinary critical and financial success. For the aspiring producer or director, formula pictures were a chance to prove one's mettle; for the distributor, they helped balance the costs of booking the big-star pictures; and for the exhibitor, they often could more than hold their own in pleasing audiences.

One producer keenly aware that films had to conform to the program picture format in order to sell, rather than please his own aesthetic nature, was Hobart Bosworth. Having a distinguished background with the Augustin Daly company of the New York stage and having appeared in pictures since 1909, this actor-producer was one of the earliest stage artists to perceive the possibilities of the new movies. One of Bosworth's friends was Bay Area author Jack London. With distributor W. W. Hodkinson, whose office was then in San Francisco, Bosworth in 1913 persuaded London to allow him to produce and to play the title role in a film version of London's *Sea Wolf*, an outdoor-adventure story that was set on San Francisco Bay. The theme provided Bosworth with the characterization of a tramp-steamer skipper—a brutal-appearing man with a heart of gold—which he continued to play in variations—and also with a colorful setting.[18] "Sea pictures are so popular," Bosworth maintained. "To thousands of people who live inland, the sea stands for romance and adventure." With his dream of films drawing from the lure of the sea—and of the West—Bosworth teamed during 1916 with the Graumans, exhibitors in San Francisco and later in Hollywood, to build a studio near San Francisco Bay with Hodkinson as distributor. Following in the momentum of *The Sea Wolf*, the initial production was to be popular San Francisco author Stewart Edward White's *Grey Dawn*. But local financial interests failed to take advantage of this promising opportunity.[19]

In 1920 Bosworth bounced back with plans to produce feature films again, following the announcement of the establishment of Pacific Studios. One of his creative projects was a costume drama based on Walter Scott's *Scottish Chiefs*. Exteriors evoking romantic highland scenes were readily available in the foothills just west of the studio in and about the Crystal Springs Lake area. Yet despite this imaginative concept and the opportunity to bring something of quality into motion pictures, Bosworth had to turn from ideals to commercialism. He could not be innovative because he found that, although businessmen liked the idea of moviemaking in San Francisco, they were unwilling to back their words with hard cash. Reluctantly surrendering his ideal of quality films, he reverted to run-of-the-mill formula films hinging on the clash of wills aboard a tramp steamer. With Max Graf as his production manager, Bosworth shot *Blind Hearts* (October 1921) and *The Sea Lion* (December 1921), using San Francisco Bay for the predominant exterior scenes. The Bosworth-Graf team also made the first film completely shot at the

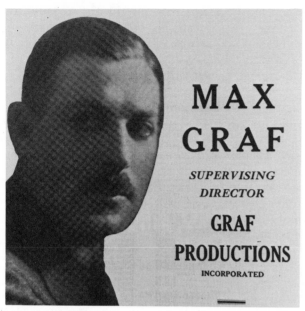

Max Graf. *(Photo permission of Academy of Motion Picture Arts and Sciences, Beverly Hills)*

Milton Sills. *(Photo from collection of Geoffrey Bell)*

new Pacific Studios, *White Hands* (December 1921), with a small role played by the later Fox film star George O'Brien. For this story, in the tradition of men against the sea, the studio's scene department provided settings of unusual visual appeal, evoking an exotic North African seaport. Desert sequences were filmed in San Francisco's Sunset District, at that time an expanse of desolate shifting sand dunes. "Algiers" sequences were filmed at an exterior set constructed at Coyote Point, just east of the studio on San Francisco Bay, with atmospheric palms, camels, lurking Arabs, and dust.[20]

In contrast to the torrid setting of *White Hands*, a subsequent Pacific Studios picture was set in the chill, frozen Northwest. This was *The Great Alone* (May 1922), produced by Isadore Bernstein, up from Hollywood, where he had been involved with a number of competently crafted films, including the first *Tarzan of the Apes*. An exterior set covering several acres on the San Mateo lot represented a Yukon settlement banked with plaster snow and matched with location scenes shot in the Sierra. In this outdoor-adventure picture, teams of husky dogs and intrepid men of the north, lashed by artificial snow (salt from the nearby Leslie Salt Flats) and driven by a blizzard (created by electric wind machines) struggle against the elements. In the climactic scene the stalwart hero finally reaches the isolated, snow-bound cabin where his beloved is held against her will, smashes in the door, confronts the villain, and finally triumphs in a free-for-all fight.[21]

The next producer for Pacific Studios was Max Graf. Before his work as production manager for Hobart Bosworth, Graf had had a decade of on-the-set movie experience: he started his motion picture career in 1911 with "Broncho Billy" Anderson's Essanay company, then in San Rafael, and continued it with Warner Brothers (at that time primarily distributors) and in New York, assisting in the production of the now-classic serial film *The Perils of Pauline* (starring Pearl White). Shortly thereafter, Graf transferred his talents to the World Film Corporation and, following that experience in film distribution, became production manager for Hobart Bosworth. In the wake of Bosworth's *White Hands*, Graf persuaded a number of San Francisco investors to finance his own unit, Graf Productions, Inc. Graf had become an expert at convincing others of the merits of his products and services, exuding assurance from the sheen of his well-oiled hair to the shine of his patent-leather shoes. On the momentum of his own production

The Forgotten Law (1922). Sills and Alec B. Francis. *(Photo permission of Museum of Modern Art—Film Stills Archive, New York)*

Edna Altemas and Jack Mulhall in *The Forgotten Law*. *(Photo permission of Museum of Modern Art—Film Stills Archive, New York)*

The Forgotten Law. Cleo Ridgley and Sills. *(Photo permission of Museum of Modern Art—Film Stills Archive, New York)*

Anna Q. Nilsson. *(Photo from collection of Geoffrey Bell)*

In *Half A Dollar Bill* (1924), Nilsson repels an unidentified intruder. *(Photo permission of Museum of Modern Art—Film Stills Archive, New York)*

Half a Dollar Bill. Raymond Hatton, William T. Carleton, Nilsson, and Frankie Darrow as "Bill." *(Photo permission of Museum of Modern Art—Film Stills Archive, New York)*

unit, his movie experience, and his persuasive manner, he was able to negotiate a contract to produce for Metro Pictures, also the distributor for ace director Rex Ingram *(The Four Horsemen of the Apocalypse, Scaramouche, The Prisoner of Zenda).* Shortly thereafter, Ingram also spurned the Hollywood system and established his own studio at Nice on the Riviera; while Graf, more patriotically, chose to produce in a coastal area far more photogenic than anything the French Riviera could show: that of California.

Max Graf presented an unusual study of the movie producer's mentality. A man of power and presence who commanded respect and who was listened to when he spoke, he had a clear vision of everything he intended to accomplish in each picture and was a perfectionist in carrying out his ideas so that he achieved results of superb quality. For just these reasons, he was not an easy man to work for, not easy to get to know, and not especially likeable. Because he was so consumed with his work and with getting to the top, he was power-hungry, and his personal life suffered—neither of his marriages endured. Putting all his creative energies into his work and on the basis of his strongly motivated and movie-centered background, Graf produced a series of audience-pleasing pictures of high professional quality. While judiciously keeping within the bounds of the program-picture format, he was able to feature players of considerable box-office appeal—such as Milton Sills, the virile star of First National's *Sea Hawk*—and to engage technicians of top quality,

The Fog (1923), starring Cullen Landis and Mildred Harris. *(Photo permission of Museum of Modern Art—Film Stills Archive, New York)*

such as cinematographer John R. Arnold, chief cameraman for MGM's great success *The Big Parade*.[22]

Among the San Francisco–based Graf productions were *Half a Dollar Bill* (January 1924), a small-town story with the "kid" angle; *The Fog* (July 1923), a sweet and light romantic comedy, the making of which was breathlessly described by newsmen to an avid public: "Filmy Clad Beauties Cavort on Lawn"; *The Forgotten Law* (November 1922), a tense, soul-stirring domestic marriage triangle drama; and *Wandering Footsteps* (October 1925), a gin-and-jazz society social comedy. These were movies made with an eye to the box office and with hopes of more lucrative productions in the future.[23]

Yet despite his shrewd management and knowledge of movie markets, Graf's work was destroyed by the very people who had promised to help him.

Estelle Taylor. *(Photo from collection of Geoffrey Bell)*

Graf in newspaper at time of false charges against him, 1924. *(Photo permission of California State Library, Sacramento)*

The trouble started during the production of *Wandering Footsteps*, starring brunette Estelle Taylor, movie siren and wife of pugilist Jack Dempsey. Production was begun in early 1924 but the picture's release was delayed until late 1925 because local investors were disturbed by rumors about various items charged to the production budget, such as the "gift" of a fur coat to Miss Taylor, and about Graf's alleged drinking after hours in the sultry beauty's apartment (those were the days of Prohibition). Investors were further alarmed by Taylor's fervent revelations to the press given under the heading: "Movie Star Explains Why Film Styles Change in Making Love." Consequently, while Graf was in New York promoting and marketing the film, the investors appropriated the books, seized the film, and sued the producer for embezzlement of funds. After nearly a year of litigation, Graf proved his innocence in court by

pointing out that such alleged "misuse of funds" or "extravagances" in the way of perquisites were standard procedures in film production to elicit better acting performances. But the time and expense of fighting this needless court action tied up all of Graf's assets and meant the loss of his movie company.[24]

As fate would have it, Graf's financial troubles were further compounded when his distributor, Metro, became involved in the merger that resulted in the formation of Metro-Goldwyn-Mayer. In the changeover, Graf lost this crucial business contact. Largely as a result of ill-advised interference by petty business interests, this creative venture failed. Yet, with his practical experience, imagination, and good taste, Max Graf could have been the salvation of the silent film production industry in Northern California.

The demise of Graf Productions precipitated a reorganization of Pacific Studios in 1924. A new company took over, headed by A. B. C. Dohrman and William J. Connery, the former described as a San Francisco capitalist; and the latter, as a Hollywood motion picture magnate. The former Pacific Studios was renamed Peninsula Studios, and the new management signed a contract for a series of

Frank E. Woods. *(Photo permission of California State Library, Sacramento)*

Beauty and the Bad Man (1925). Mabel Ballin and Forrest Stanley. *(Photo permission of Museum of Modern Art—Film Stills Archive, New York)*

Patsy Ruth Miller. *(Photo from collection of Geoffrey Bell)*

Warner Baxter. *(Photo from collection of Geoffrey Bell)*

films with Producers Distributing Corporation, an outgrowth of W. W. Hodkinson's distribution company and an affiliate of Cecil B. De Mille, then heading his own unit in Hollywood. The PDC was organized to provide efficient, nationwide distribution channels for independent producer-directors with their own ideas about what pictures should be.[25]

In the optimistic mid-1920s the PDC appeared to hold the key to dependable distribution for independent producers, and the new Peninsula Studios' management signed contracts with two movie producers with backgrounds of notable success in the entertainment world—Elmer Harris and Frank E. Woods. Elmer Harris, a native of San Francisco and a graduate of the University of California, was a professional of considerable theatrical experience who at one time had been an actor in the companies of the classic French stars Coquelin and Rejane. Turning to writing, he had served as the drama critic of the *New York Globe,* later writing such Broadway comedy successes as *So Long Letty* and *Canary Cottage.* Moving from stage to screen, he specialized in adaptations of the comedy-romance genre for movie use. Frank E. Woods had started his career on the East Coast, making a name for

Agnes Ayres. *(Photo from collection of Geoffrey Bell)*

The Awful Truth (1925). Raymond Lowney and Ayres. *(Photo permission of Museum of Modern Art—Film Stills Archive, New York)*

Baxter and Ayres in *The Awful Truth*. *(Photo permission of Museum of Modern Art—Film Stills Archive, New York)*

himself as drama critic for the *New York Dramatic Mirror* as the first serious American reviewer to write about cinema. In 1908 D. W. Griffith asked Woods to make a screen version of Tennyson's *Enoch Arden*. The film was a success, and Woods continued as a scriptwriter for Griffith for a number of years. Among his other story finds, he saw the movie potential of a novel (which also had been the basis for an unsuccessful stage play), *The Clansmen*, and had adapted it for D. W. Griffith into the picture that was retitled *The Birth of a Nation*. In time Woods became story chief for Paramount Pictures. Highly creative and original, he set keen standards for himself and his screen stories. His publicity described him as the "master craftsman of the motion picture art" and "organist of the human heart." On the basis of his experience gained from working with top figures in the industry, Woods decided to use his creative talents to produce his own films for himself in partnership with Elmer Harris.[26]

Woods also was attracted to San Francisco because he felt Hollywood was too limited and ingrown, particularly after his years in New York, and he felt that he could draw from the Bay Area cultural enrichment and fresh new approaches that would enhance his films and his career. The new partnership of Woods and Harris was offered working conditions at the Peninsula Studios more serviceable than those available in a crowded multiple-unit Hollywood studio, where they would have to compete for studio floor space and juggle shooting schedules. At San Mateo they had the advantage of the exclusive use of two capacious enclosed stages, and a lot with plenty of space, and control over their film laboratory and processing plant. With these freedoms, their combined experience, and their many contacts in Hollywood and New York, the partners were able to engage a superior professional technical crew.

Both Harris and Woods had a number of story ideas that they were eager to put into movie form. One of these was *Chalk Marks* (September 1924). Set in a small American town, the story told of a self-sacrificing schoolteacher and her blighted love. "Woods has done careful work," commended the *San Francisco Chronicle*, "and the scheme of building a story on character is new and interesting." Another was *Beauty and the Bad Man* (April 1925), a pictorially handsome adaptation of an adventure-romance by the San Francisco author Peter B. Kyne, whose stories of the West had influenced the Broncho Billy Westerns. *Moving Pic-*

ture World praised this story of gold rush days in old California for its "smooth continuity. Every foot [of film is] used to advance the story, develop characterization, or provide comedy relief." These two Woods dramas of genuine depth were balanced by light comedy-romances produced by Harris—*Let Women Alone* (January 1925), *A Wise Virgin* (August 1924), and *The Girl on the Stairs* (November 1924). The last two films featured Patsy Ruth Miller, a Hollywood starlet, fresh from her appearance opposite Lon Chaney in Universal's *Hunchback of Notre Dame*. Rare insights into the arduous demands made upon movie actresses were afforded newspaper readers with "'Patsy' Gets Cold in 'Nightie' Scene." Miller and most of the leading players in the pictures made at the San Mateo studios were drawn from Hollywood, bringing with them a "name," although most of the character actors and minor roles were drawn from Bay Area theatrical sources.[27]

This flourishing film production momentum was slowed, however—and finally halted—by a brittle blond darling of the silent screen, Agnes Ayres. Intoxicated by her earlier triumph as the object of Rudolph Valentino's ardor in *The Shiek*, Agnes Ayres was enjoying movie fan magazine adulation at Peninsula Studios as the star of the society drama *Her Market Value* (February 1925), and found time to reveal her attitude toward her work in a brittle article stating that she "Finds Art and What Public Wants Are Entirely Different." Woods next starred Ayres in the comedy-romance *The Awful Truth* (April 1925), an adaptation of a sophisticated Ina Claire stage success (later remade with éclat by Irenne Dunne and Cary Grant). In support of Ayres, Warner Baxter brought assurance and magnetism to the role of the husband in this matrimonial escapade. After the picture's showing in New York, *Moving Picture World* described it as "a bright production that is good for a number of laughs, smoothly developed and smartly directed for the more intelligent class of patrons."[28]

Yet despite these flattering showcases for her charms and heedless of the fact that her contract with Paramount Pictures had not been renewed, Agnes Ayres pouted and was unwisely advised to sue Frank Woods—who earlier had helped her when they were both with Paramount Studios—for $95,000, claiming that she had been guaranteed appearances in three pictures, that only one was released, and that she was not advertised in a manner suitable for a "star of her caliber." Although Ayres later played a featured role in Rudolph Valentino's *Son of the Shiek*, she reportedly was eventually re-

duced to demonstrating comestics in department stores.[29]

While one lawsuit by one individual might have little overall effect on a secure and well-financed organization, the strain of litigation continuing over a year was fatal to this small, independent company, which required the cooperation and understanding of all concerned to complete a work in progress. As had been the case with the previous unnecessary suit against Max Graf, a lack of commitment to a creative ideal had halted the work of a promising Bay Area film endeavor.

The anxiety of attempting to sustain production on inadequate financing had long haunted filmmakers, whether working in the feature-film or short-length movie format. Future producer Jack Warner, later one of the very successful heads of the Warner Brothers studio, began learning his craft when he was operating the All Star movie house on San Francisco's Fillmore Street, near Sutter, between 1910 and 1915. His daily contact with paying customers taught him what kinds of movies people pay to see. He also well knew that baseball attracted huge paying crowds. Seeking to combine the appeal of baseball with the movies, the youthful Warner in 1914 had invested all of his hard-earned savings to produce a baseball story, *The Bleacher Hero* (July 1914). The filming went on schedule, and he had high hopes for the results. But after waiting anxiously to view the rushes, Warner was flabbergasted and utterly crushed to find the screen completely blank: during the entire shooting of the picture, the cameraman had forgotten to remove the lens cover! Disasters in production procedure—like the camera take-up mechanism's jamming and ruining an entire reel of takes—were not uncommon. Such disheartening, unpredictable quirks tested the would-be producer, who had to quickly overcome them, or be ruined. For *The Bleacher Hero* there was no choice but costly refilming. As Warner years afterward related to the author: "When we went back to the Seal's stadium, the management refused to let us shoot, because when we were there before, the players could not concentrate on their game—so we had to go back to Golden Gate Park and build a small section of the bleachers and reshoot the film there. It was quite a task to remake the picture after the big five hundred dollars had been spent!"[30]

Not all Bay Area moviemakers had to shoot in a ballpark. During the 1920s the city of San Francisco itself was the site of a studio, which had been converted from a former riding academy. Although less imposing than the studio on the Peninsula, the city studio enjoyed a special advantage because of its proximity to Golden Gate Park, with its ideal exterior locations amidst incomparable vistas of meadows, gardens, lakes and woodlands, and a landscaped Japanese garden as well. Near at hand also, the crooked alleys and pagoda towers of Chinatown provided yet other movie backgrounds. Exotic Chinatown exteriors enlivened Benjamin B. Hampton's *Money Changers* (October 1920). The *Moving Picture World* noted that this story of drug traffic "moves with authority through many diverse phases of underworld life, holds the attention closely, and winds up in a smashing climax."[31]

One movie man of outstanding accomplishments who made his directorial debut in San Francisco was Frank Capra, with a gutsy one-reel drama set in a Calcutta waterfront bar and adapted from Rudyard Kipling's *Ballad of Fisher's Boarding House* (April 1922). To make the film distinctive, the imaginative young Capra recruited real derelicts, ruffians, and passé chorus girls for the barroom scene, instead of casting it with actors merely made up to look like these types. Even though a first film, the production turned out so well that it was bought immediately by Pathe Films for national release. Following this success, Capra be-

came the film editor (cutter) for another locally-produced series of films, the "Plum Center" comedy series, adaptations of the popular newspaper "Toonerville Comedy" comic strip with its well-known character, "Pop Tuttle." These one-reel comedies with their small town settings were shot at Belmont, just south of San Mateo and Pacific Studios. With these folksy comedy shorts, Capra took another step toward his later success in the feature-length entertainment film field, directing fast-moving comedies like *It Happened One Night* and humanistic tributes to the "little guy" such as *It's a Wonderful Life.*[32]

The next picture made at the San Francisco studio was a feature film, *The Broadway Madonna* (November 1922), under the direction of Harry Revier. Veteran Revier had started in the movies by

Dan Mason as "Pop Tuttle." *(Photo from collection of Geoffrey Bell)*

Frank Capra. *(Photo from collection of Geoffrey Bell)*

Pop Tuttle's Lost Nerve (1923). Wilna Hervey, center, Mason on platform. *(Photo permission of Museum of Modern Art—Film Stills Archive, New York)*

Roy Stewart, center, in *The Money Changers* (1920). Robert McKim at left, Claire Adams at right. *(Photo from collection of Geoffrey Bell)*

setting up a studio in a former barn on Vine Street in Hollywood. After shooting a few pictures there, he helped new arrivals Cecil B. De Mille and Jesse Lasky with their first moviemaking. The barn became the basis of the Lasky (later Paramount) studio. As a result of his experience in directing for Lasky and at the Metro and Universal studios, Revier came to know to the dime what moviegoers would pay to see. It was his no-nonsense-let's-get-moving attitude that got his pictures shot and into the can. In the University of California graduate Roy Stewart—who was well over six feet tall—Revier found a prototype of the big strong guy (the type later played so well by John Wayne) to feature in films with appropriate backgrounds of the great outdoors. One of the San Francisco–made Revier epics was *The Heart of the North* (October 1921), a melodrama which, according to the reliable *Moving Picture World*, depicted the redoubtable Stewart "racing against death . . . in a forest fire episode that will stir the blood." Another saga of the Northwest, *Life's Greatest Question* (February 1922), again featured Stewart as a muscular Moun-

The Flying Dutchman (1923). Ella Hall, center. *(Photo permission of Museum of Modern Art—Film Stills Archive, New York)*

tie. Of this Revier-directed movie the *San Francisco Chronicle* wrote that "the story holds interest from first to last."[33]

Major figures from the local theater world also brought their entertainment experience into the movies. George B. Davis, the stage manager of San Francisco's important Alcazar Theatre stock company—for many years a training ground for theater people and movie hopefuls alike—decided to use his long experience in mounting plays successful with Alcazar patrons to make movies with national appeal. His initial choice, an adaptation of a yarn by the best-seller author James Oliver Curwood, came to the screen as *Isobel, or the Trail's End* (November 1920). Its outdoorsman hero, House Peters, earlier the leading man of CMPC's 1914 success, *Salomy Jane*, "possessed just that blending of rugged strength and tenderness to interpret the role," according to the *San Francisco Chronicle* in a review of this Edwin Carewe-directed film.[34]

San Francisco's other tyro from the theater, Edward Belasco, came from a family of tremendous theatrical originality—his brother, David Belasco, was the dean of Broadway theatrical producers. Like Davis, he had a strong background in the theater. Regrettably, however, the only way he could obtain financial support was to produce routine program pictures with time-proven plots, such as *The Mysterious Witness* (June 1923), an outdoor drama; *Her Accidental Husband* (April 1923), an indoor drama; or *Enemies of Children* (October 1923), a tug-at-the-heart "kid" drama. Still, Belasco did manage to embellish his work with some distinctive touches and real style. *Her Accidental Husband* gained distinction because of its interiors, filmed at San Francisco's famed Palace Hotel, adding the texture of real marble and the sumptuousness of carved wood paneling to its settings in lieu of the routine studio pasteboard sets. Yet despite all that Davis and Belasco brought to the movies from the theater arts, their full potential went unrealized.[35]

A striking departure, however, from routine

Paul Gerson. (*Photo permission of Archives for the Performing Arts, San Francisco*)

The Aristocrat Series of the Year

B. Berger presents

Richard Holt

The Sensational "Find"
in
a series of
Romantic Thrill Comedy
Dramas

RICHARD HOLT

"Ten Days"
"Too Much Youth"
"It Can Be Done"
(Temporary Title)
"The Canvas-Kisser"
"Once in a Lifetime"
"Going the Limit"

DUKE WORNE Productions

Produced *by* Gerson Pictures Corp.

Richard Holt. (*Photo permission of California State Library, Sacramento*)

program picture fare was an adaptation from a literary classic, *The Flying Dutchman* (July 1923) which *Photoplay*, more used to reviewing shop-girl romances, described as "an unusual picture. The tragic legend of the mariner doomed to live and suffer until set free by the love of a woman who would be faithful unto death." This Lloyd B. Carleton production earned compliments from other trade journals for its picturesque Hollander settings and unusually fine photography.[36]

The major tenant at the San Francisco studio during the silent era was the Gerson Pictures Corporation, which renamed the plant the Gerson Studio. Producer Paul Gerson, born and theater-trained in England, had acted in the original New York stage production of *Ben Hur*, along with future Western movie hero William S. Hart, and also had appeared with the foremost turn-of-the-century actress Minnie Maddern Fiske in her production of *Becky Sharp*, an adaptation of Thackeray's *Vanity Fair*.

In the wake of his successful stage career, Gerson opened a drama school in Chicago with a branch in San Francisco, training, among others, Marjorie Rambeau, long a star with the Alcazar Theatre stock company in San Francisco before becoming a much-in-demand character actress in the movies. The Gerson Dramatic School supplied talent first to the California Motion Picture Corporation, and later to his own Gerson Pictures Corporation. This combination of acting academy and movie production enabled Gerson to utilize profits from the school to underwrite film production, and there were certainly many pretty girls with doting parents quite ready to pay for "schooling" in order for their darlings to appear in the movies.[37]

There are plenty of parts and characterizations in any story of Dickens, and picturesque settings as well. Gerson's dramatization of Dickens's *Cricket on the Hearth* caused even hard-boiled *Variety* to grant that this period piece about old London "should prove gratifying to Dickens's disciples. The settings are restful and expressive of mid-Victorian England, with all its quiet beauty." Undoubtedly this was a venture dear to Gerson's heart, but the majority of his feature films prudently had to comply with tried-and-true program picture formats. Using San Francisco's waterfront, piers, and bay as backgrounds, he made a number of crime melodramas, including *Waterfront Wolves* (March 1924), *Paying the Limit* (August 1924), *Three Days to Live* (April 1924), and *The Pride of the Force* (November 1925). Among those players involved were Ora Carew, Tom Santchi, and Gladys Hulette, all people with considerable Hollywood experience.[38]

The Barbary Coast (1913) playing in San Francisco.
(Photograph courtesy of Samuel Stark)

Street scene on the "Barbary Coast." *(Permission of San Francisco History Room, San Francisco Public Library)*

Gerson Pictures also shone with a series of fast-moving comedy-romances starring Richard Holt, an all-around athlete, who began in the movies working as a daredevil double and stunt man. Capitalizing on his clean-cut features, Holt worked his way up to feature roles, playing the ebullient, derring-do roles that, a decade earlier, had catapulted Douglas Fairbanks into movie fame. While none of the Gerson Pictures Corporation films starring Holt ever made the list of any year's top ten films, they were, nonetheless, adroitly fashioned to meet popular audience expectations. Among them were *Ten Days* (December 1924), *Too Much Youth* (February 1925), *Easy Going Gordon* (October 1925), and *The Boaster* (February 1927). About the latter New York's *Film Daily*, wrote: "[It was] amusing, with several new comedy angles that appeared to make a real hit with audiences. The situations are so cleverly turned and twisted, with constant introduction of new business, that it makes for really good entertainment. A good quota of laughs."[39]

Gerson's *Going the Limit* (September 1925), starring Holt, captured the spirit of the Jazz Age, with its profiled, masterful heroes straight out of Arrow Collar advertisements and its Marmon and Hudson Super Six wire-wheeled, open sport cars. The film capitalized on the freedom of the uninhibited 1920s and infused its reckless, dashing spirit with the automobile craze. "A popular combination of entertaining elements makes this first-rate fare," *Film Daily* observed. "The pursuit leads up and down San Francisco's many hills. The plot has been worked out with effective suspense and is finished off with a crackerjack, whirlwind climax." Its chase sequence, replete with flashing glimpses of San Francisco Bay, dizzying turns, and hairbreadth escapes, made a sensational windup to a clever, bright film, sparkling enough to entertain audiences on jaded Broadway, the flappers and raccoon-skin–coated undergraduates of college towns, and high school crowds with cut-down Ford runabouts as well. It was a picture that strikingly demonstrated how a filmmaker could overcome limitations in budget, production facilities, and even the lack of highly publicized stars by using *imagination*.[40]

Aside from this picture and a few others of the silent era, local moviemakers for the most part failed to take advantage of the unique resources of the Bay Area. Too often, these more than competent movie people remained blind to the treasure trove they had all about them. For example, story material was readily available from such Bay Area authors as Jack London, Ambrose Bierce, or Peter B. Kyne. Hollywood studios, not San Francisco–based companies, made highly successful movie adaptations of these writers, as well as of the works of other local writers like Kate Douglas Wiggin; Frederick O'Brien; Stuart Edward White; Gertrude Atherton; Will and Wallace Irwin; Frank, Kathleen and Charles Norris; or a struggling Dashiell Hammett—to name only a few. Not only did local producers leave untapped this vast reservoir of literary talent, but they neglected to envision the possibilities of commissioning scripts making use of the area's special flavor and romance: love stories of the Italianate wine country or Hispanic Monterey; mystery thrillers set in some turreted, forbidding Gothic-Victorian mansion; or sagas of the powerful family dynasties of the vast interior grain ranches or of San Francisco's Nob Hill. Local directors might have turned their cameras on northern California's tall timber with its derring-do lumberjacks; or on the still-surviving nineteenth-century railroads with their ornate locomotives and cars winding through snowcapped mountains; or on the rugged seacoast with its weathered fishing boats, surging seas, and sheltered coastal villages. Despite the quantities of Western props and costumes, the carriages and gear, and the rifles and plows available at the inactive Essanay studio at Niles and at the CMPC studio in San Rafael, Bay Area producers surprisingly did not even make movie Westerns—which were among the least expensive films to make, the most certain of earning a profit, and the most common in the industry. Moreover, local producers had, all about them in Northern California, the actual settings of much of early Western history. The photogenic mining towns of bonanza days were peopled with fascinating characters from bold highwayman Black Bart to racy beauty Lola Montez.

Northern California, both in existing terrain and structures, could also represent locations throughout the world. Seacoast, mountain, savanna, forest, lake, river, or valley backgrounds were in abundance. Examples of buildings, already standing, represented a wide variety of national types, in three-dimensional quality and genuine construction, offering the exacting camera eye a solidity and texture no studio sham could achieve. In nearby countryside areas, rural carpentry evoked an earlier, untouched America—the white clapboard villages of New England, the galleried towns of the Old South, the gingerbread periods of the 1870s and 1880s, the frontier streets of the Old West, the unaffected small town Main Streets of middle

America. In larger towns and cities, the civic structures and the mansions of leading citizens—with their turrets, domes, oriels, and frescoed ceilings—stood as a veritable compendium of architectural styles: the Romanesque church, the Gothic fortress, the Italian Renaissance palace, the eighteenth-century French pavillion, the English baronial hall, the classic brick Georgian mansion, and even the Spanish churrigueresque, with hints of exotic China, Japan, or India; and bits from Holland or the Rhineland as well. The very streets of San Francisco could represent many different locales in different parts of the world: London or Paris, at the city's great hotels; Naples, in North Beach; Hong Kong, in Chinatown; Wall Street, in the financial district; the Bowery, in the Tenderloin.

A rare exception to the general neglect of the area's special resources occurred in 1913 when an enterprising moviemaker filmed a documentary of San Francisco's underworld, *The Barbary Coast.* The Barbary Coast, nearby the waterfront, was a notorious sector, of which many had heard but into which few respectable people had ventured. It not only was the brothel district, but it also had a reputation for being dangerous because of its nightly fights, robberies, and shanghaiing of sailors. Yet the motion picture camera could capture the look, texture, and thrills of this alarming place and make it possible for all to see it in the safety and comfort of the movie house. Fascinated audiences, secure in a darkened theater, could see with their own eyes what had hitherto been concealed and forbidden—scenes of uninhibited couples cheek-to-cheek in dance halls, actual raids on the cribs in the crooked alleys off the notorious lower Pacific Street, and painted women plying their shameless trade. As this pioneering early documentary demonstrated, the movies could bring to the virtuous and respectable—at no risk at all—the vicarious thrill of living life to the hilt. The concept and execution of this audacious film owed much of its success to the work of its young cameraman, Hal Mohr. A native of San Francisco, Mohr, was endowed with scientific aptitude, charm, an intuitive ability to please, and extensive training and experience with the movie camera and with photographic lighting, which enabled him to capture actual evening street scenes in the Barbary Coast area after dark. "The vice area was active at night, so the problem, from a cameraman's point of view, was lighting—how to record scenes on the very slow film stock we had to work with then," Mohr explained to the author, "so I brought in arc lights and rigged them up on poles—I still don't know how I ever did it—and got my scenes that way." But he did. Mohr also was able to film scenes in the Barbary Coast's Midway Cafe showing couples dancing the disreputable Bunny Hug, and the Texas Tommy. Rather than simulating a scene on a studio set with actors, these cafe and dance scenes were among the first made in an existing interior, and, despite the difficulties of production, won unqualified praise. "I have rarely seen livelier and more graceful dancing, it was indeed poetry translated into motion," exclaimed W. Stephen Bush of the *Moving Picture World,* "I do not hesitate to commend this picture without reserve or qualification. The taking of the night scenes must have been a task of tremendous difficulty but it was done very finely indeed." Mohr went on to a distinguished career in Hollywood, winning an Academy Award for photographing Max Reinhardt's *Midsummer Night's Dream* and being elected president of the prestigious American Society of Cinematographers.[41]

During the span of the silent era, while local moviemakers, with exceptions like Mohr and Ger-

Director Rex Ingram. *(Photo from collection of Geoffrey Bell)*

Rudolph Valentino and San Francisco Bay—*Moran of the Lady Letty. (Photo permission of Museum of Modern Art—Film Stills Archive, New York)*

son, neglected their area, many of Hollywood's perceptive producers and stars realized the photogenic values of San Francisco and environs and frequently journeyed to the Bay Area with their cameras and crews for location shooting. For example, director Rex Ingram, noted for his impeccable visual taste, selected some of San Francisco's more stately beaux-arts architectural gems to provide a European atmosphere for his *Prisoner of Zenda;* Marin County shores and San Francisco's Embarcadero made authentic maritime settings for heartthrob Rudolph Valentino's *Moran of the Lady Letty;* and majestic Big Trees north of the Golden Gate were backgrounds of visual splendor for Wallace Reid's *Valley of the Giants.* San Francisco's ambience even allowed it a place in religious specta-

Rudolph Valentino and Bay Area waterfront—*Moran of the Lady Letty. (Photo permission of Museum of Modern Art—Film Stills Archive, New York)*

Wallace Reid at Big Trees north of the Golden Gate—*The Valley of the Giants. (Photo permission of Academy of Motion Picture Arts and Sciences, Beverly Hills)*

Eric Von Stroheim in San Francisco—*Greed. (Photo from collection of Geoffrey Bell)*

Greed—vintage buildings as exteriors. *(Photo from collection of Geoffrey Bell)*

Eric Von Stroheim in Carmel—*Foolish Wives. (Photo permission of Museum of Modern Art—Film Stills Archive, New York)*

Eric Von Stroheim in San Francisco filming in actual interior for *Greed. (Photo from collection of Geoffrey Bell)*

cle when it became a setting for the modern sequences in Cecil B. De Mille's first *Ten Commandments*. In a different vein altogether, cowboy hero Tom Mix rode triumphantly up Market Street at his resplendent best in the optimistic adventure film *Rough Riding Romance*. Yet another Western hero, "Strong Silent Man" William S. Hart, filmed in and around San Francisco his suspense stories *The Primal Lure*, *The Aryan*, *The Poppy Girl's Husband*, *The Cradle of Courage*, and *The Testing Block*. Carmel's sea-girt pines and promontories made settings of romance for Samuel Goldwyn's *Dark Angel*, Edwin Carewe's *Evangeline*, and Eric Von Stroheim's *Foolish Wives*. Contrastingly, San Francisco's nineteenth-century streets and structures supplied settings of convincing reality to Von Stroheim's *Greed*, a film that has become a classic in the art of creating a realistic environment.[42]

Another superstar in a position to go beyond studio sham and to insist on the absolute best in scenic effects was Mary Pickford, who filmed scenes in the Bay Area for many of her most be-

Eric Von Stroheim filming in lobby of original Orpheum in San Francisco for *Greed*. *(Photo from collection of Geoffrey Bell)*

Greed company filming in Bay Area locations. *(Photo permission of Museum of Modern Art—Film Stills Archive, New York)*

Eric Von Stroheim and company at work filming *Greed* in San Francisco. *(Photo permission of Museum of Modern Art—Film Stills Archive, New York)*

loved pictures. San Francisco's famed cable cars were part of the action in *Amarilly of Clothesline Alley.* Pacific Heights and Burlingame mansions made handsome backgrounds for *Daddy Long Legs* and *The Little Princess.* Golden Gate Park's greensward and noble groves evoked vistas of Tudor England for her *Dorothy Vernon of Haddon Hall,* while the Haddon Hall itself was a half-timber mansion in Burlingame. Sunol, Alameda County, and nearby Niles Canyon provided the middle-America rural settings for one of her greatest successes, *Rebecca of Sunnybrook Farm.*[43]

These successful Hollywood movies of the silent era benefited from the added production values of refreshing outdoor locations because their makers knew that one of the ways to attract maximum audiences was to embellish their movies with eye-

Mary Pickford and Bay Area mountain ranges—*M'Liss.* *(Photo permission of Academy of Motion Picture Arts and Sciences, Beverly Hills)*

Mary Pickford and the Pleasanton-Sunol Area—*Rebecca of Sunnybrook Farm. (Photo permission of Academy of Motion Picture Arts and Sciences, Beverly Hills)*

Mary Pickford and Niles Canyon—*Rebecca of Sunnybrook Farm. (Photo permission of Museum of Modern Art—Film Stills Archive, New York)*

appealing realistic spectacle—especially in days when most movies were routinely shot against backlot, false-front structures and artificial trees and shrubbery. Location jaunts were costly, however, so that the small producer with a limited budget had to lure the public to see his picture in other ways, the most basic of which was story material with mass appeal. Since his days as a producer at Pacific Studios, Max Graf had kept in touch with· the movie business by operating two show houses, the Aztec and the Egyptian theaters, on San Francisco's Market Street rialto.[44]

Month after month, tallying his box-office receipts, he found that rousing Irish farces consistently drew capacity crowds. Armed with this firsthand data and with the knowledge that, a continent away, *Abie's Irish Rose* held the world's record as the longest-running play on Broadway, Graf was able to obtain tentative financing in anticipation of the sure earnings promised by an Irish genre movie. The script of Graf's movie venture strung together a series of simple knockabout vaudeville skits. By early 1927 production was again in full swing at Peninsula Studios. No idealistic venture this, it was a calculated business proposition made to quickly recoup movie fortunes so that Graf could again move into producing the smooth-running romances that had long been his specialty. With hopes of quality pictures ahead, Graf produced a hasty-pudding fable of family misunderstandings, bricklayers' rivalries, and much running in and out of doors—the type of piece described in the posters of the day as a "comedy riot."

However corny in concept and pinch-penny in production, *Finnegan's Ball* was a means to an end. It was the weapon by which a small independent producer with very limited resources could get a toehold on the slippery path of movie success. In a wider view, the making of the picture served as a metaphor of the vulnerable outsider valiantly battling the entrenched giants of the moviemaking establishment, the Sears-Roebucks of the trade, who made, distributed, and showed their products in an interlocking system that kept outsiders out. Graf's effort was an affirmation of the American ideal of self-reliance—the idea that by hard work and initiative, the little guy could better his place in the world. Graf's daring movie gamble, when released in New York, played to good houses and garnered approval from that bible of the trade, *Variety:* "*Finnegan's Ball* . . . has a well balanced cast. It is a picture that will get a lot of laughs, it has plenty of good comedy, and that will get it over."[45]

But would it?

Graf's silent comedy was released in October 1927, the same month as another film that abruptly changed the history of motion pictures—*The Jazz Singer,* with Al Jolson's spontaneous, ad-libbed scene and his vibrant voice. The effect on audiences of voices apparently issuing from the lips of humans was electrifying. After such a blockbuster, a simple silent film like *Finnegan's Ball* had no chance at all. With his future staked on one picture launched only by perilous financing, the "talkies" dealt a crushing and eventually fatal blow to Max Graf. For all other moviemakers, 1927 also became a time of drastic change and peril because all movie procedures—production, distribution, and exhibition—were overturned. Sound films might have been produced at Peninsula Studios at San Mateo had its stages been soundproofed, but its location near busy railroad lines was a disadvantage at a time when the available microphones were nonselective. In addition the studio would have had to obtain sound-recording equipment, which was expensive and in short supply, and an additional crew of the much-in-demand and all-important new breed of sound technicians. In this, the small, independent producer could not possibly compete. Only the national New York–Hollywood studio combines could finance such a costly changeover, particularly when the situation was complicated by dispute among the production companies and theater owners over which of the new competing sound systems would become standard. In the mergers and reorganizations forced by the immense and costly task of reoutfitting the move industry for sound, one of the casualties was Producers Distributing Corporation, which, only a few years earlier, had promised national distribution for independent filmmaker pictures. The onset of the Depression in 1929—with economic collapse, bank closings, and widespread unemployment—put a further damper on investor willingness to finance anything as risky as the movies. The double blow of the end of the silent movie and of the financial crash of 1929 dealt the coup de grace to San Francisco's early filmmakers.

Although no footage was to run through the cameras of Bay Area filmmakers for nearly a score of years following 1927, that hiatus could not erase the record of courage, experimentation, and innovation they compiled in the era of the silent film. This half-century of creative cinematic activity began during the early 1870s, when Leland Stanford

was willing to squander a fortune on unpredictable experiments that he felt would produce significant results—though he could have had no idea that this scientific work, with the added photography of Eadweard Muybridge, would create the motion picture. The Miles brothers, through their experience with early forms of film distribution and their motion picture exchange, dreamed of the finest movie studio in the West—a dream that began to take shape in Niles, where "Broncho Billy" Anderson defined the Western movie genre, and that took an even more promising form in the California Motion Picture Corporation's quality feature-length dramatic films. Leon Douglass with his work with color films; Thomas Kimmwood Peters with his dedication to educational motion pictures; and such independents as Max Graf and Paul Gerson, whose pictures were the equal of Hollywood's fare: these were but a few of the others who made the area rich in fledgling studios and cinematic experimentation.

Through the years linking 1877 and 1927, Bay Area moviemakers pioneered and experimented in many aspects of the motion picture, preparing the way for a new generation and achieving, in retrospect, more than they themselves could have known. These courageous, tenacious individuals, often pitted against overwhelming odds, kept alive the possibilities of independent filmmaking in Northern California and, in a wider sense, throughout the entire country. Because of what they did, filmmakers of the 1970s and 1980s could push ahead into new dimensions of cinema, inspired by the same artistic daring that was present on that San Francisco springtime evening of May 1880, when the movies were born.

Whether yesterday or today, the San Francisco Area lures filmmakers with its colorful history, unexcelled setting, and rich creative opportunities. *(Photo permission of California Historical Society, San Francisco)*

Epilogue

The cinema and the city today: San Francisco's face inevitably shows the lines and blemishes that long have distorted, even mutilated, other American cities. Still, while many a Hollywood lot has closed down—the studio's treasures in props and costumes auctioned off as relics of a former time—movie companies embrace San Francisco's seductive beauty, and television cameras continue to present her charms to captivated audiences throughout the world.

But the ongoing physical attraction that San Francisco presents to movie producers is only secondary to her role as host to some of the most innovative and exciting filmmaking of our time. The light of motion picture production in the Bay Area, extinguished by 1930, was rekindled after 1945 with a burst of new creative activity. While the number of moviemakers and their works is almost beyond count, the renascent Bay Area film movement and its effect on the industry everywhere can best be understood in the work of four representative artists: Frank Stauffacher, who brought postwar filmmakers together and focused attention on their work; James Broughton, poet and filmmaker; Jordan Belson, visionary film artist par excellence; and George Lucas, world-famous for feature films like *American Graffiti* and *Star Wars.*

This movie renaissance was signaled in striking fashion in 1946 by an event presented by the San Francisco Museum of Art, the exhibition arm of the San Francisco Art Association, which had,

years earlier, also championed the world's first public presentation of motion pictures—the 1880 cinematic projection of the Eadweard Muybridge–Leland Stanford sequential illuminated photographs in motion. In September 1946, the San Francisco Museum of Art, in another motion picture first, brought before the public its landmark presentation *Art in Cinema.* This program offered film fare differing greatly from the conventional themes and stereotypes accepted in the movies up to that time. Instead of theatrical spectacles or romantic fantasies made to sell tickets at movie house box offices, here were noncommercial films crafted primarily as personal statements.[1]

With a vigor and style rarely attempted before, these were films seeking to create new ways of seeing the unseen and even making it visible to others. One such personal, unorthodox work, exhibited at *Art in Cinema* by new filmmakers James Broughton and Sidney Peterson, was *The Potted Psalm.* "The film has all the sudden changes and metaphors of dreams," exclaimed P. Adams Sitney, with its "use of distorted imagery, outrageously contrived effects . . . wild camera movements, and a montage that suggests free association." The opening shots indicated its ambiguous, even bizarre, construction. From an image of dry weeds the camera panned to a hilltop view of San Francisco and then to a grave marked Mother, across which a caterpillar crawled. The camera then settled on a bust of a male on a tomb and then cut to a similar profile of the protagonist's face.[2]

135

Movie critics from the San Francisco newspapers of 1946, apparently nonplussed by such flouting of accepted norms, ignored these newsworthy films, choosing instead to fill their columns with respectful accounts of the overblown costume romance then before Hollywood's cameras—*Forever Amber*. One newsman, however, Alfred Frankenstein, later a distinguished art critic and curator, had the perception to tackle the uncharted. In October 1946, Frankenstein wrote about *The Potted Psalm* and the program as a whole:

> You can see San Francisco transmogrified through the poetic and image-making eyes of Sidney Peterson and James Broughton into a place of such strangeness, wild action, and still terror, as exists nowhere else

except in the dreaming mind of every human being. . . . What has been created so far is a large body of experimental film which has a curiously epic quality and appeal.
  The epic is a medium of adventure. From its beginning it suggests a long unfoldment of curious experiences, strange incidents, and fantastic happenings. Such an unfoldment is provided by the experimental films at the museum, even when they are extremely short. As a famous character far from unknown to the cinema once remarked, "In a small way, it's colossal."[3]

Although mayhap Sam Goldwyn, the "famous character" alluded to by Frankenstein, did not have the esoteric film in mind, the films shown at *Art in Cinema* did prove to have a stature that was nothing less than colossal. Although movie executives of the day, like Goldwyn, initially spurned these small noncommercial, experimental films, Hollywood itself was in time to be challenged and enriched by the vitality, immediacy, and intensity of these provocative, poetic, and personal films. Although before 1946 there had been showings of film as art, rather than as entertainment, very few had an influence as immediate and long-lasting as this one.

Art in Cinema (repeated, by popular demand, in 1947) was important, not only because of its artistic content, but also because it took place at the right time and place. The aftermath of World War II brought a sense of release from wartime restrictions and sufferings and, at the same time, a need for new openness in thought. A cultural cross-fertilization from the influx of people from all over America, Europe, and Asia into the Bay Area engendered new attitudes and an awakened interest in a wide range of ideas, concepts, philosophies, and

theories. Recharged with energy, San Francisco found itself an influential center of new thought. This artistic dynamism—later evident in the beat generation of Jack Kerouac and Allen Ginsberg—had its original and most enduring expression in the "San Francisco school" of filmmakers.[4]

"New, vast audiences saw ideological, documentary, educational, and training subjects for the first time and developed a taste for experimental and noncommercial techniques," wrote film historian Lewis Jacobs about the postwar emergence of interest in film itself. "Thousands of filmmakers were developed in the various branches of the service. Many of these, having learned to handle picture and sound apparatus, [began] to use their skills to seek out, through their own experiments, the artistic potentialities of the medium." After release from the service, many of these neophyte filmmakers settled in the Bay Area and became interested in the creative potential of the medium because of the 1946 *Art in Cinema* presentation.[5]

Frank Stauffacher, the organizer of *Art in Cinema*, was then a successful graphic artist in San Francisco. His entire previous life, it would seem, had been a preparation for this event. He had always loved the movies and had studied stage and cinema design, along with other visual arts, under a scholarship at the Art Center in Los Angeles. Returning to San Francisco, he established his own firm, where he made a number of advertising films for his clients. As an amateur in the true sense of the word, he also made personal films, reflecting his identification with the avant-garde films of Europe and America. From this work, Stauffacher attained a firsthand knowledge of the problems involved in transposing visual, poetic, and dramatic concepts into cinema. Among the best known of his films are *Sausalito* (1948) and the evocative *Notes on the Port of St. Francis* (1952), with its visual rhythms of ships against clouds, light-dappled water, and fog swirling in poetic counterpoint.[6]

Inspired to share his own intense feelings about new cinema with others, Stauffacher persuaded the San Francisco Museum of Modern Art to provide facilities for film showings on the order of those at the Museum of Modern Art in New York. According to film historian Jacobs, he was "actually the first in this country to assemble, document, and exhibit on a large scale a series of strictly avant-garde films."[7]

Art in Cinema was especially notable because of Stauffacher's organization of the material and his bringing together and juxtaposing so many varied films that previously had been scattered or unobtainable. He organized ten programs, each illustrating one phase of film as art: "Some Precursors," "The French Avantgarde," "Continental Avantgarde," "Nonobjective Form Synchronized with Music," "The Animated Film as an Art Form," "Contemporary Experimental Films in America," "Fantasy into Documentary," "Experiments in the Fantastic and the Macabre," "Poetry in Cinema," and "The Surrealists."

The presentations were enlivened by Stauffacher's insightful introductions and enthusiastic program notes. In addition to the screen fare itself, Stauffacher brought to the symposium many of the filmmakers themselves. Some were immigrants with European reputations, such as Hans Richter and Man Ray. Among the Americans was Maya Deren, who presented her film *Meshes of the Afternoon* (1943), which, made in collaboration with Alexander Hammid, was a dreamlike picture generally considered to mark the initiation of the new American noncommercial cinema movement. Among others present were John and James Whitney from Los Angeles, who, since 1941, had been synchronizing abstract visual images on film with electronic sounds, the ebb and flow of color and design counterpointing the sound track in exquisite harmony. The Whitney films, with their audiovisual music, have continued to astonish and delight audiences ever since.

The body of filmmakers assembled at *Art in Cinema* were able to speak personally about the meaning of their works and about what was involved in making a film—the grueling work, the endless trials, the disappointments, the dedication, and, most important, the emotional rewards. Adding brio to the occasion were viewers from San Francisco's art world and intelligentsia—poets, dramatists, authors, painters, composers, musicians, museum curators, librarians, educators, psychologists. Out of this mix of intellectual elite and innovative filmmakers—spurred by the stimulation of the extraordinary images exhibited on the screen—emerged a rich and lively interchange of ideas. Local artists also were encouraged to experiment with the movie camera and, in turn, to exhibit their films. It was a watershed moment.[8]

For many years afterward, Frank Stauffacher remained a catalyst for Bay Area and West Coast personal filmmaking.

One of the young artists presented by Frank Stauffacher was James Broughton, who had coproduced with Sidney Peterson (then a San Francisco resident) *The Potted Psalm,* the subject of so much comment at that time. After 1946 Broughton remained as one of the foremost filmmakers of the "San Francisco school," making a number of short films preoccupied with the absurdities of human existence. Among the most widely known is *Mother's Day* (1948), with its dual themes of an adult reaching back into childhood and of the childish behavior of adults. The cameraman was Frank Stauffacher, and the technician in charge of props and costumes was a new film enthusiast, Pauline Kael, later one of America's most renowned film critics. In 1953, under the sponsorship of the British Film Institute, Broughton filmed a comic fantasy, *The Pleasure Garden,* on the grounds of the Crystal Palace, London, in which figures dressed in frivolous party costumes, in contrast to others in somber black, swirled in absurd arabesques against backgrounds of crumbling Victorian grandeur, expressive, as Sitney observed, of the "cyclic and ritualistic nature of human events and antagonisms."[9]

During these and following years Broughton was also active in writing, reciting, and printing plays and poetry. He resumed active filmmaking with a work commissioned by the Royal Film Archive of Belgium—*The Bed* (1968). Since then, he has produced a new film each year. One example is *Nuptiae* (1969), which possesses a rare charm. It is almost as if the film called itself into being with the spontaneity characteristic of much experimental filmmaking. When a friend filmed Broughton's wedding in 1961, with its contrasting scenes of the formal, classical splendor of San Francisco's City Hall and those of the very informal and motley celebrations along the Marin County seashore following the wedding, no one intended to use this record of the event as the basis for a poetic film. Yet Broughton later wove this footage together into a tapistry of ritual, myth, and symbolism with a sound track made up of fragments of the marriage service and a poem Broughton had written for the occasion.

Even among experimental films, Broughton's are unique. *Nuptiae*'s sense of joy, for example, is a refreshing change from the gloom characterizing so many of the humorless, contemporary, "socially conscious" films made by others. "It's easy to do something topical, or to depress an audience," Broughton declared, "they're depressed enough already. I only want to make celebrational films—I believe in Delightments, Incitements, Enlightenments." Broughton's films have won prizes at festivals throughout the world. He has received an individual grant from the National Endowment for the Arts, and twice he has been awarded Guggenheim Fellowships. He is the only established American poet consistently engaged in filmmaking.[10]

Another San Franciscan who was originally inspired by *Art in Cinema*, yet who has a totally different approach to his medium, is Jordan Belson. Belson's art is acclaimed by both critic and craftsman as representing the high point of the visionary film. While profound in content, his works are capable of being experienced on many levels so that they may also be enjoyed purely for their sensuous visual delights. Their genesis is the individual emotional ecstasy arising from an intense response to the world outside the self and to the wonder of human existence: *Momentum* (1969) inquires into the nature of the center of our solar system; *World* (1971) explores the creation and evolution of a planet; *Cycles* (1975) reviews the organic interrelation of planetary and human cycles; *Infinity* (1979) studies the multiple planes on which humans live; and *Light* (1974) examines the full range of the light spectrum—from infrared to ultraviolet. These amazing cinematic experiences offer a breathtaking variety of effects—organic washes of colors endlessly gathering, evolving, receding, and returning in yet other forms like flashing jewels, explosions of vivid color, or iridescent ocean waves. Through constantly changing rainbows, sunrises, or sunsets, the films transport viewers into regions glorious with luminations—from planets and stars and beyond into even more awe-inspiring vistas of outer space.

Belson synthesizes visual effects with sounds to achieve such a perfect harmony that the spectator cannot be sure whether he is seeing or hearing the presentation. The rise and fall of Belson's own breathing, for instance, forms much of the sound track of *Samadhi* (1967), the rhythms of breathing creating an aural counterpart to the visual images of circular forms undergoing a series of transformations, as the circles and spheres revolve to fill the entire frame with their luminosity, suggesting the ultimate fusion of breath and mind, the union of subject and object.

Belson has been most active in the years since 1965. Drawing from both Western scientific disciplines and Eastern metaphysics, his films have gone through a continuous process of evolution. *Reentry* (1965), for example, was inspired by the United States space program, while such a film as *Meditation* (1972) explores the ecstasy—or blissful tranquility—of inward contemplation. Yet these works make no claim to scientific validity, nor to

being accurate representations of any Buddhist, Hindu, or other religious doctrines. In these both timely and timeless films, a starry galaxy can be seen undergoing a life cycle similar to that of a human being in its birth, youth, maturity, and eventual death, so that from the wondrous perspectives of outer space, life here on earth takes on a different meaning.

Using the image-making film equipment as an extension of the mind, Belson considers cinema to be a means of discovering and clarifying what is most essential in life. As Belson once remarked to the author, "Finally, we reach a point where there is virtually no separation between science, observation, philosophy—and art." Because the Belson films do not tell linear stories nor depict dramatic plots enacted by humans, they are sometimes categorized as abstract. But the word *abstract* is a bleak, one-dimensional way to describe such gorgeous fusions of color and motion, of sound effects and celestial music—or to express the richness of content and the sense of cosmic destiny. With poetic brevity, his films run from six to ten minutes, though each, when shown, seems to have its own time-span, not measured in chronological time. These are works aimed more and more at individual appreciation, rather than theatrical presentation before large audiences, the usual target of most filmmakers.[11]

Belson's ultimate aim is videotape presentations, which can be run and rerun at home, like symphonic records or tapes. Such wider audiences may respond to Belson, as has art critic Thomas Albright, because of his "ability to express an essentially intellectual concept in terms that remain as emotionally intense as they are sensually splendid—in other words, to transform mysticism into art."[12]

The originality of Jordan Belson's work is emblematic of the evolution of cinema over the past three decades. These changes have been brought about because of a new perception by the public and by filmmakers of what cinema should be, because of economic readjustments in the industry, and because of technological advances in motion picture equipment. Just as the spoken word captured on a sound track completely altered film production methods after 1927, so new motion picture cameras, lenses, film stock, lighting equipment, and sound recording systems effected equally sweeping changes after 1945. With this advanced, and far more portable, adaptable and sophisticated equipment, it became possible to shoot exteriors in adverse conditions, such as dusk or inclement weather, and to film interiors with existing lighting or with minimal, supplemental lighting. Audio systems were also completely transformed so that sound and dialogue could be recorded on location despite even heavy background noises. As a result, moviemakers were released from confining and cumbersome studio methods and could enjoy the artistic freedom of filming on authentic, outdoor locations and within existing buildings. Their productions gained new texture and visual excitement in ways that utterly changed and greatly broadened the horizons of both commercial entertainment movies and poetic, personal films.

Prior to the postwar era, any film made as art had to be produced with the ponderous thirty-five millimeter equipment, which was not only prohibitively expensive even to rent, let alone buy, but also could only be operated by costly professional technicians. But after 1945, the new, far less expensive, and vastly simplified sixteen millimeter sight and sound systems enabled filmmakers in San Francisco—or Seattle or St. Paul—to obtain results formerly possible only with big-studio paraphernalia. With affordable sixteen millimeter equipment, it became possible to make a personal film for the cost of a two-week vacation—or, perhaps, of a new automobile—and to make it not primarily as a money-making proposition, but as a creative expression. The result has been an explosion of individual filmmaking and of film festivals exhibiting new cinema all over the United States and the world.

Many of the experimental filmmakers grew up in homes with private movie equipment and thus had the opportunity to view all manner of films. During their formative years they became familiar with a wide variety of cinematic styles—from traditional masters like D. W. Griffith to such iconoclasts as Luis Buñuel or Stan Brakhage—and so could bring to their own work a rich and varied heritage. In an age open to the intuitive, their imaginations have been able to range unfettered. After 1945, reflecting and contributing to a democratic environment, many men and women began making films, dissolving the distinction between amateur and professional moviemaking. "Filmmaking styles have changed since the days of Stauffacher," notes Clyde B. Smith and Robert M. Sitton of the University of California Extension Media Center, "but the spirit of Art in Cinema programs lives on."[13]

Not only was the form of the art film given new dimensions, but the theatrical motion picture—formerly produced almost entirely within Hollywood's concrete sound stages—could now be produced virtually anywhere. In a way that was not heretofore possible, moviemaking became commercially feasible in the Bay Area after 1945. During the earlier 1915–1945 period, the New York–Hollywood studio corporations held most of the winning cards. After 1945, they did not. These major studio corporations lost their monopoly on moviemaking equipment; were forced to divest themselves of their coast-to-coast theater chains, which had guaranteed a profitable marketing of their products; and, because of the dual threat of foreign film and television competition, could no longer maintain assembly-line production methods at the studios. The name *Hollywood* became associated less and less with a geographical location and more and more with a state of mind. In fact, with moviemaking freed from the confines of the studio lot, many Hollywood directors found Northern California a favorite movie location. Since the mid-1940s there has hardly been a time that a feature film was not being shot somewhere in the Bay Area. Alfred Hitchcock started the trend with his *Shadow of a Doubt* (Santa Rosa, Sonoma County), *Vertigo* (San Francisco), and *The Birds* (Bodega Bay, Marin County). And, many, many television programs and commercial spots have been, and continue to be, shot locally.[14]

Just as more and more movie location units come to the Bay Area, a number of professionals choose to live there and commute, when required, to Hollywood, New York, or other centers of activity. Stimulated and refreshed by the same ambience that sustains local film artists like Belson and Broughton, many moviemakers reside in San Francisco itself; others, notably actor-director Clint Eastwood, live in, and draw inspiration from, nearby scenic regions. According to director Philip Kaufman, "Everyone works harder and is more devoted to film here. Los Angeles . . . may be more 'professional,' but there's not the same commitment to the movie. The difference is that, up here, people push you to make it better." Director Michael Ritchie finds that he has more opportunity for creative work in Marin County, close to nature, observing, "There are no meaningless meetings, you gain time for yourself and your family and for thinking."[15]

John Korty's Marin County production company has achieved a reputation of high distinction in both motion pictures and in television, attracting admiring audiences for feature films, including *Crazy Quilt* (1966), *Funnyman* (1968), and *River-run* (1969), and for its television specials *The Auto-*

biography of *Miss Jane Pittman* (1974), *Who Are the DeBolts, and Where Did They Get Nineteen Kids?* (1978), and *Christmas without Snow* (1980). *Pittman* won Emmy and Director's Guild awards, and *DeBolts* won an Emmy and an Academy Award. A masterpiece of the documentary genre, *DeBolts* has for its subjects the pathos and hard-won triumphs of physically disabled children. Without telling his audience what to think, for instance, Korty won hearts through such means as an unadorned sequence in which a one-legged newspaper boy hops up and down stairs, proud to be able to earn his way like other youngsters.[16]

In the field of the feature-length theatrical entertainment film, few can equal the commercial and artistic success of George Lucas. The Lucasfilm center of activity also is in Marin County, where woodland and marine vistas, valleys, meadows, and gardens have long lured photographers. Fittingly, the Lucas headquarters are not far from the site that the California Motion Picture Corporation chose for its studio some sixty years earlier. An early member of the Zoetrope studio facilities in San Francisco, headed by Francis Ford Coppola, Lucas quickly and certainly established his own cinematic style and artistry. Early stepping stones to his later major movie achievements include *THX-1138* (1970) and *American Graffiti* (1973). *THX-1138* presented a bleak view of future society, where humans are reduced to robots existing without sunlight in underground living and working spaces filled with ominous echoes. For his futuristic settings, Lucas made creative use of BART (Bay Area Rapid Transit) subway tunnels and of the Frank Lloyd Wright Marin County Civic Center, north of San Rafael. In visualizing a very different type of story of middle America, Lucas found his settings for *American Graffiti* along Marin County back roads; downtown Petaluma, Sonoma County; and at a San Francisco drive-in restaurant. This imaginatively photographed picture examined the youth society of the 1950s, dominated, corrupted, and insulated by the shallow comforts of mass-produced gadgets, fast foods, and blaring radios. Much of the atmosphere was created by lovingly documented visuals of fish-tail automobiles, neon lights, and drive-ins, neatly edited to the rhythms of Top 40 rock-and-roll music to create a touching picture of the mating rituals of youth. With *American Graffiti,* Lucas succeeded in capturing both the poignancy of American small-town life and the mystique of the automobile, which, half a century earlier, had been the subject of the San Francisco–made movies

Chalk Marks (1924), by Frank E. Wood, and *Going the Limit* (1925), by Paul Gerson.

Shifting the setting from small towns to outer space, Lucas carried his young characters into new and far different regions with his *Star Wars* (1977) and *The Empire Strikes Back* (1980). Like Jordan Belson, Lucas has a mythical vision, though each imaginatively interprets this vision differently for differing artistic ends. In *Star Wars* youthful adventurers from a planet only marginally habitable escape into an interstellar region where machines enhance, rather than diminish, life. In both pictures, the stirring music and eerie electronic sounds of the galactic environment are counterpoints to the everyday, casual language of the protagonists; in both pictures, the ultimate in cinematography and sound recording produce special effects that are not merely used to astonish but are organic elements of the story development, emphasizing dramatic moments, advancing the plot, and linking blocks of story material. Continuing these exciting qualities in *The Raiders of the Lost Ark* (1981), producer Lucas also recaptures in the process the thrill-a-minute magic of the Saturday matinee movie fare initiated so long before by G. M. Anderson with his wildly popular Broncho Billy Westerns. Today, with *The Return of the Jedi* (1983), Lucas sustains this serial tradition in one of the most far-reaching projects in movie history.[17]

In his cinematic presentations George Lucas has stretched the imagination of his audiences; he has made the incredible visual and almost tangible. Drawing from the deep wells of symbol, myth, fairy tale, legend, and dream, he has restated their themes and has channeled their energies into new, fresh, and humane forms, appealing to a very wide range of people. Lucas has made his films with his personal stamp, while at the same time utilizing the advantages of the commercial establishment for financing, marketing, and distribution. Although long considered incompatible, both business acumen and aesthetic vision have been united in George Lucas's impressive transmutation of the personal film into the popular film. Minimizing the esoteric aspects of the personal, poetic, iconoclastic film, the Lucasfilm productions have reaffirmed the special values of the film as art and have used them to enrich and revitalize the mainstream of mass entertainment. Although the artistic and commercial aspects of the motion picture have long been antithetical, here they are united.

In terms of tangible resources—laboratories, studios, offices, and centers for advanced technology—Lucas's northern California motion picture facility reactivates the spirit of the Miles Brothers operation some seventy-five years earlier. The Lucasfilm animation and special effects unit, Industrial Light and Magic, is a striking blend of expert business management, precise science, and soaring imagination. Its elaborate sound equipment, animation stands, computerized motor control systems, and editing rooms equal or surpass any other similar installation in the entire world. Here, in artistic coordination on an international scale, special scenes were completed for the *Star Wars* picture saga and *The Raiders of the Lost Ark* to blend with major filming for these pictures done at the EMI-Elstree Studio in London. Lucas currently plans to supplement Industrial Light and Magic with another cinematic center on secluded, sylvan acreage in central Marin County, which will contain all other Lucasfilm activities. "I'm trying to create the optimum working environment," Lucas explains, "to bring together a group of filmmakers who are friends, and give us a place to work." Here, in congenial surroundings, other directors and producers will have an opportunity to plan, design and edit their films, film artists like Korty, Ritchie, or Kaufman; Carrol Ballard *(The Black Stallion);* Harold Barwood and Matthew Robbins *(Dragonslayer);* Irvin Kersher *(The Empire Strikes Back);* and Stephen Spielberg *(E.T.—The Extra-Terrestrial).*[18]

Nor does the story stop here. Looking further into the future, Lucas envisions computerized digital printing, editing, and sound-mixing video technology, which is expected to make obsolete the present-day motion picture systems, with its risks of torn sprockets or loss of sync, and the ever-present hazard of damage to the fragile film itself. Already a staff of specialists from such computer centers as the California Institute of Technology's Jet Propulsion Laboratory are working on this new video system, which will free Lucasfilm and other Bay Area filmmakers from reliance on Hollywood film laboratories for the printing of the thousands of copies of movie prints and from dependence on the big-studio movie cartels, which now control distribution of the theatrical entertainment film. The circle is complete: the motion picture, invented in the Bay Area over a century ago, has returned to its place of origin, and the inspired saga of the *"picture that moves"* is infused with new vitality. Beginning in 1946, new American cinema was galvanized by the presentations of Frank Stauffacher, who shocked audiences and moviemakers out of their lethargy. It has been revitalized by such individualists as James Broughton, has achieved some of its most consummate artistic expression in the visionary films of Jordan Belson, and has fostered the record-breaking and ground-breaking feature films of George Lucas. All of these individuals have contributed importantly to major phases in the development of contemporary cinema. As the spiritual descendants of the pioneering filmmakers of the Bay Area, they stand at the apex of a full century of experimentation—going back to the entertainment feature films of Paul Gerson, Frank E. Woods, Max Graf, and Beatriz Michelena, and the innovative color films of Leon Douglass; to the prototype movie Westerns of "Broncho Billy" Anderson; to the living-motion photographs and first motion picture show of Eadweard Muybridge and Leland Stanford.

Today's Bay Area filmmakers carry on this long and adventurous tradition of motion picture activity, extending from the 1870s to the 1980s. It is not surprising that film production is continuing in Northern California, with particular focus on San Francisco. The region has always been sympathetic to the artistic temperament. Its romantic and dramatic setting, its meeting of land and water, its fusion of East and West, its swirl of maritime trade from ports of call the world over: these elements have all engendered vital creative currents. Its literature, theater, music, and paintings; its wine making—even its sourdough French bread—all have a zest and flavor not attainable elsewhere. No less so, its filmmakers have expressed themselves through their individualist cast of mind and artistic vision. San Francisco's unique blending of all these elements with her long tradition of experimentation promises centuries of creative cinematic activity from the filmmakers of tomorrow who are spawned by the time-tested marriage of the Golden Gate and the Silver Screen.

APPENDIX A

Titles and Production Data of Silent Films Produced in Northern California, 1897–1930*

SHORT FILMS

Travel and Actuality Films by Various Producers

Thomas Edison Company

Arrest in Chinatown (October 1897)
Fisherman's Wharf, San Francisco (?) (October 1897)
Hotel Del Monte, Monterey (October 1897)
Hotel Vendome, San Jose, Cal. (October 1897)
Lick Observatory, Mt. Hamilton, California (October 1897)
Lurline Baths, San Francisco (?) (October 1897)
Stanford University, California (October 1897)
Surf at Monterey (October 1897)
Sutro Baths, San Francisco (September 1897)
Sutro Baths, No. 1, San Francisco (October 1897)
Mount Tamalpais R.R., No. 1 (March 1898)
Mount Tamalpais R.R., No. 2 (March 1898)
Mount Taw [sic] R.R., No. 3 (March 1898)
Parade of Chinese, San Francisco (?) (March 1898)
Jeffries and Ruhlin Sparring Contest at San Francisco (1901)
Bird's Eye View of San Francisco, Cal., from a Balloon (January 1902)
Cable Road in San Francisco (January 1902)
Fishing at Faralone Island (January 1902)
Panoramic View of Mt. Tamalpais (January 1902)
Panoramic View of the Golden Gate (January 1902)
Panoramic View of Mt. Tamalpais between Bow Knot and McKinley Cut (January 1902)

American Mutoscope and Biograph Company

Panorama, Union Square, San Francisco (June 1903)
Panorama of Beach and Cliff House, San Francisco (September 1903)
Scenes in San Francisco (May 1906)
Views in San Francisco (May 1906)
Wawona, Big Tree (April 1908)

Miles Brothers Company

Nelson-Britt Prize Fight (September 1905)
No Bill Peddlers Allowed (1905)
A Trip down Mt. Tamalpais (April 1906)
Head-on Collision at Brighton Beach Race Track (July 1906)
Gans-Nelson Contest; Goldfield, Nevada (September 1906)

*For some films, especially early short films, little or no information is available about casts and production credits. When a credit is probable but not verified, the entry is followed by a question mark. Sources vary considerably in the spelling of names and in the dating of films and events; in each case, only the version deemed most likely to be correct is given.

O'Brien-Burns Contest; Los Angeles, Cal. (November 1906)
Shriners' Conclave at Los Angeles, Cal. (May 1907)
Jim Jeffries on His California Ranch (June 1907)
International Contest for the Heavyweight Championship—Squires vs. Burns; Ocean View, Cal. (July 1907)
Panorama, Crowds at Squires-Burns International Contest from Center of Ring, Colma (July 1907)
Panorama, Crowds at Squires-Burns International Contest from Moving Picture Stand (July 1907)
Squires, Australian Champion, in His Training Quarters (1907)

Progressive Film Producers of America

The Barbary Coast (November 1913)
    Producer: Sol Lesser
    Camera: Hal Mohr

Story Films by Essanay Film Manufacturing Company

Westerns Starring Gilbert M. Anderson as "Broncho Billy"

Shanghaied (March 1909)
The Road Agents (March 1909)
A Tail of the West (April 1909)
The Indian Trailer (May 1909)
A Mexican's Gratitude (May 1909)
The Black Sheep (June 1909)
Ten Nights in a Barroom (June 1909)
A Maid of the Mountains (August 1909)
The Best Man Wins (November 1909)
Judgment (November 1909)
His Reformation (December 1909)
The Ranchman's Rival (December 1909)
The Spanish Girl (December 1909)
The Heart of a Cowboy (December 1909)
A Western Maid (January 1910)
The Outlaw's Sacrifice (January 1910)
The Cowboy and the Squaw (February 1910)
The Mexican's Faith (February 1910)
The Fence at Bar Z Ranch (March 1910)
The Girl and the Fugitive (March 1910)
The Flower of the Ranch (April 1910)
The Ranger's Bride (April 1910)
The Mistaken Bandit (April 1910)
The Cowboy's Sweetheart (April 1910)
A Vein of Gold (April 1910)
The Sheriff's Sacrifice (May 1910)
The Cowpuncher's Ward (May 1910)
The Brother, the Sister, and the Cowpuncher (May 1910)
Away Out West (June 1910)
The Ranchman's Feud (June 1910)
The Bandit's Wife (June 1910)
The Forest Ranger (June 1910)
The Bad Man's Last Deed (July 1910)
The Unknown Claim (July 1910)

Trailed to the Hills (July 1910)
Broncho Billy's Redemption (July 1910)
Under Western Skies (August 1910)
An Indian Girl's Love (August 1910)
The Girl on Triple X Ranch (August 1910)
The Dumb Half-Breed's Defense (August 1910)
The Deputy's Love (August 1910)
The Millionaire and the Ranch Girl (September 1910)
The Pony Express Rider (September 1910)
The Tour's Remembrance (September 1910)
    Also with: Ethel Clayton
Patricia of the Plains (October 1910)
The Bearded Bandit (October 1910)
Pals of the Range (October 1910)
The Silent Message (October 1910)
A Westerner's Way (November 1910)
The Marked Trail (November 1910)
The Little Prospector (November 1910)
A Western Woman's Way (November 1910)
Circle C Ranch Wedding Present (December 1910)
A Cowboy's Vindication (December 1910)
The Tenderfoot Messenger (December 1910)
The Bad Man's Christmas Gift (December 1910)
A Gambler of the West (December 1910)
The Girl of the West (January 1911)
The Border Ranger (January 1911)
The Two Reformations (January 1911)
Carmenita, the Faithful (February 1911)
The Bad Man's Downfall (February 1911)
The Cattleman's Daughter (February 1911)
The Outlaw and the Child (February 1911)
On the Desert's Edge (March 1911)
The Faithful Indian (March 1911)
The Romance on Bar Q Ranch (March 1911)
    Also with: Arthur Mackley
A Thwarted Vengeance (March 1911)
Across the Plains (April 1911)
The Sheriff's Chum (April 1911)
The Indian Maiden's Lesson (April 1911)
The Bad Man's First Prayer (April 1911)
What a Woman Can Do (April 1911)
The Puncher's New Love (May 1911)
The Lucky Card (May 1911)
Forgiven in Death (June 1911)
The Tribe's Penalty (June 1911)
The Hidden Mine (June 1911)
At the Break of Dawn (July 1911)
The Sheriff's Brother (July 1911)
    Also with: Arthur Mackley (?)
The Corporation and the Ranch Girl (July 1911)
The Backwoodsman's Suspicion (July 1911)
The Outlaw Samaritan (July 1911)
The Two Fugitives (July 1911)
The Two-Gun Man (August 1911)
The Ranchman's Son (August 1911)
A Pal's Oath (August 1911)
Spike Shannon's Last Fight (August 1911)
A Western Girl's Sacrifice (September 1911)
The Millionaire and the Squatter (September 1911)

The Strike at the Little Johnny Mine (September 1911)
An Indian's Sacrifice (September 1911)
The Cowpuncher's Law (September 1911)
The Power of Good (September 1911)
The Sheriff's Decision (October 1911)
    Also with: Arthur Mackley (?)
The Stage Driver's Daughter (October 1911)
A Western Redemption (October 1911)
The Forester's Plea (October 1911)
The Outlaw's Deputy (November 1911)
The Girl Back East (November 1911)
The Cattle Rustler's Father (November 1911)
The Desert Claim (November 1911)
The Mountain Law (December 1911)
A Frontier Doctor (December 1911)
A Cowboy Coward (December 1911)
Broncho Billy's Christmas Dinner (December 1911)
Broncho Billy's Adventure (December 1911)
A Child of the West (January 1912)
The Tenderfoot Foreman (January 1912)
    Also with: Edna Fisher
The Sheepman's Escape (January 1912)
The Loafer (January 1912)
The Oath of His Office (January 1912)
Broncho Billy and the Schoolmistress (February 1912)
The Deputy and the Girl (February 1912)
    Also with: Edna Fisher
The Prospector's Legacy (February 1912)
    Also with: Roy Clement (?)
The Ranch Girl's Mistake (March 1912)
    Also with: Vedah Bertram
A Romance of the West (March 1912)
The Bandit's Child (March 1912)
The Deputy's Love Affair (March 1912)
An Arizona Escapade (March 1912)
A Road Agent's Love (April 1912)
    Also with: Arthur Mackley, Julia Mackley
Broncho Billy and the Girl (April 1912)
Under Mexican Skies (April 1912)
    Also with: Vedah Bertram
The Indian and the Child (April 1912)
The Cattle King's Daughter (April 1912)
    Also with: Hal Angus (?)
Broncho Billy and the Bandits (May 1912)
The Dead Man's Claim (May 1912)
The Sheriff and His Man (May 1912)
The Desert Sweetheart (May 1912)
Broncho Billy and the Indian Maid (June 1912)
Broncho Billy's Bible (June 1912)
    Also with: Emory Johnson
Broncho Billy and the Schoolmarm's Kid (June 1912)
    Also with: Vedah Bertram, Brinsley Shaw
On El Monte Ranch (June 1912)
A Child of the Purple Sage (June 1912)
Western Hearts (June 1912)
    Also with: David Kirkland, Frederick Church, Evelyn Selbie
Broncho Billy's Gratitude (June 1912)
The Foreman's Cousin (June 1912)

On the Cactus Trail (July 1912)
    Also with: Vedah Bertram
Broncho Billy's Narrow Escape (July 1912)
A Story of Montana (July 1912)
The Smuggler's Daughter (July 1912)
    Also with: Arthur Mackley, Vedah Bertram, Hal Angus, Frederick Church
A Wife of the Hills (July 1912)
A Moonshiner's Heart (July 1912)
Broncho Billy's Pal (July 1912)
    Also with: Arthur Mackley, Vedah Bertram, Brinsley Shaw, Lee Willard (?)
The Loafer's Mother (August 1912)
The Little Sheriff (August 1912)
    Also with: Hal Angus
Broncho Billy's Last Holdup (August 1912)
On the Moonlight Trail (August 1912)
Broncho Billy's Escapade (August 1912)
Broncho Billy for Sheriff (August 1912)
The Ranchman's Trust (September 1912)
A Woman of Arizona (September 1912)
    Also with: Hal Angus
Broncho Billy Outwitted (September 1912)
    Also with: Vedah Bertram
An Indian Sunbeam (September 1912)
Love on Tough Luck Ranch (October 1912)
The Shotgun Ranchman (October 1912)
    Also with: Emory Johnson (?)
The Outlaw's Sacrifice (October 1912)
    Also with: Hal Angus, True Boardman
The Tomboy on Bar Z (October 1912)
The Ranch Girl's Trial (October 1912)
The Mother of the Ranch (November 1912)
The Ranchman's Anniversary (November 1912)
The Dance at Silver Gulch (November 1912)
Broncho Billy's Heart (November 1912)
The Boss of Katy Mine (November 1912)
An Indian's Friendship (November 1912)
Broncho Billy's Mexican Wife (November 1912)
    Also with: Reina Valdez
The Western Girls (December 1912)
Broncho Billy's Love Affair (December 1912)
    Also with: Evelyn Selbie, Brinsley Shaw
The Prospector (December 1912)
Broncho Billy's Promise (December 1912)
    Also with: Bessie Sankey
The Sheriff's Luck (December 1912)
    Also with: Arthur Mackley (?)
The Reward for Broncho Billy (December 1912)
The Sheriff's Inheritance (December 1912)
    Also with: Arthur Mackley (?)
The Miner's Bequest (January 1913)
Broncho Billy and the Maid (January 1913)
Broncho Billy and the Outlaw's Mother (January 1913)
Broncho Billy's Brother (January 1913)
The Sheriff's Child (January 1913)
    Also with: Arthur Mackley
Broncho Billy's Gun Play (January 1913)
The Sheriff's Story (January 1913)

Also with: Arthur Mackley (?)
The Making of Broncho Billy (February 1913)
    Also with: Harry Todd
The Ranchman's Blunder (February 1913)
    Also with: Arthur Mackley, Bessie Sankey
Broncho Billy's Last Deed (February 1913)
    Also with: Brinsley Shaw
Broncho Billy's Ward (February 1913)
Where the Mountains Meet (February 1913)
Across the Great Divide (February 1913)
Broncho Billy and the Sheriff's Kid (February 1913)
    Also with: Baby Audrey Hanna, Arthur Mackley
The Accusation of Broncho Billy (April 1913)
Broncho Billy and the Rustler's Child (April 1913)
The Story the Desert Told (May 1913)
    Also with: Arthur Mackley
The Crazy Prospector (May 1913)
Two Western Paths (May 1913)
The Ranch Girl's Partner (May 1913)
Broncho Billy's Grit (May 1913)
A Widow of Nevada (May 1913)
Broncho Billy and the Express Rider (May 1913)
The New Sheriff (May 1913)
The Last Shot (June 1913)
Broncho Billy's Capture (June 1913)
    Also with: Evelyn Selbie, Frederick Church
The Ranch Feud (June 1913)
The Rustler's Spur (June 1913)
Across the Rio Grande (June 1913)
    Also with: Brinsley Shaw, Evelyn Selbie
Broncho Billy's Strategy (June 1913)
This Life We Live (July 1913)
    Also with: Arthur Mackley
At the Lariat's End (July 1913)
    Also with: Frederick Church, Bessie Sankey
The Daughter of the Sheriff (July 1913)
Broncho Billy and the Western Girls (July 1913)
    Also with: Evelyn Selbie
The Heart of a Gambler (July 1913)
Two Ranchmen (July 1913)
The Dance at Eagle Pass (July 1913)
The Western Law that Failed (February 1913)
The Influence of Broncho Billy (March 1913)
A Montana Mix-Up (March 1913)
    Also with: Arthur Mackley, Gladys Fields
Broncho Billy and the Squatter's Daughter (March 1913)
Broncho Billy and the Step Sisters (March 1913)
The Housekeeper of Circle C (March 1913)
    Also with: Arthur Mackley
Broncho Billy's Sister (March 1913)
The Sheriff's Honeymoon (March 1913)
    Also with: Arthur Mackley (?)
Broncho Billy's Gratefulness (March 1913)
The Sheriff's Son (April 1913)
Broncho Billy's Way (April 1913)
The Sheriff's Wife (April 1913)
    Also with: Arthur Mackley, Julia Mackley
Broncho Billy's Reason (April 1913)

Director: Lloyd Ingraham
Camera: Rollie Totheroh
Story: Josephine Rector
Also with: Frederick Church, Josephine Rector
Broncho Billy and the Schoolmarm's Sweetheart (July 1913)
The Call of the Plains (July 1913)
The Tenderfoot Sheriff (August 1913)
Their Promise (August 1913)
    Also with: Frederick Church
The Edge of Things (August 1913)
    Also with: Evelyn Selbie
Broncho Billy and the Navajo Maid (August 1913)
The Man in the Cabin (August 1913)
    Also with: Evelyn Selbie
The Sheriff of Cochise (August 1913)
Broncho Billy's Mistake (August 1913)
A Western Sister's Devotion (August 1913)
    Also with: Evelyn Selbie
The Episode of Cloudy Canyon (August 1913)
Broncho Billy's Conscience (September 1913)
    Also with: Marguerite Clayton
Bonnie of the Hills (September 1913)
    Also with: Marguerite Clayton
Broncho Billy Reforms (September 1913)
The Broken Parole (September 1913)
The Redeemed Claim (September 1913)
Days of the Pony Express (September 1913)
Why Broncho Billy Left Bear Country (September 1913)
    Also with: Marguerite Clayton
The Belle of the Siskiyou (October 1913)
    Also with: Marguerite Clayton
The Struggle (October 1913)
Love and the Law (October 1913)
    Also with: Frederick Church, Marguerite Clayton
Broncho Billy's Oath (October 1913)
    Also with: Marguerite Clayton
A Borrowed Identity (October 1913)
    Also with: Marguerite Clayton
Broncho Billy Gets Square (October 1913)
The Kid Sheriff (October 1913)
    Also with: Frederick Church, Marguerite Clayton
Broncho Billy's Elopement (October 1913)
The Greed for Gold (October 1913)
    Also with: Marguerite Clayton
The Doctor's Duty (November 1913)
    Also with: Marguerite Clayton
The Rustler's Step-Daughter (November 1913)
    Also with: True Boardman, Evelyn Selbie
Broncho Billy's Secret (November 1913)
The New Schoolmarm of Green River (November 1913)
A Cowboy Samaritan (November 1913)
    Also with: Marguerite Clayton (?)
The End of the Circle (November 1913)
Broncho Billy's First Arrest (November 1913)
The Naming of the Rawhide Queen (November 1913)
    Also with: True Boardman, Evelyn Selbie, Harry Todd, Roy Clement
A Romance of the Hills (December 1913)

Broncho Billy's Squareness (December 1913)
The Three Gamblers (December 1913)
    Also with: Marguerite Clayton
The Trail of the Snake Band (December 1913)
Children of the Forest (December 1913)
Broncho Billy's Christmas Deed (December 1913)
Through Trackless Sands (January 1914)
The Hills of Peace (January 1914)
    Also with: Frederick Church, Marguerite Clayton,
      Carl Stockdale
The Story of the Old Gun (January 1914)
The Cast of the Die (January 1914)
    Also with: Frederick Church, Harry Todd, David
      Kirkland, Josephine Rector
Broncho Billy, Guardian (January 1914)
    Also with: Victor Potel, Marguerite Clayton(?)
A Night on the Road (January 1914)
Broncho Billy and the Bad Man (January 1914)
What Came to Bar Q (January 1914)
    Also with: Frederick Church
Broncho Billy and the Settler's Daughter (January 1914)
A Gambler's Way (February 1914)
    Also with: True Boardman, Harry Todd, Emory
      Johnson, Rena Valdez, Josephine Rector
Broncho Billy and the Red Man (February 1914)
    Also with: Lee Willard, Harry Todd
The Weaker's Strength (February 1914)
The Calling of Jim Barton (February 1914)
    Also with: True Boardman, Emory Johnson, Carl
      Stockdale
The Arm of Vengeance (February 1914)
The Conquest of Man (March 1914)
    Also with: True Boardman
The Warning (March 1914)
    Also with: Marguerite Clayton
The Interference by Broncho Billy (March 1914)
Single-Handed (March 1914)
    Also with: True Boardman, Carl Stockdale
The Atonement (March 1914)
    Also with: Carl Stockdale
Broncho Billy's True Love (March 1914)
Dan Cupid, Assayer (April 1914)
    Also with: Carl Stockdale
The Treachery of Broncho Billy's Pal (April 1914)
Broncho Billy and the Rattler (April 1914)
    Also with: Carl Stockdale
Broncho Billy, Gunman (April 1914)
Broncho Billy's Close Call (May 1914)
    Also with: True Boardman, Roy Clement, Harry
      Todd, Marguerite Clayton(?)
Broncho Billy's Sermon (May 1914)
Broncho Billy's Leap (May 1914)
Broncho Billy's Cunning (May 1914)
Broncho Billy's Duty (June 1914)
Broncho Billy and the Mine Shark (June 1914)
Broncho Billy, Outlaw (June 1914)
    Also with: Evelyn Selbie, Carl Stockdale, Harry
      Todd
Broncho Billy's Jealousy (June 1914)

Broncho Billy's Punishment (July 1914)
Broncho Billy and the Sheriff (July 1914)
    Also with: Marguerite Clayton, True Boardman,
      Carl Stockdale
Broncho Billy Puts One Over (July 1914)
    Also with: Marguerite Clayton, Carl Stockdale
Broncho Billy and the Gambler (July 1914)
The Squatter's Gal (August 1914)
Broncho Billy's Fatal Joke (August 1914)
Broncho Billy Wins Out (August 1914)
Broncho Billy's Wild Ride (August 1914)
    Also with: Harry Todd, Victor Potel, True Board-
      man(?)
Broncho Billy's Indian Romance (August 1914)
Broncho Billy, the Vagabond (September 1914)
Broncho Billy, A Friend in Need (September 1914)
Broncho Billy Butts In (September 1914)
The Strategy of Broncho Billy's Sweetheart (September
    1914)
Broncho Billy Trapped (October 1914)
Broncho Billy and the Greaser (October 1914)
    Also with: Marguerite Clayton, Lee Willard
Broncho Billy Rewarded (October 1914)
Broncho Billy, Favorite (October 1914)
    Also with: Marguerite Clayton, Carl Stockdale
Broncho Billy's Mother (October 1914)
Broncho Billy's Mission (November 1914)
Broncho Billy's Decision (November 1914)
Broncho Billy's Scheme (November 1914)
Broncho Billy's Double Escape (November 1914)
The Tell-Tale Hand (November 1914)
    Also with: Marguerite Clayton, Lee Willard, True
      Boardman
Broncho Billy's Judgment (December 1914)
Broncho Billy's Dad (December 1914)
Broncho Billy's Christmas Spirit (December 1914)
Broncho Billy and the Sheriff's Office (December 1914)
    Story: Frank Blighton
Broncho Billy and the Escaped Bandit (January 1915)
Broncho Billy and the Claim Jumper (January 1915)
    Also with: Marguerite Clayton
Broncho Billy and the Sisters (January 1915)
Broncho Billy and the Baby (January 1915)
    Also with: Evelyn Selbie, Lee Willard(?)
Broncho Billy and the False Note (January 1915)
Broncho Billy's Greaser Deputy (February 1915)
Broncho Billy's Sentence (February 1915)
    Also with: Virginia Eames, Carl Stockdale, Ernest
      van Pelt, Evelyn Selbie, True Boardman
Broncho Billy and the Vigilante (February 1915)
    Also with: Lee Willard, Harry Todd, Victor Potel
Broncho Billy's Vengeance (March 1915)
Broncho Billy's Teachings (March 1915)
    Also with: Roy Clement
The Western Way (March 1915)
The Outlaw's Awakening (March 1915)
Ingomar of the Hills (April 1915)
Andy of the Royal Mounted (April 1915)
The Other Girl (May 1913)

Also with: Marguerite Clayton, Lee Willard

The Revenue Agent (May 1915)
Also with: Marguerite Clayton, Lee Willard

*The Bachelor's Burglar** (May 1915)
Also with: Marguerite Clayton

Broncho Billy's Word of Honor (June 1915)

Broncho Billy and the Land Grabber (June 1915)

The Little Prospector (July 1915)

Broncho Billy Well-Repaid (July 1915)
Also with: Marguerite Clayton, Lee Willard

*The Bachelor's Baby** (July 1915)
Also with: Marguerite Clayton

Broncho Billy and the Posse (July 1915)

Broncho Billy's Surrender (July 1915)
Also with: Marguerite Clayton

Broncho Billy's Protégé (August 1915)
Also with: Marguerite Clayton

Broncho Billy Steps In (August 1915)
Also with: Marguerite Clayton

Broncho Billy's Marriage (August 1915)
Also with: Marguerite Clayton

Her Return (August 1915)
Also with: Marguerite Clayton

Broncho Billy Begins Life Anew (September 1915)
Also with: Marguerite Clayton, Lee Willard, Lloyd Bacon

Broncho Billy and the Lumber King (September 1915)
Also with: Marguerite Clayton, Lee Willard, Lloyd Bacon

The Convict's Threat (September 1915)
Also with: Marguerite Clayton, Lee Willard, Harry Todd

Broncho Billy and the Card Sharp (September 1915)
Also with: Lloyd Bacon, Lee Willard, Harry Todd, Florence Cato

An Unexpected Romance (September 1915)
Also with: Marguerite Clayton, Lee Willard, Harry Todd

Broncho Billy Misled (October 1915)
Also with: Marguerite Clayton, Lloyd Bacon, Lee Willard

Broncho Billy, Sheepman (October 1915)
Also with: Marguerite Clayton, Lee Willard

Suppressed Evidence (October 1915)
Also with: Marguerite Clayton, Lee Willard, Leona Anderson, Ella McKenzie

Broncho Billy's Parents (October 1915)
Also with: Marguerite Clayton

Broncho Billy Evens Matters (October 1915)

Broncho Billy's Cowardly Brother (October 1915)
Also with: Marguerite Clayton, Lloyd Bacon, Harry Todd, Lee Willard

Broncho Billy's Mexican Wife (November 1915)

The Indian's Narrow Escape (November 1915)

Broncho Billy's Love Affair (November 1915)
Also with: Ruth Saville, Lee Willard

*The Burglar Godfather** (December 1915)
Also with: Lloyd Bacon, Lee Willard

The Escape of Broncho Billy (December 1915)

Also with: Ruth Saville, Rodney Hildebrand, Lee Willard

A Christmas Revenge (December 1915)
Also with: Marguerite Clayton, Lloyd Bacon

Broncho Billy and the MacGuire Gang (December 1915)

Broncho Billy and the Revenue Agent (January 1916)

The Book Agent's Romance (January 1916)
Also with: Ruth Saville, Lee Willard, Lloyd Bacon, Eva Heazlett

Dramas Starring Gilbert M. Anderson

Take Me Out to the Ball Game (July 1910)

The Good for Nothing (May 1914)
Also with: Victor Potel, Carl Stockdale, Lee Willard

When Love and Honor Called (January 1915)
Story: Frank Blighton
Also with: Marguerite Clayton

The Tie That Binds (April 1915)

His Regeneration (May 1915)
Also with: Lee Willard, Marguerite Clayton, Hazel Applegate, Charles Chaplin

The Wealth of the Poor (June 1915)
Also with: Marguerite Clayton

Her Realization (June 1915)
Also with: Marguerite Clayton

Wine, Women, and Song (November 1915)
Also with: Lloyd Bacon, Lee Willard, Harry Todd

Her Lesson (January 1916)
Also with: Ruth Saville, Lloyd Bacon, Rodney Hilderbrand, Eva Heazlett

The Man in Him (February 1916)
Also with: Ruth Saville, Lee Willard

Comedies by Essanay Stock Players

Augustus Carney as "Alkali Ike"
Victor Potel as "Slippery Slim"
Margaret Joslyn as "Sophie Clutes"

Won by a Hold Up (January 1910)

Western Chivalry (February 1910)

The Ranch Girl's Legacy (March 1910)

A Ranchman's Wooing (March 1910)

The Bad Man and the Preacher (April 1910)

The Little Doctor of the Foothills (May 1910)

The Desperado (July 1910)

The Cowboy's Mother-in-Law (October 1910)

The Count and the Cowboys (January 1911)

Alkali Ike's Auto (May 1911)

The Infant at Snakeville (June 1911)

Mustang Pete's Love Affair (July 1911)

Broncho Billy's Last Spree (September 1911)
Also with a guest appearance by Gilbert M. Anderson

Alkali Ike's Love Affair (February 1912)

*Possibly a crook drama, not a Western.

A Western Kimono (February 1912)
The Ranch Widower's Daughter (March 1912)
Alkali Ike Bests Broncho Bill (March 1912)
Alkali Ike's Boarding House (April 1912)
Alkali Ike's Bride (May 1912)
      Also with: Augustus Carney, Josephine Rector, Emory Johnson
A Western Legacy (May 1912)
Alkali Ike Plays the Devil (August 1912)
Alkali Ike's Pants (September 1912)
Alkali Ike Stung (October 1912)
Alkali Ike's Close Shave (November 1912)
Alkali Ike's Motorcycle (December 1912)
Alkali Ike in Jayville (January 1913)
The Misjudging of Mr. Hubby (March 1913)
Alkali Ike's Homecoming (April 1913)
Alkali Ike's Mother-in-Law (May 1913)
Alkali Ike's Misfortunes (May 1913)
Alkali Ike and the Hypnotist (June 1913)
Alkali Ike's Gal (August 1913)
Hard-Luck Bill (September 1913)
Alkali Ike and the Wildman (October 1913)
Sophie's Hero (November 1913)
Sophie's New Foreman (December 1913)
That Pair from Thespia (December 1913)
A Snakeville Courtship (December 1913)
The Awakening at Snakeville (January 1914)
Snakeville's New Doctor (January 1914)
Sophie Picks a Dead One (February 1914)
Snakeville's Fire Brigade (February 1914)
Sophie's Birthday Party (March 1914)
A Hot Time in Snakeville (March 1914)
The Coming of Sophie's Mother (April 1914)
Snakeville's New Sheriff (April 1914)
High Life Hits Slippery Slim (April 1914)
Slippery Slim and the Stork (April 1914)
Pie for Sophie (April 1914)
A Snakeville Epidemic (May 1914)
Slippery Slim's Strategem (May 1914)
A Snakeville Romance (May 1914)
Sophie Starts Something (May 1914)
Sophie Pulls a Good One (June 1914)
A Snakeville Volunteer (June 1914)
The Wooing of Sophie (June 1914)
Sophie Finds a Hero (June 1914)
Sophie Gets Stung (July 1914)
Slippery Slim, Diplomat (July 1914)
Snakeville's New Waitress (July 1914)
Slippery Slim's Inheritance (July 1914)
Snakeville's Home Guard (July 1914)
Slippery Slim's Dilemma (August 1914)
Slippery Slim and His Tombstone (August 1914)
Slippery Slim and the Claim Agent (August 1914)
Slippery Slim and the Fortune Teller (August 1914)
When Macbeth Came to Snakeville (September 1914)
Snakeville's Most Popular Lady (September 1914)
Sophie's Legacy (September 1914)
Slippery Slim and the Green-Eyed Monster (September 1914)

Slippery Slim Gets Cured (October 1914)
When Slippery Slim Met the Champion (October 1914)
Snakeville's Peace Maker (October 1914)
Slippery Slim, the Mortgage, and Sophie (October 1914)
Snakeville and the Corset Demonstrator (October 1914)
Slippery Slim and the Impersonator (November 1914)
Sophie and the Man of Her Choice (November 1914)
A Horse on Sophie (November 1914)
Snakeville's Reform Wave (November 1914)
Sophie's Fatal Wedding (December 1914)
Sophie's Sweetheart (December 1914)
Snakeville's Blind Pig (December 1914)
Slippery Slim Gets Square (December 1914)
Snakeville's Rising Sons (December 1914)
The Battle of Snakeville (January 1915)
When Slippery Slim Went for the Eggs (January 1915)
Sentimental Sophie (January 1915)
When Slippery Slim Brought the Cheese (January 1915)
Sophie's Home Coming (February 1915)
Slim the Brave and Sophie the Fair (February 1915)
Snakeville's Beauty Parlor (February 1915)
Sophie Changes Her Mind (February 1915)
Slippery Slim's Wedding Day (March 1915)
Mustang Pete's Pressing Engagement (March 1915)
Two Bold, Bad Men (March 1915)
A Coat Tale (April 1915)
Sophie's Fighting Spirit (April 1915)
The Undertaker's Uncle (April 1915)
How Slippery Slim Saw the Show (May 1915)
Sophie and the Faker (June 1915)
Others Started, but Sophie Finished (July 1915)
Snakeville's Twins (July 1915)
The Bell Hop (August 1915)
The Tale of a Tire (August 1915)
The Drug Clerk (August 1915)
Versus Sledge Hammers (September 1915)
Snakeville's Hen Medic (September 1915)
    Featuring: Ben Turpin
    Also with: Harry Todd, Robert McKenzie
Snakeville's Weak Woman (October 1915)
    Also with: Harry Todd, Robert McKenzie
When Snakeville Struck Oil (October 1915)
    Also with: Harry Todd, Robert McKenzie
The Night Sophie Graduated (November 1915)
    Also with: Harry Todd, Robert McKenzie
Snakeville's Eugenic Marriage (November 1915)
    Also with: Robert McKenzie, Bell Mitchell
Too Much Turkey (November 1915)
    Featuring: Ben Turpin
    Also with: Ruth Saville, Carrie Turpin
It Happened in Snakeville (November 1915)
    Featuring: Ben Turpin
    Also with: Harry Todd
The Merry Models (December 1915)
    Featuring: Ben Turpin
    Also with: Harry Todd, Carrie Turpin
Snakeville Champion (December 1915)
    Featuring: Ben Turpin
    Also with: Lloyd Bacon

Comedies Starring Charles Chaplin

A Night Out (February 1915)
  Also with: Edna Purviance, Ben Turpin, Fred Goodwins, Leo White, Bud Jamison
The Champion (March 1915)
  Also with: Edna Purviance, Leo White, Lloyd Bacon, Bud Jamison, with a courtesy guest appearance by Gilbert M. Anderson
In the Park (March 1915)
  Also with: Edna Purviance, Leo White, Lloyd Bacon, Bud Jamison
A Jitney Elopement (April 1915)
  Also with: Edna Purviance, Leo White, Lloyd Bacon, Fred Goodwins, Paddy McGuire, Bud Jamison
The Tramp (April 1915)
  Also with: Edna Purviance, Leo White, Lloyd Bacon, Fred Goodwins, Paddy McGuire

Story Films by Various Producers

United Keanograph Studio

Through the Portals of the Past (July 1914)
  Producer: James Keane
  Director: James Keane
  Cast: Carlotta De Felice

Liberty Studio

His Masterpiece (September 1915)
  Cast: Sadie Lindblom, with Emory Johnson
The Woman Who Laughs (September 1915)
  Cast: Sadie Lindblom
Rosie's Victory (September 1915)
  Cast: Sadie Lindblom
Her Devoted Son (September 1915)
  Cast: Sadie Lindblom (?), with Emory Johnson
Nolan's Wedding (October 1915)
  Cast: Sadie Lindblom
The Birthmark (October 1915)
  Cast: Emory Johnson, Marguerite Clayton
The Unexpected Reward (November 1915)
  Cast: Sadie Lindblom
School Boy's Memories, or Kids at School (November 1915)
  Cast: Harry Fisher, Dorothy Brown, Charles James, Lotte Chase
Jean (November 1915)
  Cast: Sadie Lindblom

Montague (Gerson) Studio Drama

The Ballad of Fultah Fisher's Boarding House (April 1922)
  Producer: Walter Montague
  Director: Frank Capra (first film)
  Camera: Roy Wiggins

  Story: Rudyard Kipling's *Fultah Fisher's Boarding House*
  Adaptation: Frank Capra and Walter Montague
  Location: San Francisco waterfront
  Distributor: Pathe Exchange, Inc.

Montague (Gerson) Studio Comedies

  Company: Gerson Pictures Corp.
  Director: Robert Eddy
  Story: A. H. Giebler
  Other
    Locale: Belmont, San Mateo County
  Properties, later Editor:
               Frank Capra
  Cast: Dan Mason ("Pop Tuttle"), Wilna Hervey, with Oliver J. Eckhart, Helen Howell

Pop Tuttle's One-Horse Play (August 1922)
Pop Tuttle's Tack-Tics (August 1922)
Pop Tuttle's Movie Queen (September 1922)
Pop Tuttle's Clever Catch (October 1922)
Pop Tuttle, Fire Chief (November 1922)
Pop Tuttle's Grass Widow (December 1922)
Pop Tuttle's Long Shot (December 1922)
Pop Tuttle, Deteckative (December 1922)
Pop Tuttle's Polecat Plot (February 1923)
Pop Tuttle's Lost Control (February 1923)
Pop Tuttle's Lost Nerve (March 1923)
Pop Tuttle's Russian Rumour (May 1923)

Banner Studio Comedies

Curing Bill (September 1915)
  Cast: Bill Stinger, Myrtle Pippin
In and Out (September 1915)
  Cast: Sadie Lindblom
Dusty's Finish (September 1915)
Innocent Kidnapper (October 1915)
From Smith to Smyth (October 1915)
The Movie Nut (October 1915)
Love Finds Its Way (October 1915)
You Never Can Tell (October 1915)
Teasing Tiny (October 1915)
  Cast: Bill Stinger, Harry Siegel
Plaid Coat (October 1915)
The Axeman (November 1915)
Won by a Nose (November 1915)
Sammy, the Cub Reporter (November 1915)
Aunt Tillie's Elopement (November 1915)
His Middle Name Was Trouble (December 1915)
The Spooners (December 1915)

Independent Production

The Eye of India (June 1919) (Color)
  Director: Mark J. Branstein

FEATURE FILMS

California Motion Picture Corporation Studio

Dramas Starring Beatriz Michelena

Salomy Jane (November 1914)
Producer: Alexander Beyfuss
Director: George E. Middleton and William Nigh
Camera: Arthur Powelson and Frank Padilla
Story: Adapted from Bret Harte's *Salomy Jane* and the play of the same name by Paul Armstrong (1907)
Locations: Monte Rio, Sonoma County; Lagunitas, Marin County
Also with: House Peters, Andrew Robson, Clarence Arper, William Nigh, William Pike, Jack Holt
Distributor: ALCO Film Corp.

Mrs. Wiggs of the Cabbage Patch (December 1914)
Producer: Alexander Beyfuss
Director: George E. Middleton and William Nigh
Camera: Arthur Powelson
Story: Adapted from the novel by Alice Hegan Rice and the play by Anne C. Flexner
Locations: San Rafael, Marin County
Also with: House Peters, Blanche Chapman, Andrew Robson, William Pike, Jack Holt, Belle Bennett
Distributor: World Film Corp.

Mignon (January 1915)
Producer: Alexander Beyfuss
Director: George E. Middleton and William Nigh
Camera: Arthur Powelson
Story: Adapted from the opera libretto by Barbier and Carre, based on Goethe's poem *Wilhelm Meister*
Locations: Bothin Estate, Ross, Marin County; Angel Island
Also with: House Peters, William Pike, William Nigh, Clara Byers, Belle Bennett, Andrew Robson
Distributor: World Film Corp.

The Lily of Poverty Flat (April 1915)
Producer: Alexander Beyfuss
Director: George E. Middleton
Story: Adapted from Bret Harte's *Her Letter, His Answer,* and *Her Last Letter*
Locations: Lagunitas, Marin County; Boulder Creek, Santa Cruz County
Also with: Frederic Lewis, Andrew Robson, James Leslie, Clarence Arper, Rolph Winters, Clara Byers
Distributor: World Film Corp.

Minty's Triumph (June 1915)

Producer: Alexander Beyfuss
Director: George E. Middleton
Story: Adapted from Bret Harte's poem *Minty's Triumph*
Locations: Boulder Creek, Santa Cruz County; Marin County
Also with: William Pike, Myrtle Newman, Clarence Arper(?)
Distributor: World Film Corp.

Salvation Nell (October 1915)
Producer: Alexander Beyfuss
Director: George E. Middleton
Camera: Robert Carson
Story: Adapted from the play by Edward Sheldon
Locations: San Rafael, Marin County; San Francisco
Also with: William Pike, Andrew Robson, Clarence Arper, James Leslie, Myrtle Newman
Distributor: World Film Corp.

The Rose of the Misty Pool (late 1915)
Producer: Alexander Beyfuss
Director: George E. Middleton
Camera: Robert Carson(?)
Story: Charles Kenyon
Locations: San Rafael, Marin County; San Francisco
Also with: Harold Meade, Myrtle Newman
Distributor: No record of picture's release

The Unwritten Law (January 1916)
Producer: Alexander Beyfuss
Director: George E. Middleton
Camera: Robert Carson
Locations: Bothin Residence, Ross, Marin County
Also with: William Pike, Andrew Robson, Irene Outrim, Clarence Arper, Myrtle Newman, Felice Rix
Distributor: States Rights

The Woman Who Dared (July 1916)
Producer: Alexander Beyfuss
Director: George E. Middleton
Camera: Robert Carson
Locations: San Rafael, Marin County
Also with: William Pike, Andrew Robson, Clarence Arper, Albert Morrison, James Leslie, Rolph Winters, Irene Outrim
Distributor: Ultra Pictures Corp. (New York)

Just Squaw (March 1919)
Producer: Beatrice Michelena and George E. Middleton
Director: George E. Middleton
Camera: Frank Padilla and John Pender
Locations: Boulder Creek, Santa Cruz; Lake Lagunitas, Marin County
Also with: William Pike, Andrew Robson, Albert Morrison, Katherine Angus
Distributor: Exhibitors Mutual

The Heart of Juanita (December 1919)
Producer: Beatrice Michelena and George E. Middleton
Director: George E. Middleton
Camera: Frank Padilla and John Pender
Story: Leslie T. Peacocke, and Earle Snell
Locations: Boulder Creek, Santa Cruz County; Lagunitas, Camp Taylor, Marin County
Also with: William Pike, Andrew Robson, Irene Outrim, Albert Morrison, Clarence Arper

The Flame of Hellgate (February 1920)
Producer: Beatrice Michelena and George E. Middleton
Director: George E. Middleton
Camera: Frank Padilla and John Pender
Story: Earle Snell
Locations: Boulder Creek, Santa Cruz County
Also with: William Pike, Clarence Arper, Albert Morrison, Cliff Thompson, Katherine Angus, Jack Millerick

Dramas by Various Producers

The Pageant of San Francisco (December 1914)
Company: Pageant Film Co.
Producer: California Motion Picture Corporation
Director: Earle Emlay, William Nigh (?)
Story: A. Mackay Sutherlund
Locations: Marin County; San Francisco; Bay Area
Cast: Ralph Phelps(?), Nicholas A. Covarrubias(?)
Distributor: Alliance Film Corp.

The Finger of Justice (July 1918)
Company: Morality Film Co.
Producer: Reverend Paul Smith
Director: Louis W. Chaudet
Camera: Ray Duehm or Lewis C. Hutt(?)
Story: Grace M. Sanderson
Locations: San Francisco; Marin County
Cast: Crane Wilbur, Velma Whitman, Mae Gaston

The Vigilantes (August 1918)
Company: Bear State Film Co.
Director: Earle Emlay
Cast: George Skaff

Cupid Angling (September 1918)
Company: Leon Douglass Natural Color Motion Picture Co.
Producer: Leon Forrest Douglass
Director: Louis W. Chaudet
Camera: Robert L. Carson
Story: Leon Forrest Douglass
Locations: Marin County
Cast: Ruth Roland, Albert Morrison
Distributor: W. W. Hodkinson

The Price Woman Pays (November 1919)
Company: J. Frank Hatch Enterprises

Producer: J. Frank Hatch
Director: George Terwillegar
Camera: Robert L. Carson
Story: J. Frank Hatch
Cast: Lois Wilson, Frances Burnham, William Scott
Distributor: Hatch–St. Regent

The Kingdom of Human Hearts (April 1921)
Company: Christian Philosophical Institute
Producer: Wilbert Leroy Cosper
Camera: Ray Duehm or Lewis C. Hutt(?)
Story: Wilbert Leroy Cosper
Locations: Marin County
Cast: Hugh Metcalfe, Lona Good, Jack Gray, Sylvia Edney, Richard Lancaster, Jean Traig, Seldy Roach, Ed Russell, Thora Lorraine
Distributor: States Rights

United Keanograph Studio

Money (November 1914)
Producer: James Keane
Director: James Keane
Camera: George Scott
Story: James Keane
Locations: Marin County; San Francisco
Cast: Mat Snyder, Carlotta DeFelice, Norbert Gillis, Elizabeth Stewart, George Chesebro, E. A. Warren
Distributor: World Film Corp.

Pacific (Peninsula) Studios

Dramas by Various Producers*

The Sea Lion (December 1921)
Company: Hobart Bosworth Productions
Producer: Max Graf
Director: Rowland V. Lee
Camera: J. O. Taylor
Story: Emilie Johnson
Locations: Freighter *Oregon*, on San Francisco Bay
Cast: Hobart Bosworth, Bessie Love, Emory Johnson, Jack Curtis, Harry Kearley, Carol Holloway, Charles Clary, Florence Carpenter, Richard Morris, J. Gordon Russell
Distributor: First National

Blind Hearts (December 1921)
Company: Hobart Bosworth Productions
Producer: Associated Producers
Director: Rowland V. Lee
Camera: J. O. Taylor

*For synopses and additional production data of Bay Area films of the 1920s, much of it supplied by the author, see *American Film Institute Catalog, Feature Films, 1921–1930* (R. R. Bowker, 1971).

Story: Emilie Johnson
Locations: San Francisco Bay; San Quentin
            Prison, Marin County
Cast: Hobart Bosworth, Madge Bellamy,
            Robert McKim, Colette Forbes,
            William Conklin, Wade Boteler,
            Irene Blackwell
Distributor: First National

White Hands (December 1921)
Company: Hobart Bosworth–Wid Gunning
Producer: Max Graf Productions
Director: Lampert Hilyar
Story: C. Gardner Sullivan
Locations: San Francisco waterfront; Coyote
            Point, San Mateo County
Cast: Hobart Bosworth, Elinor Fair,
            Freeman Wood, Robert McKim,
            George O'Brien, Al Kaufman,
            Muriel Frances Dana, Jimmie Sturia
Distributor: FBO

The Great Alone (May 1922)
Company: West Coast Films Corp.
Producer: Isadore Bernstein
Director: Jacques Jaccard
Camera: Frank B. Good
Story: Jacques Jaccard
Cast: Monroe Salisbury, Maria Draga, Wal-
            ter Long, Lura Ansen, Alfred Allen,
            George Waggoner, Jimmie Sturia
Distributor: American Releasing Corp.

The Forgotten Law (November 1922)
Company: Metro Pictures
Producer: Max Graf Productions
Director: James W. Horne
Camera: John S. Stumar, A.S.C.; Asst. Frank
            Heiser
Story: Adapted from Caroline Abbott Stan-
            ley's *Modern Madonna*
Cast: Milton Sills, Cleo Ridgley, Jack
            Mulhall, Alec B. Francis, Ednah Al-
            temas, Walter Long, Alice Hollister,
            Muriel Dana, Lucretia Harris, Jim-
            mie Sturia, Leo A. Keith

The Man Alone (February 1923)
Company: Motion Picture Utility Co.
Producer: Hobart Bosworth
Director: William Clifford
Camera: J. O. Taylor
Story: Effie G. Whitehorn
Locations: Amador County; San Francisco Bay;
            San Francisco; Piedmont, Alameda
            County
Distributor: Anchor Films
Cast: Hobart Bosworth

The Fog (July 1923)
Company: Metro Pictures
Producer: Max Graf
Director: Paul Powell
Camera: John R. Arnold

Story: William Dudley Pelley
Locations: San Francisco; San Mateo County
Cast: Mildred Harris, Cullen Landis, Louise
            Fazenda, Ralph Lewis, Louise Dres-
            ser, David Butler, Ethel Wales,
            Frank Currier, Marjorie Prevost,
            Edward Phillips, Ann May
Distributor: Metro Pictures

Half a Dollar Bill (January 1924)
Company: Metro Pictures
Producer: Max Graf, for Graf Productions
Director: W. S. Van Dyke
Camera: Andre Barlatier
Story: Original by Curtis Benton, adapted by
            Max Graf
Locations: San Francisco Bay
Cast: Anna Q. Nilsson, William T. Carle-
            ton, Frankie Darro, Raymond Hat-
            ton, Alec B. Francis, George Mac-
            Quarrie, Mitchell Lewis, Rosa Gore
Distributor: Metro Pictures

The Wise Virgin (August 1924)
Company: Peninsula Studios
Producer: Frank E. Woods and Elmer Harris
Director: Lloyd Ingraham
Camera: Joseph B. Walker
Story: Elmer Harris
Locations: San Francisco; San Mateo County
Cast: Patsy Ruth Miller, Matt Moore,
            Edythe Chapman, Leon Barry, Lucy
            Fox, Charles A. Stevenson, James
            Neill
Distributor: Producers Distributing Corp.

Chalk Marks (September 1924)
Company: Peninsula Studios
Producer: Frank E. Woods and Elmer Harris
Director: John G. Adolfi
Camera: Joseph B. Walker
Story: Frank E. Woods
Locations: San Francisco; San Mateo County
Cast: Marquerite Snow, Rex Lease, Helen
            Ferguson, Ramsay Wallace, June El-
            vidge, Prisilla Bonner, Joseph D.
            Templet, Lydia Knott, Harold Hol-
            land
Distributor: Producers Distributing Corp.

The Girl on the Stairs (November 1924)
Company: Peninsula Studios
Producer: Frank E. Woods and Elmer Harris
Director: William Worthington
Story: Adapted from story by Winston Bouve
Locations: San Francisco; San Mateo County
Cast: Patsy Ruth Miller, Niles Welch, Shan-
            non Day, Bertram Brasby, Freeman
            Wood, Michael Clark, Aline Pretty,
            George Perrola
Distributor: Producers Distributing Corp.

Let Women Alone (January 1925)
Company: Producers Distributing Corp.

Producer: Frank E. Woods and Elmer Harris
Director: Paul Powell
Story: Adapted from Viola Brothers Shore's *On the Shelf*
Locations: San Francisco; San Mateo County
Cast: Pat O'Malley, Wanda Hawley, Noah Berry, J. Farrell MacDonald, Ethel Wales, Harris Gordon, Betty Jane Snowden

Her Market Value (February 1925)
Company: Producers Distributing Corp.
Producer: Paul Powell
Director: Paul Powell
Story: Adapted from stage play *Her Market Price*
Locations: San Francisco; San Mateo County
Cast: Agnes Ayres, Anders Randolf, Taylor Holmes, Hedda Hopper, Edward Earle, George Irving

The Awful Truth (April 1925)
Company: Peninsula Studios
Producer: Frank E. Woods and Elmer Harris
Director: Paul Powell
Camera: Joseph Dubray
Story: Adapted from Arthur Richman's stage play
Locations: San Francisco; Truckee
Cast: Agnes Ayres, Warner Baxter, Phillips Smalley, Raymond Lowney, Winifred Bryson, Carrie C. Ward
Distributor: Producers Distributing Corp.

Beauty and the Bad Man (April 1925)
Company: Peninsula Studios
Producer: Frank E. Woods and Elmer Harris
Director: William Worthington
Story: Adapted from Peter B. Kyne's *Corn-flower Classie's Concert*
Locations: San Mateo County
Cast: Mabel Ballin, Forrest Stanley, Russel Simpson, Andre De Beranger, Edna Mae Cooper, James Gordon
Distributor: Producers Distributing Corp.

Wandering Footsteps (October 1925)
Company: Graf Productions
Director: Phil Rosen
Camera: Lyman Broening
Locations: San Francisco
Cast: Estelle Taylor, Bryant Washburn, Alec B. Francis, Eugenie Besserer, Ethel Wales, Phillips Smalley, Frankie Darro, Sidney Bracey
Distributor: Harry Ginsberg, for Banner Productions

The Sea Wolf (June 1926)
Company: Ralph W. Ince Corp.
Producer: Ralph W. Ince and John C. Flinn
Director: Ralph W. Ince
Story: Jack London
Cast: Ralph W. Ince, Claire Adams, Mitchell Lewis, Theodore Von Eltz, Snitz Edwards
Distributor: Producers Distributing Corp.

Finnegan's Ball (February 1927)
Company: Pallas Photoplay
Producer: Max Graf
Director: James P. Hogan
Story: Adapted from a Murray and Mack farce
Locations: Spring Valley Lakes, San Mateo County
Cast: Blanche Mehaffey, Cullen Landis, Charles McHugh, Aggie Herring, Mack Swain, Wescott Clarke, Kewpie Mogan, Mimi Finnegan
Distributor: First Division–Pallas

Montague (Gerson) Studio

Dramas by Various Producers

The Heart of the North (October 1921)
Company: Quality Films
Producer: George H. Davis
Director: Harry J. Revier
Camera: Lee Humiston
Story: Edward V. Dowling
Locations: San Francisco; Marin County; Truckee
Cast: Roy Stewart, Louise Lovely, George Morell, Henry Van Meter, Roy Justi, William L. West, Betty Marvin, George O'Brien
Distributor: Joe Brandt–CBC

Life's Greatest Question (February 1922)
Company: CBC
Producer: George H. Davis
Director: Harry J. Revier
Story: Harry J. Revier
Locations: San Francisco; Marin County
Cast: Roy Stewart, Louise Lovely, Dorothy Valerga, Harry Van Meter, Eugene Burr
Distributor: Joe Brandt–CBC

The Broadway Madonna (November 1922)
Company: R-C Pictures Corp.
Director: Harry J. Revier
Story: Harry J. Revier
Locations: San Francisco; Burlingame, San Mateo County
Cast: Dorothy Revier, Jack Connolly, Harry Van Meter, Juanita Hansen, Lee Williard, Eugene Burr, Lydia Knott
Distributor: FBO

The Flying Dutchman (July 1923)
Company: R-C Pictures Corp.
Producer: Lloyd B. Carleton
Director: Lloyd B. Carleton; Asst. W. Bradley Ward
Camera: Andre Barlatier

Story: Based on ancient legend
Locations: Bay Area
Cast: Lawson W. Butt, Ella Hall, Walter Law, Lola Luxford, Edward Coxen
Distributor: FBO

The Cricket on the Hearth (August 1923)
Company: Gerson Pictures Corp.
Producer: Paul Gerson
Director: Lorimer Johnston
Camera: Silvano Balboni
Story: Adapted from Charles Dickens's novel
Cast: Paul Gerson, Virginia Brown Faire, Josef Swickard, Fritzie Ridgway, Lorimer Johnston, Margaret Landis, Joan Standing, Paul Moore
Distributor: Selznick

Waterfront Wolves (March 1924)
Company: Gerson Pictures Corp.
Producer: Paul Gerson
Director: Tom Gibson
Camera: George Crocker
Story: Tom Gibson
Cast: Ora Carew, Jay Morley, Hal Stephens, Dick La Reno, Eddie O'Brien, Stanley Sandford, Emma Muncy, Fernedo Galvez, James Lono
Distributor: Renown Films

Getting Her Man (April 1924)
Company: Gerson Pictures Corp.
Producer: Paul Gerson
Director: Tom Gibson (?)
Cast: Ora Carew, Jay Morley, Hal Stephens
Distributor: Renown

Three Days to Live (April 1924)
Company: Gerson Pictures Corp.
Producer: Paul Gerson
Director: Tom Gibson
Story: Tom Gibson
Locations: San Francisco
Cast: Ora Carew, Jay Morley, Dick La Reno, Hal Stephens, Helen Howell, James Lono
Distributor: Gerson-SR

Paying The Limit (August 1924)
Company: Gerson Pictures Corp.
Producer: Paul Gerson
Director: Tom Gibson
Camera: George Crocker
Story: Tom Gibson
Locations: San Francisco
Cast: Ora Carew, Jay Morley, Helen Howell, Eddie O'Brien, Stanley Sandford, Hal Stephens, Arthur (or George) Wellington, Dick La Reno
Distributor: Gerson-SR

Ten Days (December 1924)
Company: Gerson Pictures Corp.
Producer: Paul Gerson
Director: Duke Worne

Story: Arthur Hoerl
Locations: San Francisco
Cast: Richard Holt, Hazel Keener, Joseph Girard, Victor Potel, Hal Stephens, Lloyd Potter, W. Mollenhauer, Carmelita Tellos
Distributor: Berthold Berger–Independent

Too Much Youth (February 1925)
Company: Gerson Pictures Corp.
Producer: Paul Gerson
Director: Duke Worne
Camera: Roland Price
Story: Grover Jones
Locations: San Francisco
Cast: Richard Holt, Sylvia Breamer, Walter Perry, Harris Gordon, Eric Mayne, Charles K. French, Joseph Belmont
Distributor: Berthold Berger

The Canvas Kisser (June 1925)
Company: Gerson Pictures Corp.
Producer: Paul Gerson
Director: Duke Worne
Camera: Alfred Gosden
Cast: Richard Holt, Ruth Dwyer, Garry O'Dell

Going the Limit (September 1925)
Company: Gerson Pictures Corp.
Producer: Paul Gerson
Director: Duke Worne
Camera: Alfred Gosden
Story: Grover Jones
Locations: San Francisco
Cast: Richard Holt, Ruth Dwyer, Hal Stephens, Miriam Fouche, Robert Cosgriff, Garry O'Dell, Robert Drumm, G. E. Kelly
Distributor: Gerson-SR

Easy Going Gordon (October 1925)
Company: Gerson Pictures Corp.
Producer: Paul Gerson
Director: Duke Worne
Story: Grover Jones
Locations: San Francisco
Cast: Richard Holt, Katharine McGuire
Distributor: Gerson-SR

Once in a Lifetime (October 1925)
Company: Gerson Pictures Corp.
Producer: Paul Gerson
Director: Duke Worne
Camera: Ernest Smith
Cast: Richard Holt, Mary Milford, Jack O'Brien

The Pride of the Force (November 1925)
Company: Gerson Pictures Corp.
Producer: Paul Gerson
Director: Duke Worne
Story: Arthur Hoerl
Locations: San Francisco
Cast: Tom Santschi, Gladys Hulette, Edythe

Chapman, James Morrison, Crawford Kent, Joe Girard
Distributor: Rayart

In Search of a Hero (September 1926)
Company: Gerson Pictures Corp.
Producer: Paul Gerson
Director: Duke Worne
Cast: Richard Holt, Jane Thomas, Jimmy Harrison, Al Kaufman, Claire Vinson.
Distributor: Aywon

The Waster (September 1926)
Company: Gerson Pictures Corp.
Cast: Richard Holt

The Reckless Mollycoddle (January 1927)
Company: Gerson Pictures Corp.
Cast: Richard Holt

The Boaster (February 1927)
Company: Gerson Pictures Corp.
Producer: Paul Gerson
Director: Duke Worne
Camera: Grover Jones
Story: Grover Jones
Locations: San Francisco
Cast: Richard Holt, Gloria Grey
Distributor: Gerson-SR

Unverified Studios

The Money Changers (October 1920)
Company: Federal Photoplays of California
Producer: Benjamin B. Hampton
Director: Jack Conway
Camera: Harry Vallejo
Story: Adapted from Upton Sinclair's book
Locations: Chinatown, San Francisco
Cast: Roy Stewart, Claire Adams, Robert McKim, Audrey Chapman, George Webb, Edward Peil, George Hernandez
Distributor: Pathe Exchange

Isobel, or *The Trail's End* (November 1920)
Company: George H. Davis
Producer: George H. Davis
Director: Edwin Carewe; Asst. J. L. Pollock
Camera: Robert B. Kerrle
Story: Adapted from James Oliver Curwood's *Trail's End*
Cast: House Peters, Jane Novak, Edward Peil, Dick La Reno
Distributor: St. Regent

A Motion to Adjourn (November 1921)
Company: Roy Stewart
Producer: Ben Wilson
Director: Roy Clement
Story: Adapted from Peter B. Kyne's story
Cast: Roy Stewart, Marjorie Daw, Norval McGregor, Sidney D. Albrook, Harry Rattenburg, Evelyn Nelson, Charles King, Bill White, Jim Welsh, William Carroll
Distributor: Arrow Film Corp.

The Innocent Cheat (January 1922)
Company: Arrow Film Corp.
Producer: Ben Wilson
Director: Ben Wilson
Camera: Harry W. Gerstad
Story: Peter B. Kyne
Cast: Roy Stewart, Kathleen Kirkham, Sidney de Grey, George Hernandez, Rhea Mitchell, Joseph Girard
Distributor: Arrow Film Corp.

Fools of Fortune (July 1922)
Company: Golden State Films
Director: Louis William Chaudet
Camera: King Gray
Story: Adapted from W. C. Tuttle's *Assisting Ananias*
Cast: Frank Dill, Marguerite De La Motte, Russell Simpson, Tully Marshall, Frank Brownlee, Thomas Ricketts, Lillian Langdon
Distributor: American Releasing Corp.

Her Accidental Husband (April 1923)
Company: Belasco Productions
Producer: Edward Belasco
Director: Dallas M. FitzGerald
Story: Lois Zellner
Locations: Palace Hotel, San Francisco
Cast: Miriam Cooper, Mitchell Lewis, Kate Lester, Forrest Stanley, Richard Tucker, Maude Wayne, Consuelo Kalem
Distributor: CBC

The Mysterious Witness (June 1923)
Company: Belasco Productions
Producer: Edward Belasco
Director: Seymour Zeliff
Story: Adapted from Eugene Manlove Rhodes's *Stepsons of Light*
Cast: Robert Gordon, Elinor Fair, Jack Connolly, Nan Wright, J. Wharton James
Distributor: FBO

Enemies of Children (October 1923)
Company: Fisher Productions
Producer: Victor B. Fisher
Director: Lillian Ducey
Camera: Glen MacWilliams, John Miehle
Story: Adapted from George Gibbs's novel *Youth Triumphant*
Cast: Virginia Lee Corbin, Anna Q. Nilsson, William Boyd, Eugenie Besserer, George Seigman, Claire McDowell, Lucy Beaumont, Joseph Dowling, Raymond Hatton, Ward Crane
Distributor: Mammoth Films

Loving Lies (January 1924)
  Company: Associated Authors
  Producer: Thompson Buchanan, Frank E.
              Woods, Elmer Harris, Charles W.
              Thomas
  Director: W. S. Van Dyke
  Story: Adapted from Peter B. Kyne's *Harbor
              Bar*
  Cast: Monte Blue, Evelyn Brent, Ethel
              Wales, Andy Waldron, Joan Lowell,
              Charles Gerrard, Ralph Faulkner,
              Tom Kennedy
  Distributor: Allied Producers and Distributors
              Corp.

No More Women (February 1924)
  Producer: Elmer Harris
  Director: Lloyd Ingraham
  Story: Elmer Harris
  Cast: Matt Moore, Madge Bellamy, Clarence
              Burton, Kathleen Clifford, George
              Cooper, H. Reeves Smith, Stanhope
              Wheatcroft
  Distributor: Allied Producers and Distributors
              Corp.

Midnight Limited (February 1926)
  Company: Gerson Pictures Corp.
  Producer: Paul Gerson
  Director: Oscar Apfel
  Camera: Ernest Smith
  Cast: Richard Holt, Gaston Glass, Wanda
              Hawley, Eric Mayne
  Distributor: Rayart

Somebody's Mother (March 1926)
  Company: Gerson Pictures Corp.
  Producer: Paul Gerson
  Director: Oscar Apfel
  Cast: Mary Carr, Rex Lease

Perils of the Coast Guard (March 1926)
  Company: Gerson Pictures Corp.
  Producer: Paul Gerson
  Director: Oscar Apfel
  Cast: Cullen Landis, Dorothy Dwan
  Distributor: Rayart

The Call of the Klondike (June 1926)
  Company: Gerson Pictures Corp.
  Producer: Paul Gerson
  Director: Oscar Apfel
  Camera: Alfred Gosden
  Cast: Gaston Glass, Dorothy Dwan, Earl
              Metcalfe, Sam Allen
  Distributor: Rayart

The Last Alarm (June 1926)
  Company: Gerson Pictures Corp.
  Producer: Paul Gerson
  Director: Oscar Apfel
  Cast: Rex Lease, Wanda Hawley, Maurice
              Costello, Florence Turner, Theodore
              Von Eltz, Helen Howell
  Distributor: Rayart

The Flight of the Southern Cross (February 1929)
  Producer: G. Allan Hancock
  Theme: Documentation of historic hydroplane
              flight, Oakland—Australia—San
              Francisco

APPENDIX B
Hollywood Silent Films about, or Filmed in, Northern California

SHORT FILMS

The Luck of Roaring Camp (June 1917)
Director: Irvin Willat
Story: Bret Harte

Mabel and Fatty Viewing the World's Fair at San Francisco (April 1915)
Company: Keystone
Producer: Mack Sennett
Cast: Mabel Normand and Fatty Arbuckle

The Man from Tiajuana (1917)
Company: Kalem
Director: James W. Horne
Cast: Art Accord, Marin Sais, Jack Hoxie

Hello 'Frisco (July 1925)
Company: Universal
Director: Slim Summerville

FEATURE FILMS

San Francisco

Streets, Parks, Mansions, Neighborhoods

Madame Butterfly (November 1915)
Company: Famous Players–Lasky
Story: John Luther Long, David Belasco

Cast: Mary Pickford

Amarilly of Clothesline Alley (March 1918)
Company: Famous Players–Lasky
Director: Marshall Neilan
Story: Frances Marion
Cast: Mary Pickford

The Poppy Girl's Husband (March 1919)
Company: William S. Hart Productions
Cast: William S. Hart

A Petal on the Current (July 1919)
Company: Universal
Director: Tod Browning

Rough Riding Romance (August 1919)
Company: Fox Films
Cast: Tom Mix

The Cradle of Courage (July 1920)
Company: William S. Hart Co.
Cast: William S. Hart

Always Audacious (October 1920)
Company: Famous Players–Lasky
Director: James Cruze
Cast: Wallace Reid

The Testing Block (November 1920)
Company: William S. Hart Co.
Director: Lampert Hillyer
Cast: William S. Hart

Prisoners of Love (January 1921)
Company: Goldwyn

Dinty (February 1921)
Company: Marshall Neilan

Cast: Wesley Barry, Wallace Beery

Men-Women-Marriage (March 1921)
  Company: Allan Holubar

The Heart Line (June 1921)
  Company: Pathe
  Story: Gelett Burgess

Dynamite Smith (October 1924)
  Company: Thomas H. Ince Corp.
  Director: Ralph Ince
  Cast: Charles Ray, Wallace Beery, Bessie
               Love

Big Town Roundup (June 1921)
  Company: Fox Films
  Cast: Tom Mix

Don't Neglect Your Wife (July 1921)
  Company: Goldwyn Pictures
  Story: Gertrude F. Atherton

Fifty Candles (December 1921)
  Company: Hodkinson
  Director: Irvin Willat

Gray Dawn (February 1922)
  Company: Benjamin B. Hampton
  Director: Jean Hersholt
  Story: Stewart Edward White

Island Wives (March 1922)
  Company: Vitagraph
  Cast: Corinne Griffith

In the Name of the Law (July 1922)
  Company: Robinson-Cole
  Director: Emory Johnson

The Prisoner of Zenda (July 1922)
  Company: Metro Pictures
  Director: Rex Ingram
  Cast: Ramon Novarro, Alice Terry

Never Say Die (August 1922)
  Company: Associated Exhibitors
  Cast: Douglas MacLean

Abysmal Brute (April 1923)
  Company: Universal
  Other
    Locale: Sierra
  Cast: Reginald Denny

The Shock (April 1923)
  Company: Universal
  Director: Lambert Hillyer
  Cast: Lon Chaney

The Drivin' Fool (September 1923)
  Company: St. Regent

Ten Commandments (December 1923)
  Company: Paramount
  Director: Cecil B. De Mille
  Cast: Richard Dix, Theodore Roberts

Through the Dark (January 1924)
  Company: Goldwyn
  Story: Frances Marion
  Other
    Locale: San Quentin Prison
  Cast: Hobart Bosworth, Colleen Moore

Dorothy Vernon of Haddon Hall (April 1924)

Company: United Artists
  Other
    Locale: Mansion in Burlingame
  Cast: Mary Pickford

Little Robinson Crusoe (September 1924)
  Company: Metro-Goldwyn-Mayer
  Cast: Jackie Coogan

Dynamite Smith (October 1924)
  Company: Thomas H. Ince
  Director: Ralph Ince
  Cast: Charles Ray, Wallace Beery, Bessie
               Love

Soft Shoes (January 1925)
  Company: Producers Distributing Corp.
  Director: Lloyd Ingraham
  Cast: Harry Carey

Excuse Me (January 1925)
  Company: Metro-Goldwyn-Mayer
  Cast: Norma Shearer, Conrad Nagel

Greed (February 1925)
  Company: Metro-Goldwyn-Mayer
  Director: Eric Von Stroheim
  Cast: Jean Hersholt, Zazu Pitts, Gibson
               Gowland

If I Marry Again (February 1925)
  Company: First National
  Cast: Hobart Bosworth

Ridin' Pretty (February 1925)
  Company: Universal

Proud Flesh (April 1925)
  Company: Metro-Goldwyn-Mayer
  Director: King Vidor
  Other
    Locale: Sierra

The Last Edition (October 1925)
  Company: Robinson-Cole
  Director: Emory Johnson

The Shadow of the Law (January 1926)
  Company: Associated Exhibitors
  Cast: Clara Bow

Lawless Trails (February 1926)
  Company: Goodman

The Little Irish Girl (March 1926)
  Company: Warner Brothers

The Non-Stop Flight (March 1926)
  Company: Film Booking Office
  Director: Emory Johnson

Miss Nobody (June 1926)
  Company: First National

Everybody's Acting (November 1926)
  Company: Paramount
  Director: Marshall Neilan

The Buckaroo Kid (November 1926)
  Company: Universal
  Story: Peter B. Kyne
  Cast: Hoot Gibson

A Little Journey (January 1927)
  Company: Metro-Goldwyn-Mayer

Three Hours (March 1927)

ast: Hobart Bosworth
an of the Lady Letty (February 1922)
ompany: Famous Players–Lasky
ast: Rudolph Valentino
ned (October 1922)
ompany: J. Parker Read, Jr.
irector: Irvin Willat
ping Fast (May 1923)
ompany: Fox Films
ast: Tom Mix
* at Nothing* (February 1924)
ompany: Aywon
ged Water (August 1925)
ompany: Paramount
irector: Irvin Willat
ther
    Locale: Sausalito, Marin County
er the Twain Shall Meet (September 1925)
ompany: Metro-Goldwyn-Mayer
tory: Peter B. Kyne
* Wedding Song* (November 1925)
ompany: Producers Distributing Corp.
re Pay—Less Work (July 1926)
ompany: Fox Films
tory: Peter B. Kyne
od Ship (July 1927)
ompany: Columbia
ast: Hobart Bosworth
nghaied (October 1927)
ompany: Film Booking Office
irector: Ralph Ince
er the Storm (April 1928)
ompany: Columbia
ast: Hobart Bosworth
lship Bronson (May 1928)
ompany: Gotham-Lumas
ast: Noah Beery
* Fleet's In* (September 1928)
ompany: Paramount
ast: Clara Bow
terfront (September 1928)
ompany: First National
ast: Jack Mulhall, Dorothy Mackaill
ks of New York (September 1928)
ompany: Paramount
irector: Josef Von Sternberg
marine (November 1928)
ompany: Columbia
roducer: Irvin Willat
irector: Frank Capra
ast: Jack Holt
nghai Rose (February 1929)
ompany: Rayart
ast: Irene Rich

Bay Area Estates and Gardens

* Little Princess* (October 1917)

Company: Artcraft
Director: Marshall Neilan
Cast: Mary Pickford
Daddy Long Legs (May 1919)
Company: First National
Director: Marshall Neilan
Cast: Mary Pickford
Eyes of Youth (December 1919)
Company: Equity
Cast: Clara Kimball Young, Milton Sills,
          Rudolph Valentino
Little Lord Fauntleroy (November 1921)
Company: Mary Pickford Productions
Cast: Mary Pickford
The Woman Who Walked Alone (June 1922)
Company: Paramount
Director: George Medford
Cast: Milton Sills
The Impossible Mrs. Bellew (October 1922)
Company: Paramount
Cast: Gloria Swanson
Name the Man (January 1924)
Company: Goldwyn
Cast: Hobart Bosworth, Patsy Ruth Miller
The Magic Garden (January 1927)
Company: Film Booking Office

Small Towns and Farms

Rebecca of Sunnybrook Farm (September 1917)
Company: Artcraft
Director: Marshall Neilan
Cast: Mary Pickford
The Dawn of Understanding (November 1918)
Company: Vitagraph
Story: Bret Harte
The Testing Block (November 1920)
Company: William S. Hart Productions
Cast: William S. Hart
Peck's Bad Boy (June 1921)
Company: First National
Cast: Jackie Coogan
Our Leading Citizen (June 1922)
Company: Paramount
Story: George Ade
Cast: Thomas Meighan, Lois Wilson, Theo-
          dore Roberts
The Woman He Loved (October 1922)
Company: American Releasing
The Freshman (July 1925)
Company: Pathe
Cast: Harold Lloyd
A Woman of the World (December 1926)
Company: Paramount
Cast: Pola Negri

Company: First National
Cast: Corinne Griffith
Frisco Sally Levy (April 1927)
    Company: Metro-Goldwyn-Mayer
The Jazz Singer (October 1927)
    Company: Warner Brothers
    Cast: Al Jolson, Warner Oland
San Francisco Nights (January 1928)
    Company: Lumas Film Corporation
    Cast: Mae Busch
Burning Daylight (March 1928)
    Company: First National
    Story: Jack London
    Cast: Milton Sills
Outcast (November 1928)
    Company: First National
    Cast: Corinne Griffith
The Trail of '98 (January 1929)
    Company: Metro-Goldwyn-Mayer
    Director: Clarence Brown
The Duke Steps Out (March 1929)
    Company: Metro-Goldwyn-Mayer
    Director: James Cruze
Smilin' Guns (March 1929)
    Company: Universal
    Cast: Hoot Gibson

Chinatown and Barbary Coast

City of Dim Faces (July 1916)
    Director: George H. Medford
    Story: Frances Marion
    Cast: Sessue Hayakawa
The First Born (November 1920)
    Company: Hayakawa-Robinson-Cole
    Cast: Sessue Hayakawa
Where Lights Are Low (December 1920)
    Company: Robinson-Cole
    Cast: Sessue Hayakawa
Outside the Law (January 1921)
    Company: Universal
    Director: Tod Browning
    Cast: Lon Chaney
A Tale of Two Worlds (March 1921)
    Company: Goldwyn
    Director: Frank Lloyd
    Cast: Wallace Beery
Shame (July 1921)
    Company: Fox Films
    Cast: John Gilbert, Anna May Wong
The Night Rose (December 1921)
    Company: Goldwyn
    Cast: Lon Chaney
Bits of Life (October 1921)
    Company: First National
    Director: Marshall Neilan
    Cast: Lon Chaney
East Is West (October 1922)
    Company: First National

Cast: Warner Oland, Constanc
Purple Dawn (May 1923)
    Company: Aywon Film Corporatioı
    Cast: Bessie Love
A Man of Action (June 1923)
    Company: Thomas H. Ince
The Man Who Came Back (August 1924)
    Company: Fox Films
    Cast: George O'Brien, Doroth
Poison (August 1924)
    Company: William Steiner
The Roughneck (November 1924)
    Company: Fox Films
    Cast: George O'Brien
Speed Wild (May 1925)
    Company: Film Booking Office
Paths to Paradise (June 1925)
    Company: Paramount
    Director: Clarence Badger
Camille of the Barbary Coast (Novembeı
    Company: Associated Exhibitor
    Cast: Mae Busch
The Arizona Sweepstakes (January 1926)
    Company: Universal
    Cast: Hoot Gibson
The Border Sheriff (April 1926)
    Company: Universal
    Cast: Jack Hoxie
A Trip to Chinatown (June 1926)
    Company: Fox Films
    Cast: Anna May Wong
Old San Francisco (May 1927)
    Company: Warner Brothers
    Cast: Warner Oland, Dolores
Chinese Parrot (October 1927)
    Company: Universal
    Director: Paul Leni
    Cast: Hobart Bosworth, Anna
The Hawk's Nest May 1928)
    Company: First National
    Cast: Milton Sills
Midnight on the Barbary Coast (May 19ː
    Company: Associated Independent

Waterfront

Guile of Women (January 1921)
    Company: Goldwyn
    Cast: Will Rogers
Partners of the Tide (March 1921)
    Company: W. W. Hodkinson
    Adaptation: Irvin Willat
Cappy Ricks (October 1921)
    Company: Paramount
    Story: Peter B. Kyne
    Cast: Thomas Meighan, Agneː
Blind Hearts (October 1921)
    Company: Associated
    Director: Rowland V. Lee

Monterey and Carmel

Foolish Wives (February 1922)
  Company: Universal
  Director: Eric Von Stroheim
Dark Angel (September 1925)
  Company: Goldwyn-First National
  Director: George Fitzmaurice
  Story: Frances Marion
  Cast: Ronald Colman, Vilma Banky
Primrose Path (September 1925)
  Company: Arrow
  Cast: Clara Bow
A Woman of the Sea (Privately exhibited 1926)
  Company: Produced by Charles Chaplin
  Director: Josef Von Sternberg
  Cast: Edna Purviance
Notorious Lady (April 1927)
  Company: First National
  Cast: Lewis Stone
Rose of the Golden West (October 1927)
  Company: First National
  Director: George Fitzmaurice
  Cast: Gilbert Roland
Evangeline (July 1929)
  Company: United Artists
  Director: Edwin Carewe
  Cast: Dolores Del Rio

Sacramento Area: Plains and Rivers

Cameo Kirby (October 1923)
  Company: Fox Films
  Director: John Ford
  Cast: John Gilbert
California in '49 (November 1924)
  Company: Arrow
  Director: Jacques Jaccard
The Flaming Forties (December 1924)
  Company: Producers Distributing Corporation
  Story: Bret Harte
  Cast: Harry Carey
The Devil's Cargo (February 1925)
  Company: Paramount
  Director: Victor Fleming
  Cast: Wallace Beery
The Splendid Road (December 1925)
  Company: First National
  Director: Frank Lloyd
  Cast: Anna Q. Nilsson, Lionel Barrymore
Uncle Tom's Cabin (November 1927)
  Company: Universal
Steamboat Bill, Jr. (May 1928)
  Company: United Artists
  Cast: Buster Keaton

Mountains and Big Trees

The Aryan (April 1916)

Company: Triangle—Thomas H. Ince
Cast: William S. Hart
The Primal Lure (May 1916)
  Company: Triangle—Thomas H. Ince
  Cast: William S. Hart
The Half Breed (July 1916)
  Story: Bret Harte
  Cast: Douglas Fairbanks
A Romance of the Redwoods (May 1917)
  Company: Artcraft
  Director: Cecil B. De Mille
  Cast: Mary Pickford
The Narrow Trail (October 1917)
  Company: William S. Hart
  Cast: William S. Hart
M'liss (April 1918)
  Company: Famous Players–Lasky
  Director: Marshall Neilan
  Story: Bret Harte
  Cast: Mary Pickford
Valley of the Giants (July 1919)
  Company: Paramount
  Director: James Cruze
  Story: Peter B. Kyne
  Cast: Wallace Reid
Bare Knuckles (March 1921)
  Company: Fox Films
The Sky Pilot (May 1921)
  Company: First National
  Director: King Vidor
  Cast: Colleen Moore
The Silent Call (November 1921)
  Company: First National
  Cast: Strongheart, the Wonder Dog
A Question of Honor (March 1922)
  Company: First National
  Director: Edwin Carewe
I Am the Law (June 1922)
  Company: First National
  Director: Edwin Carewe
Over the Border (June 1922)
  Company: Paramount
  Director: Penrhyn Stanlaws
The Girl Who Ran Wild (September 1922)
  Company: Universal
  Director: Rupert Julian
  Story: Bret Harte
The Frozen North (August 1922)
  Company: Buster Keaton Productions
  Cast: Buster Keaton
The Balloonatic (January 1923)
  Company: Buster Keaton Productions
  Cast: Buster Keaton
Salomy Jane (August 1923)
  Company: Paramount
  Director: George Medford
  Story: Bret Harte
Tiger Rose (November 1923)
  Company: Warner Brothers

Story: David Belasco
Cast: Lenore Ulric

Deeds of Daring (January 1924)
  Company: Aywon

The Gold Rush (August 1925)
  Company: United Artists
  Director: Charles Chaplin
  Cast: Charles Chaplin

Find Your Man (August 1924)
  Company: Warner Brothers
  Cast: Rin-Tin-Tin

The Golden Princess (October 1925)
  Company: Paramount
  Story: Bret Harte

The Everlasting Whisper (October 1925)
  Company: Fox Films
  Other
    Locale: San Francisco
  Cast: Tom Mix

Flower of the Night (October 1925)
  Company: Paramount
  Other
    Locale: San Francisco
  Cast: Pola Negri

The Man from Red Gulch (November 1925)
  Company: Producers Distributing Corp.
  Story: Bret Harte

Cast: Harry Carey

Tonio, Son of the Sierra (December 1925)
  Company: George H. Davis(?)

Devil's Dice (October 1926)
  Company: Banner
  Other
    Locale: San Francisco

Flashing Fangs (September 1926)
  Company: Film Booking Office

The General (December 1926)
  Company: United Artists
  Director: Buster Keaton
  Cast: Buster Keaton

Wizard of the Saddle (January 1928)
  Company: Film Booking Office

The Crash (October 1928)
  Company: First National
  Cast: Milton Sills

Taking a Chance (November 1928)
  Company: Fox
  Story: Bret Harte

The Drifter (March 1929)
  Company: RKO
  Cast: Tom Mix

Betrayal (May 1929)
  Company: Paramount
  Cast: Emil Jennings, Gary Cooper

APPENDIX C
Personnel of Essanay Film Manufacturing Company, Western Unit

Star:	Gilbert M. Anderson	Jay Hanna
Sheriff:	Arthur Mackley	Rodney Hilderbrant
	Lee Willard	Paul Hurst
Leading Men:	Roy Clement	Harry Keenan
	True Boardman	David Kirkland
Juveniles:	Frederick Church	Robert Lawlor
	Emory Johnson	Julia Mackley
Leading Ladies:	Vedah Bertram	Charles Murray
	Marguerite Clayton	Ray "Kite" Robinson
	Virginia Eames (Mrs. True Boardman)	W. S. Russell
	Gladys Fields	Brinsley Shaw
	Edna Fisher	Carl Stockdale
	Josephine Rector	Harry Todd
	Bessie Sankey	Margaret Todd
	Ruth Saville	Ernest Van Pelt
	Evelyn Selbie	Comedians: Billy Armstrong
	Reina Valdez	Wallace Beery
Cowboys:	George ("Tex") Briggs	Augustus Carney
	Bill Cato	Charles Chaplin
	Al Herman	Fred Goodwins
	Jack Holt (?)	Bud Jamison
	Frank Pimental	Margaret Joslyn
	"Spider" Roach	Paddy McGuire
	Carl Stockdale	Robert McKenzie
	"Red" Watson	Bell Mitchell
Characters:	Leona Anderson	Victor Potel
	Hal Angus	Edna Purviance
	Lloyd Bacon	Patrick Rooney
	"Colonel" Elder	Ruth Saville
	Lillian Elder	Slim Summerville

Ben Turpin
Leo White
And Shep, the Collie

Directors: Gilbert M. Anderson
Wallace Beery
Roy Clement
Lloyd Ingraham
Robert Lawlor
Arthur Mackley

Cameramen: Jesse "Jess" J. Robbins
Rolland "Rollie" Totheroh
Joseph M. Morgan

Studio Staff
  Business Manager: Jack O'Brien
  Scenario Editor: Josephine Rector
  Set Construction: Lorin "Larry" Abrott
  Properties: "Colonel" Elder

APPENDIX D
Personnel of California Motion Picture Corporation

Star:	Beatriz Michelena		Jim Ross
Leading Man:	House Peters; later, William Pike		Marin Sais
Heavy:	Andrew Robson		George Skaff
Stock Players:	Katherine Angus		Joe Snell
	Clarence Arper		Moira Wallace
	Belle Bennett		Rollin Warwick
	Clara Byers	Directors:	George E. Middleton
	Don Nicholas A. Covarrubias		William Nigh
	Earle Emlay		Earle Emlay
	Harold Entwhistle	Cameramen:	Robert Carson
	Nina Herbert		Frank Padilla
	Frank Hollins		Arthur Powelson
	Jack Holt		John Pender
	Ernest Joy		J. C. Gasberg (stills)
	James Leslie		Mortimer "Mo" Snow, Harry Jones
	Harold Meade		(assistant cameramen)
	D. Mitsuras	Studio Staff	
	Jack Millerick	Manager:	Alexander Beyfuss; later, George E.
	Albert Morrison		Middleton
	Myrtle Newman	Scenario:	Charles Kenyon, Leslie T. Peacocke
	William Nigh	Laboratory:	Lewis Hutt
	Irene Outrim	Cutter:	Ruby Gasberg
	Mat Snyder	Art Director:	Edwin B. Willis
	Cliff Thompson	Carpenters:	Alex Keegan, Ludwig ("Ludy")
	Jeff Williams		Johansen
	Rolph Winters	Painter:	Harry Grimm
Special		Properties:	Rolph Winters, Al Burrell
Engagement:	Blanche Chapman	Electrician:	Jean Bogel
	Frederick Lewis	Stables:	Jack Millerick
	John Lord	Accounting:	Grace Nicholson
	Felice Rix	Secretary:	Lillian Johansen

APPENDIX E
Personnel of Various Bay Area Independent Companies

Stars and Feature Players

Claire Adams
Agnes Ayres
Mabel Ballin
Warner Baxter
Noah Beery
Madge Bellamy
Monte Blue
Hobart Bosworth
William Boyd
Evelyn Brent
Miriam Cooper
Louise Dresser
Louise Fazenda
Helen Ferguson
Alec B. Francis
Ella Hall
Juanita Hansen
Mildred Harris
Raymond Hatton
Wanda Hawley
Richard Holt
Hedda Hopper
Gladys Hulette
Ralph W. Ince
Emory Johnson
Cullen Landis

Bessie Love
Louise Lovely
J. Farrell MacDonald
Tully Marshall
Dan Mason
Robert McKim
Patsy Ruth Miller
Matt Moore
Jack Mulhall
Anna Q. Nilsson
Jane Novak
George O'Brien
Pat O'Malley
House Peters
Ruth Roland
Monroe Salisbury
Tom Santschi
Milton Sills
Marguerite Snow
Forrest Stanley
Roy Stewart
Estelle Taylor
Bryant Washburn
Crane Wilbur
Lois Wilson

Supporting and Character Actors

Eugenie Besserer
Wade Boteler
Sylvia Breamer
Winnifred Bryson
David Butler
Lawson W. Butt
Ora Carew
William T. Carleton
Edythe Chapman
Jack Connolly
Virginia Lee Corbin
Edward A. Coxen
Frankie Darrow
Marjorie Daw
Andre DeBeranger
Marguerite DeLaMotte
June Elvidge
Elinor Fair
Virginia Brown Faire
Joseph W. Girard
Gaston Glass
Robert Gordon
Gloria Grey
Wilna Hervey

Alice Hollister
Taylor Holmes
Helen Howell
Walter Law
Rex Lease
Kate Lester
Mitchell Lewis
Ralph Lewis
Blanche Mehaffey
Jay Morley
Victor Potel
Anders Randolf
Dorothy Revier
Cleo Ridgley
George Siegman
Russell Simpson
Phillips Smalley
Mack Swain
Josef Swickard
Theodore VonEltz
Ethel Wales
Niles Welch
Freeman Wood

Directors, Producers and
Exhibiters

John G. Adolfi
Peter Bacigalupi
Edward Belasco
Isadore Bernstein
Hobart Bosworth
Frank Capra
Lloyd B. Carleton
Jack Conway
George H. Davis
Leon F. Douglass
Robert Eddy
Dallas M. FitzGerald
Paul Gerson
Tom Gibson
Max Graf
Sid Grauman
Benjamin B. Hampton
Elmer Harris
Jack Hawks
Lampert Hilyar
W. W. Hodkinson
James P. Hogan
James W. Horne
Ralph W. Ince

Lloyd Ingraham
Jacques Jaccard
Emilie Johnson
Emory Johnson
Lorimer Johnston
James M. Keane
Rowland V. Lee
Sol Lesser
Sadie Lindblom
Earl C. Miles
Walter Montague
Henry Nasser
Thomas K. Peters
Paul Powell
Harry J. Revier
Phil Rosen
Al Santell
Paul Smith
W. S. Van Dyke
Jack L. Warner
Frank E. Woods
Duke Worne
William Worthington

Cinematographers

John R. Arnold
Silvano Balboni
Andre Barlatier
Lyman Broening
George Crocker
Joseph Dubray
Raymond A. Duhem
Harry W. Gerstad
Alfred Godsen
Frank B. Good
King Gray
Lee Humiston
Glen MacWilliams
Hal Mohr
Roland Price
John S. Stumar
J. O. Taylor
Harry Vallejo
Blake Wagner
Joseph B. Walker

APPENDIX F
Current Sources of Silent Films

Today, extremely few films of the silent era remain. A number of films produced before 1912 were deposited in the Library of Congress, and prints have been struck from them in recent times. Following 1912, however, silent films, including most feature films, survived only rarely and by chance. Determined efforts are being made to salvage the often rapidly decomposing nitrate film stock both in the U.S. and Europe. The following are among the most notable American film archives:

1. Library of Congress, Motion Picture Section
2. International Museum of Photography, George Eastman House; Rochester, New York
3. The American Film Institute; Washington, D.C.
4. Museum of Modern Art; New York, N.Y.
5. University of California at Los Angeles, Film Archives

The following are among companies that sell or rent prints of films from the silent era:

1. Blackhawk Films; Davenport, Iowa
2. Em Gee Film Library; Greater Los Angeles, California
3. Film Classic Exchange; Los Angeles, California
4. Historical Films (Kemp Niver); Hollywood, California
5. Hollywood Film Exchange; Hollywood, California
6. Reel Images; Monroe, Connecticut
7. Westcoast Films; San Francisco, California

A rare collection of newsreels, travel, and other actuality films of early Bay Area and Central and Northern California is available from Bert Gould/Bay Area Archive, San Francisco, California.

The following films on motion picture history were directed by the author:
First (Motion) Picture Show (23 minutes, color, videotape)
    Theme: Origins of the motion picture
    Distributor: University of California Extension Media Center, Berkeley
The Movies Go West (13 minutes, color, videotape)
    Theme: Origins of the Western cowboy film
    Distributor: University of California Extension Media Center, Berkeley
Those Daring Young Film Makers by the Golden Gate (23 minutes, color)
    Theme: Origins of the theatrical feature film
    Distributor: Museum of Modern Art, New York

Notes

CHAPTER 1

1. For more information on Stanford's agricultural experiments and his engineering and industrial dynamism that provided a matrix for the motion picture, see George T. Clark, *Leland Stanford, War Governor of California, Railroad Builder and Founder of Stanford University,* pp. 3–363; and Norman E. Tutorow, *Leland Stanford: Man of Many Careers,* pp. 3–183.

2. These experiments with the photography of living motion are discussed in "The Stride of a Trotting Horse," *Pacific Rural Press* (San Francisco, Calif.), 22 June 1878; "How a Horse Trots," *Scientific American,* 27 July 1878, p. 52; and J. D. B. Stillman, *The Horse in Motion,* pp. 123–27.

3. For a review of the limited photographic techniques available in the 1870s, see Helmut Gernsheim, *A Concise History of Photography,* pp. 9–41, 57–168; Beaumont Newhall, *The History of Photography, from 1839 to the Present Day,* pp. 9–118; and Peter Pollack, *The Picture History of Photography,* pp. 12–237.

4. For perceptive insights into the photographic career of Muybridge, see Anita V. Mozley, "Introduction," Robert B. Haas, "Eadweard Muybridge, 1830–1904," and Mozley, "Photographs by Muybridge, 1872–1880; Catalogue and Notes on the Work," *Eadweard Muybridge: The Stanford Years, 1872–1882,* ed. Anita V. Mozley, pp. 7–9, 11–35, 37–83.

5. The Muybridge scandal and trial are described in "A Startling Tragedy. Harry Larkyns Shot Dead by Muybridge, the Artist. Sequel to a Shocking Domestic Scandal," *San Francisco Chronicle,* 19 October 1874; and "Not Guilty. End of the Muybridge Trial," *Napa Daily Register* (Napa, Calif.), 6 February 1875.

6. "A Wonder of the Century. Instantaneous Photographs of a Trotter in Fast Motion," *San Francisco Morning Call,* 16 June 1878; "Set at Rest. The True Action of a Horse in Trotting Determined," *San Francisco Chronicle,* 16 June 1878; H. C. Peterson, "The Birthplace of the Motion Picture," *Sunset: The Pacific Monthly,* November 1915, pp. 909–15; Beaum-

ont Newhall, "Muybridge and the First Motion Picture," *Image,* January 1956, pp. 4–11. An 1878 photographic series by Muybridge of the horse "Sallie Gardner" (copy negative No. 18676-54) is in the Stanford University Museum of Art, Stanford, Calif.

7. For a discussion of the effects of the Stanford-Muybridge photographs of the visual arts, see Françoise Forster-Hahn, "Marey, Muybridge and Meissonier; The Study of Movement in Science and Art," in *Eadweard Muybridge: The Stanford Years, 1872–1881,* ed. Anita V. Mozley, pp. 85–109; W. I. Homer and J. Talbot, "Eakins, Muybridge and the Motion Picture Process," *Art Quarterly,* Summer 1963, pp. 194–216.

8. "The Stride of a Trotting Horse," *Pacific Rural Press* (San Francisco, Calif.), 22 June 1878; "The Science of the Horse's Motions," *Scientific American,* 19 October 1878, cover.

9. Joseph Pennell and Georges Guéroult quoted by Forster-Hahn, pp. 103–5.

10. *American Queen,* 29 July 1882, cover; *Punch,* 1 April 1882, p. 156; J. L. E. Meissonier and Auguste Rodin quoted by Forster-Hahn, pp. 91–105.

11. "How Governor Stanford converted Meissonier. The Great Horse Painter Finds that He Has Been in Error as to the Horse all His Life," *Daily Record-Union* (Sacramento, Calif.), 23 July 1881.

12. B. E. Lloyd, *Lights and Shades in San Francisco,* pp. 490–91.

13. For more information about early nineteenth century discoveries in optics and the ensuing devices to illustrate them, see D. L. Emblen, *Peter Mark Roget,* pp. 184–86; C. W. Ceram, *Archaeology of the Cinema,* pp. 1–140; John L. Fell, *A History of Films,* pp. 2–9; Mozley, pp. 72–74.

14. These rudimentary experiments with animation and projection are discussed in Thomas Coulson, "Philadelphia and the Development of the Motion Picture," *Journal of the Franklin Institute,* July, 1956, pp. 1–16.

15. The possibilities of combining the Stanford-Muybridge photographs of living motion with the zoetrope were early suggested in the article, "A Horse's Motion Scientifically Determined," *Scientific American,* 19 October 1878, p. 241. The

original motion picture projector of 1879–1880, first called the "Zoogyroscope" and later the "Zoopraxiscope," is now in the Central Library, Kingston-upon-Thames, England; a version of the projector demonstrating its mechanics is in the International Museum of Photography, George Eastman House, Rochester, New York; a full-scale working model is in the collection of the Stanford University Museum of Art; the locations of these projectors are noted in Mozley, pp. 71–72.

16. For the attractions playing in San Francisco on 4 May 1880, see "Amusements," *San Francisco Chronicle*, 4 May 1880. For general background on San Francisco and the arts, see Julia C. Altrocci, *The Spectacular San Franciscans*; Cora M. Older, *San Francisco, Magic City;* and Oscar Lewis, *Bay Window Bohemia; An Account of the Brilliant Artistic World of Gaslit San Francisco.*

17. "The Zoogyroscope. Photographs Illustrating Animals in Motion," *San Francisco Morning Call*, 5 May 1880. For other descriptions of the event, see "Moving Shadows," *San Francisco Chronicle*, 5 May 1880; and "Muybridge's Zoogyroscope," *Scientific American*, 5 June 1880, p. 353.

18. Lawton's gymnastic performances before the cameras at Palo Alto are described in "Men in Motion," *San Francisco Chronicle*, 9 August 1879.

19. "Mr. Muybridge's Photographs of Animals in Motion," *Scientific American Supplement*, 28 January 1882, pp. 5058–59. "G. A. S." (Geo. A. Sala), "Echoes of the Week," *Illustrated London News*, 18 March 1882, p. 251.

20. "Leland Stanford's Gift to Art and to Science," *San Francisco Examiner*, 6 February 1881; *Figaro*, 27 November 1881, quoted by Haas, p. 26.

21. The impact of Muybridge and his motion pictures in England is discussed in "G. A. S.," "Echoes of the Week," and "The Attitudes of Animals in Motion," *Illustrated London News*, 18 March 1882, pp. 251, 267.

22. Leland Stanford to J. D. B. Stillman, 23 October 1882, Stanford University Archives, Stanford, Calif.

23. "Leland Stanford's Gift to Art and to Science," *San Francisco Examiner*, 6 February 1881.

24. *Alta California* (San Francisco, Calif.), 5 May 1880, quoted in Haas, p. 26.

CHAPTER 2

1. "Essanay Firm With Fifty-two Employees Choose This Spot as Most Suitable for Pictures," *Township Register* (Niles, Calif.), 6 April 1912.

2. Anderson's efforts to test community commitment to Essanay is described in Alice Phillips, "Movie Days at Niles," *Advance-Star* ("Peninsula Living" section)(San Mateo, Calif.), 1 May 1971, an article based on recollections of Niles residents.

3. Anderson's recollections of the formation of Essanay are expressed in a tape recorded interview with Lawrence Lipton, c. 1958, which is in the Special Collections, University of California Research Library, Los Angeles. For more information about Anderson and the origins of the Essanay company, see Terry Ramsaye, *A Million and One Nights*, pp. 417, 421, 443, 444; William K. Everson, *A Pictorial History of the Western Film*, pp. 14–22.

4. The nomadic early activities of Essanay are recorded in "Will Make Pictures in Mexico," *The Moving Picture World*, 18 September 1909, p. 381 (hereafter cited as *World*); "Essanay Company Out West," *World*, 4 December 1909, p. 801;

Richard V. Spencer, "Los Angeles Letter," *World*, 4 February 1911, p. 253; "Motion Picture Troupe Leave Los Gatos," *Los Gatos Mail* (Los Gatos, Calif.), 9 February 1911; "Moving Picture Company Here," *Redlands Daily Review* (Redlands, Calif.), 7 February 1911; "To Use Indians in the Pictures," *Redlands Daily Review*, 11 February 1911; "Motion Pictures True to Life," *Redlands Daily Facts*, (Redlands, Calif.) 8 February 1911; "More Cowboys for Film Co.," *Redlands Daily Facts*, 20 February 1911; "Thrilling Story of Border Life Told for Motion Films," *Redlands Daily Facts*, 23 February 1922; "Essenay [sic] Pictures Co. to Operate Here," *Marin County Journal* (San Rafael, Calif.), 1 June 1911; "Splendid Exhibition of Rough Riding," *Marin County Journal*, 29 June 1911; "*Man from Mexico*—Show by Essanay Film Co.," *Marin County Journal*, 28 September 1911; "Splendid Celebration—Specially Fine Parade," *Marin County Journal*, 26 October 1911; "Essanay Co.—Banqueted," *Marin County Journal*, 7 December 1911.

5. For more information about the early history of the Niles area, see "History of Washington Township (Alameda County, Calif.)," The Women's Club of Washington Township, 1904, Oakland History Room, Oakland Public Library, Oakland, Calif.; Donald Parkhurst, "A Study of a Small, Rural American Community, Niles, California, and Its Relation to a Major Industry, 1912–1916," (M.A. diss., California State University, Hayward, 1977).

6. Hal Angus (Essanay actor in Niles), interviews by author, 1972–75.

7. Owen Wister, *The Virginian, A Horseman of the Plains*, p. 4. For more information on the affects of the American West on the public imagination, see Russel B. Nye, *The Unembarrassed Muse: The Popular Arts in America*, pp. 280–304; Henry Nash Smith, *Virgin Land: The American West as Symbol and Myth*, pp. 3–260; John C. Cawelti, *The Six-Gun Mystique.*

8. Catherine Hoover, "Pantoscope of California," *California Historical Courier*, July 1978, p. 3; John Burke, *Buffalo Bill, the Noblest Whiteskin*, pp. 96–271.

9. For discussions about the theatrical genre of melodrama, see David Grimsted, *Melodrama Unveiled: American Theater and Culture, 1800–1850;* Frank Rayhill, *The World of Melodrama*, pp. 230–39, 297–305; A. Nicholas Vardac, *Stage to Screen*, pp. 1–198; John Fell, "Motive, Mischief and Melodrama: The State of Film Narrative in 1907," *Film Quarterly*, Spring 1980, pp. 30–37.

10. Anderson, interview by Lipton; Everson, pp. 14–22; Ramsaye, pp. 416–19.

11. For evidence of early Essanay activities in Niles, see "Essanay Company to Build Cottages," *Washington Press* (Washington Township, Alameda County, Calif.), 12 April 1912; "Notes from the Essanay Western Company at Niles," *World*, 9 November 1912, p. 555; James S. McQuade, review of *The Smuggler's Daughter*, *World*, 16 July 1912, p. 233.

12. For descriptions of the Essanay studio, see Hal Angus, interviews; Alton R. Cummings, "Essanay Film Manufacturing Company: California Historical Sites and Landmarks, Alameda County Series," mimeographed, 1937, California State Library, Sacramento; "Essanay's New Studios," *World*, 11 July 1914, pp. 266–67; "Essanay Western Plant," *World*, 10 July 1915, pp. 237–38.

13. The estimate of Anderson's total film output is based on the author's tabulation of titles of Essanay releases from *World* and other contemporary journals, January 1909 to April 1916.

14. Anderson quoted by Bob Thomas, "Pioneer Recalls

1903 Film Venture," *Oakland Tribune* (Oakland, Calif.) 21 February 1958.

15. Anderson quoted by Thomas. Review of *Broncho Bill's* [*sic*] *Redemption, World*, 13 August 1910, p. 35. Some of the inconclusive questions of the origins of the name "Broncho Billy" are discussed in Mrs. John F. Drew (niece of Peter B. Kyne), interview by author, 1972; Peter B. Kyne Papers, University of Oregon Library, Eugene; Ivan Gaddis, "The Origins of 'Broncho Billy,'" *Motion Picture Magazine*, March 1916, pp. 99–101; George Pratt, "The Posse Is Ridin' Like Mad," *Image*, April 1958, pp. 76–85; Anderson, interview by Lipton.

16. The range of Anderson's characterization is conveyed in a review of *Broncho Billy's Pal, World*, 30 July 1912, p. 453; Edward Wagonknecht, *The Movies in the Age of Innocence*, pp. 49–51; Everson, p. 20.

17. Lewis Jacobs, *The Rise of the American Film: A Critical History With an Essay Experimental Cinema in America 1921–1947*, pp. 143–44.

18. Review of *Sheepman's Escape, World*, 6 January 1912, p. 44.

19. The photograhic quality of Essanay films is discussed in Timothy J. Lyons, ed., "Roland H. Totheroh Interviewed," *Film Culture*, Spring 1972, p. 230; Fred J. Balshofer and Arthur C. Miller, *One Reel a Week*, pp. 55, 78–79; review of *Western Hearts, World*, 15 June 1912, p. 931; review of *Broncho Billy's Bible, World*, 1 June 1912, p. 735.

20. James S. McQuade, review of *Tell-Tale Hand, World*, 19 November 1914, p. 1366.

21. For more information about Josephine Rector, see Bill Strobel, "Niles Days as Film Capital," *Oakland Tribune*, 21 May 1958; information on *Dance at Silver Gulch* was drawn from a poster, collection of the author.

22. Angus, interviews. *Movies Go West* (1974) is distributed by the Extension Media Center, University of California, Berkeley.

23. Review of *Broncho Billy's Surrender, New York Dramatic Mirror*, 4 August 1915, p. 33.

24. Leon Solon is quoted in Phillips. For other recollections of Essanay players, see Ray Hubbard, "When the Movies Came from Niles," television script prepared c. 1965 for Broadcast House, Washington, D.C.; "Essanay Western Plant," *World*, 10 July 1915, pp. 237–38; "The King of the Movies," *San Francisco Chronicle*, 6 January 1914.

25. For more information about Essanay comedies, see "Essanay Western Plant," *World*, 10 July 1915, pp. 237–38; Parkhurst; Phillips.

26. "Charles Chaplin as 'The Souse,' Karno's London Comedians: A Night in a London Club," advertisement for Empress Vaudeville Theater, *San Francisco Examiner*, 6 October 1913.

27. Charles Chaplin, *My Autobiography*, pp. 128–71.

28. Roger Manvell, *Chaplin*, p. 94; Denis Gifford, *Chaplin*, pp. 63–65.

29. For Anderson's theatrical endeavors, see "*Merry Gambol* at Gaiety—Marie Dressler is Whopping Success," *San Francisco Examiner*, 3 February 1914; "Another Climax in Gaiety Scrap," *San Francisco Chronicle*, 10 March 1914; "Marie Dressler and Gilbert M. Anderson, the 'Broncho Billy' of the Movies, Appearing in a New Comedy-Drama—Before U.S. Attorney," *San Francisco Examiner*, 11 March 1914. Although Dressler appeared in stage shows produced by Anderson, no evidence has been found by the author of her appearance in any films produced at Niles by Anderson and released by Essanay.

30. For Bill Cato's recollection, see Hubbard.

31. For reflections on the demise of Essanay's Niles studio, see Gladys Priddy, "Essanay Lot Gone, Not Its Guiding Hand," *Chicago Tribune*, 21 December 1947; Theodore R. Smith, "Niles' Last Hope for World Movie Fame Dies As Old Essanay Studio Is Torn Down," *San Francisco News*, 22 July 1933; Hubbard; Parkhurst; Phillips.

CHAPTER 3

1. Review of *Salomy Jane, New York Dramatic Mirror*, 4 November 1914, p. 30; Walter Anthony, review of *Salomy Jane, San Francisco Chronicle*, 27 October 1914.

2. Peter Milne, review of *Salomy Jane, Motion Picture News*, 7 November 1914, p. 41.

3. "*Salomy Jane*, America's Greatest Picture Play," souvenir program from Alcazar Theater, San Francisco, 1914, collection of author.

4. "Beatriz Michelena, Greatest and Most Beautiful Artist Now Appearing in Motion Pictures," *Moving Picture World*, 2 January 1915, pp. 34–35 (hereafter cited as *World*).

5. California Motion Picture Corporation, articles of incorporation, 16 September 1913, Office of the Secretary of State, Sacramento, Calif.; "Motion Picture Concern Is Backed by Millions," *San Francisco Chronicle*, 6 January 1914.

6. For more information about Payne, see "California Motion Picture Corporation," *World*, 10 July 1915, p. 252; "Form Big Motion Picture Concern," *San Francisco Chronicle*, 17 September 1913; "Herbert Payne at Wheel of his Simplex Car," *San Francisco Examiner*, 28 September 1913; "In the World of Society: Splendor, Social Perfection in Wedding of Mr. and Mrs. Herbert Payne," *San Francisco Examiner*, 4 February 1914.

7. For more information about Beyfuss, see "Alex E. Beyfuss Enters General Publicity Field," *San Francisco Chronicle*, 8 December 1909; "$250,000 Film of *Kismet* to be Made in San Rafael, Announcement Brought from New York by Alex E. Beyfuss, Vice President and General Manager of the California Motion Picture Corporation," *San Francisco Examiner*, 16 February 1916.

8. For more information about Middleton, see George E. Middleton, interviews by author, 1965–67; Irving Ackerman (movie exhibitor in San Francisco and classmate of Middleton), interviews by author, 1970–75; Lillian Johansen (CMPC secretary-stenographer), interviews by author, 1970–75; "George E. Middleton," *World*, 17 June 1916, p. 2044.

9. For examples of these early films, see the historic film collection at Bert Gould's Bay Area Archive, San Francisco.

10. For a facsimile of the CMPC logo created by George E. Middleton, see the collection of the author.

11. Jesse L. Lasky, *I Blow My Own Horn*, p. 96.

12. Charles Ray, "Confessions Made by a Star-Producer," *Photoplay*, November 1924, p. 57.

13. For descriptions of the CMPC studio, see "Picture People Want Marin Scenery," *Marin County Journal* (San Rafael, Calif.), 26 March 1914; "San Francisco," *World*, 4 July 1914, p. 89; "California Motion Picture Corporation," *World*, 10 July 1915, p. 252.

14. For more information on CMPC's Boulder Creek facility, see Josephine McCracklin, "Bret Harte in 'The Movies,'" *Overland*, June 1915, pp. 486–87; "California Motion Picture Corporation," *World*, 10 July 1915, p. 252; William S. Hart, *My Life, East and West*, pp. 220–21; "Pioneer Movie in the Making," *San Francisco Examiner*, 23 June 1917.

15. "Nicholas A. Covarrubias," *San Francisco Examiner*, 25 November 1924; "San Rafael—Movie Capital of Old," *Independent Journal* (San Rafael, Calif.), 23 July 1949; photograph of Dan Bart, History Department, Wells Fargo Bank, San Francisco.

16. For representative titles of releases of *Golden Gate Weekly*, see listing, *World*, 27 December 1913, p. 1570. For more information on Ishi, see Theodora Kroeber, *Ishi in Two Worlds;* still photographs of Ishi are in Lowie Museum of Anthropology, University of California, Berkeley, Calif.

17. Information on the CMPC technical staff is drawn from Rolph Winters (CMPC properties man), interviews by author, 1965; Letty Etzler (niece of Frank Padilla), interviews by author, 1973; George Skaff (actor, CMPC and Alcazar Theater stock company), interviews by author, 1975; Johansen, interviews; "San Rafael—Movie Capital of Old," *Independent-Journal* (San Rafael, Calif.) 9 July, 16 July, 23 July 1949.

18. For discussions of Daly's *Under the Gaslight*, see Martin Felheim, *The Theatre of Augustin Daly*, pp. 47–59; Arthur H. Quinn, *A History of American Drama*, Vol. I, pp. 11–12. For an excellent discussion of the relationship between stage techniques and early film techniques, see A. Nicholas Vardac, *Stage to Screen*, pp. 1–198.

19. "Painting the Lily—and Improving It," *Motion Picture Mail* (New York), 4 March 1916.

20. Review of *The Pageant of San Francisco, World*, 10 April 1915, p. 244.

21. For evidence of Roberts, Rambeau, Lytell, Barriscale, Stanley, Taylor, Lowe, Brady, and Boland, see Edmond M. Gagey, *The San Francisco Stage*, pp. 172, 218; for Chaney, see Alcazar Theater program, 15 January 1912, archives of California Historical Society, San Francisco; for Gilbert, Hersholt, Wilson, and Rich, see Hal C. Herman, ed., *How I Broke into the Movies*, pp. 11, 47, 85, 101; for Butler, see the *Blue Book of the Screen*, pp. 40–41; for Pringle and Fay, see Jack L. Warner, *My First Hundred Years in Hollywood*, p. 75; for Von Stroheim, see Thomas Q. Curtiss, *Von Stroheim*, pp. 23–31.

22. For further evidence of Michelena's career and appeal, see "Beatriz Michelena, Prominent in List of Artists—Prima Donna Soprano and Light Opera Star—to Sing at Mechanics Fair," *San Francisco Examiner*, 23 September 1913; "Beatriz Michelena," *World*, 28 February 1914, p. 1071; "Beatriz Michelena the Beautiful and Celebrated Prima Donna," *World*, 4 July 1912, p. 12; photograph of Michelena, *New York Dramatic Mirror*, 9 December 1914, cover; photograph of Michelena, *New York Dramatic Mirror*, 29 January 1916, cover; photograph of Michelena, *New York Dramatic Mirror*, 13 May 1916; "Michelena's Moods Cost Firm $35,000—Temperamental Unreasonableness," *San Francisco Examiner*, 3 February 1917; Hal Angus (actor with Essanay company), interviews by author, 1972–75; Johansen, interviews; Winters, interviews.

23. For evidence of filmed versions of Norris's stories, see *Motion Pictures, 1912–1939: Index*, Copyright Office, Library of Congress, p. 119.

24. "Jack Holt," *Blue Book of the Screen*, pp. 116–17.

25. Review of *Mrs. Wiggs of the Cabbage Patch, World*, 9 January 1915, p. 199.

26. For discussions of these films, see review of *Lily of Poverty Flat, World*, 1 May 1915, p. 739; review of *A Phyllis of the Sierra, Photoplay*, July 1915, p. 96; review of *Heart of Juanita, World*, 13 December 1919, p. 855; the reference to *Passion Flower* is drawn from Middleton interviews; review of *Just Squaw, World*, 10 May 1919, p. 934; review of *Flame of Hellgate, World*, 20 March 1920, p. 2007. For more informa-

tion about these and other CMPC releases, see Harry C. Donoho, "San Francisco Pictures Win Wide Praise," *San Francisco Chronicle*, 4 December 1920.

27. Quinn, pp. 108–14.

28. Review of *Salvation Nell, New York Dramatic Mirror*, 25 August 1915, p. 28; review of *Mignon, New York Dramatic Mirror*, 20 January 1915, p. 38.

29. Edwin M. Royle, review of *Unwritten Law, Billboard* (New York), 12 February 1916. For another evaluation of Michelena's acting, see *The Film Renter & Moving Picture News* (London), 4 September 1920.

30. Review of *Woman Who Dared, The Film Renter & Moving Picture News* (London), 4 September 1920. For descriptions of other Michelena vehicles, see review of *Mignon, World*, 23 January 1915, p. 499; review of *Salvation Nell, World*, 28 August 1915, p. 1493; "Company Forced to Abandon Great Production of *Faust*," *San Francisco Examiner*, 3 February 1917; review of *Woman Who Dared, World*, 15 July 1915, p. 473.

31. For discussions of Michelena's performances in these pictures, see review of *Mrs. Wiggs of the Cabbage Patch, World*, 9 January 1915, p. 199; review of *Unwritten Law, World*, 22 January 1916, p. 618; review of *Unwritten Law, New York Dramatic Mirror*, 22 January 1916, p. 28.

32. Patrick Kearney's comments about *Woman Who Dared* quoted in "Northern California Films Are Praised," *San Francisco Chronicle*, 16 July 1916; "F. R. B." review of *Unwritten Law* from *Motion Picture Mail* (New York), 15 January 1916.

33. For Fell's observation about De Mille, see John L. Fell, *A History of Films*, pp. 107–8.

34. For more information about World Film Corporation, see "World Film Gets Calif. M. P. Corp. Product," *World*, 12 December 1914, p. 1528; Harvey Denkin, "Shubert Film: the Giant that Never Was," *The Passing Show*, Summer 1981, Newsletter of the Shubert Archive, New York; Terry Ramsaye, *A Million and One Nights*, pp. 712–64.

35. For Michelena's view of the financial crisis, see Margaret I. MacDonald, "Beatriz Michelena Speaks," *World*, 7 April 1917, p. 105.

36. For more information about the Middleton-Michelena company and its films, see "Pioneer Movie in the Making, Beatriz Michelena [and] Company Working on Stirring Drama of Early California. Beatriz Michelena has launched a new motion picture enterprise," *San Francisco Examiner*, 23 June 1917; "Mayor Rolph Brings Beatriz Michelena to City Hall," *San Francisco Examiner*, 29 July 1919; Etzler, interviews; Johansen, interviews; Middleton, interviews; Winters, interviews.

37. For more information about Hodkinson's career, see Lewis Jacobs, *The Rise of the American Film: A Critical History With an Essay Experimental Cinema in America 1921;1947*, pp. 93, 167; Fell, p. 82; Lasky, pp. 121–22; Ramsaye, pp. 628–31, 633, 639, 679, 710.

38. For more information about the three films produced by the Middleton-Michelena company, see review of *Heart of Juanita, World*, 13 December 1919, p. 855; review of *Just Squaw, World*, 10 May 1919, p. 934; "*Just Squaw* Just Such a Production as Bret Harte Might Have Devised," *San Francisco Examiner*, 28 July 1919; review of *Flame of Hellgate, World*, 20 March 1920, p. 2007; review of *Flame of Hellgate, Film Daily*, 29 February 1920.

39. *Those Daring Young Film Makers by the Golden Gate* (1979) is in the collection of the Museum of Modern Art, New York.

40. "Clubman Admits He Is Bankrupt—Herbert Payne,

32," *San Francisco Call,* 16 September 1918; "Herbert Payne, 56, Committed Suicide Today," *San Francisco Chronicle,* 9 May 1938; "Alex Beyfuss Takes Own Life, 38," *San Francisco Examiner,* 10 January 1925; "Beatriz Michelena, Motion Picture Star, with Company of Thirty, Sailed Last Week for a Tour of Central and South America," *San Francisco Chronicle,* 10 July 1927.

CHAPTER 4

1. J. Laurence Toole, "S. F. Blue Book Written in as Movie Cast" (abridged), *San Francisco Examiner,* 29 November 1920.

2. Roger Ferri, review of *Her Accidental Husband, Moving Picture World,* 24 March 1923, p. 444 (hereafter cited as *World*); review of *Awful Truth, New York Times,* 2 July 1925.

3. For more information on motion pictures in San Francisco in the 1890s, see "San Francisco, Cal., Dates Back to the Year 1894," *World,* 15 July 1916, p. 399.

4. *Cineograph* program, July 1898, California Historical Society, San Francisco.

5. Terry Ramsaye, *A Million and One Nights,* 427. For more information on the Miles brothers, see Ramsaye, pp. 401–2, 427; "Miles Brothers Made Early Start," *World,* 15 July 1916, pp. 399–400; John L. Fell, *A History of Films,* p. 17; Lewis Jacobs, *The Rise of the American Film: A Critical History With an Essay Experimental Cinema in America, 1921–1947,* pp. 52–53.

6. For examples of such early films, see the historic film collection at Bert Gould's Bay Area Archive, San Francisco.

7. *A Trip Down Mt. Tamalpais* is available from Kemp Niver's Historical Films, Hollywood, Calif.

8. "Miles Brothers, Pioneers. A Bit of History of the Firm Which Built the First Motion Picture Studio on the Coast," *World,* 10 July 1915, p. 248.

9. "Miles Brothers, Pioneers," *World,* 10 July 1915, p. 248.

10. John Hoffman, "When Pictures Came to Life," *American Cinematographer,* February 1974, p. 184; Exactus Photo-Film Corporation, miscellaneous papers donated by Samuel Stark, File Bo55, Special Collections, Stanford University Libraries, Stanford, Calif.

11. "Five-Act Show is 'Made in Alameda,'" *Alameda Times-Star* (Alameda, Calif.), 14 August 1916; "Alameda's Bid for Movies," *Alameda Times-Star,* 6 January 1928.

12. "Motion Pictures in Color. New Process Exhibited Here," *New York Times,* 15 February 1918; review of *Cupid Angling, San Francisco Chronicle,* 15 June 1918. For more information on the career of Douglass, see Leon Douglass, untitled autobiography, mimeographed, c. June 1940, Douglass family, Menlo Park, Calif.; "Douglass, Leon," *National Cyclopaedia of American Biography,* 1961; "The Recipe of Leon F. Douglass for Changing Fortune's Frown into a Smile," *Sunset Magazine,* November 1921 pp. 44–66; "Color Movies Latest from L. F. Douglass," *San Francisco Examiner,* 18 June 1916; "Color Photography Puts Dame Nature on Screen, *San Francisco Chronicle,* 18 June 1918; "New Camera Brings Wonder Film Effects," *San Francisco Chronicle,* 29 January 1922; "Inventor Gets Movie Recognition. Menlo Park Man Perfects Lenses to Facilitate Camera Tricks—Used in *Phantom of the Opera,*" *San Francisco Chronicle,* 14 October 1924; "Loss to Science, L. F. Douglass, 71, Inventor," *San Francisco Chronicle,* 8 September 1940.

13. Reverend Smith is quoted in Maude C. Pilkington, "The Finger of Justice," *Sunset, the Pacific Monthly,* December 1917, pp. 24–25. For reactions to the film, see review of

Finger of Justice, World, 6 July 1918, p. 112; review of *Finger of Justice, Photoplay,* June 1918, p. 92.

14. The statements of officials in Washington, D.C. and Seattle, Washington are quoted in "*The Finger of Justice* Is Approved," *World,* 17 August 1918, pp. 980–81. For more information on the censorship action, see "The Parson Presents," "The Censor in Action," and "Replies to Mrs. O'Grady," *New York Times,* 30 June, 7 July, and 8 July 1918.

15. Hodkinson is quoted in "Picture Pioneer W. W. Hodkinson," *Variety,* 3 June 1971. For more information on his career, see William W. Hodkinson, career summary, mimeographed, c. 1971, archives of the Academy of Motion Picture Arts and Sciences, Beverly Hills, Calif.; Fell, p. 82; Jacobs, pp. 93, 167; Ramsaye, pp. 628–749; "$6,000,000 Studio for San Francisco, Cal., Hodkinson Among Backers," unidentified press clipping date-stamped 1 June 1918, collection of L. Kenneth Wilson, Menlo Park, Calif.; "Distributor of Independent Films in S.F.," *San Francisco Chronicle,* 13 June 1923.

16. Eliason is quoted in "San Francisco Light Declared Best for Films," *San Francisco Chronicle,* 13 June 1919; the Civic League is quoted in "Civic League Plans Increased Motion Picture Industry," *San Francisco Chronicle,* 8 April 1920; "Motion Picture Plant to Go Up in San Mateo," *San Francisco Chronicle,* 26 August 1920. For other reports of the promotional activities, see "Movie Studio Sought for S.F.," *San Francisco Chronicle,* 26 November 1918; "Twenty Movie Firms May Locate in San Francisco," *San Francisco Chronicle,* 29 May 1919; "San Francisco Discussed as Movie Capital," *San Francisco Chronicle,* 20 June 1919; "San Francisco to the Fore As Motion Picture Center," *San Francisco Chronicle,* 19 January 1921; "Our Motion Picture Industry," *San Francisco Chronicle,* 1 September 1921.

17. For more information about the Pacific Studios, see "The Invasion of San Francisco," illustrated brochure of Pacific Studios Corp., c. 1922, California Historical Society, San Francisco; Pacific Studios Corp., prospectus and stock offering, 1 September 1920, collection of author; "Work Begins on Movie Studio in San Mateo," *San Francisco Chronicle,* 16 September 1920; "Dedicating Moving Picture Studio in San Mateo, Draws 10,000," *San Francisco Chronicle,* 15 November 1920; "Northern California's Latest Modern Motion Picture Studio," *San Francisco Chronicle,* 16 February 1922.

18. For additional information on Bosworth, see "Bosworth, Hobart," *Who's Who in California, 1928–1929; Blue Book of the Screen,* p. 27; Ramsaye, p. 630; George C. Warren, "Celebrated Screen Stars Make Headquarters in this City," *San Francisco Chronicle,* 5 February 1922.

19. "Picture Star Making New Films on Bay," *San Francisco Chronicle,* 3 April 1921. For the Hodkinson-Bosworth endeavor, see "San Mateo Gets Moving Pictures," *San Francisco Chronicle,* 14 June 1916; "San Mateo May Become Film City," *San Francisco Chronicle,* 27 June 1916.

20. For reactions to the Bosworth film, see review of *White Hands, World,* 11 February 1922, p. 663; review of *White Hands, San Francisco Chronicle,* 9 January 1922. For information about Bosworth's films in production, see "Technical Staff Opens Film Plant," *San Francisco Chronicle,* 15 August 1921; "Motion Picture Filming Begins in San Mateo," *San Francisco Chronicle,* 16 August 1921; "Realism Unreal to San Francisco," *San Francisco Chronicle,* 11 September 1921; "Bay Shots in Bosworth's New Picture," *San Francisco Chronicle,* 10 April 1922.

21. For reactions to Bernstein's film, see review of *Great Alone, World,* 24 June 1922, p. 735; review of *Great Alone,*

Photoplay, September 1922, p. 108; review of *Great Alone, San Francisco Chronicle*, 25 March 1922. For information about Bernstein's film in production, see "Rock Salt Flies to Furnish San Mateo Blizzard," *San Francisco Chronicle*, 29 January 1922.

22. For more information on Graf's career, see "Chronicle Newsboy Now Movie Magnate," *San Francisco Chronicle*, 15 April 1923; "S.F. Chronicle Lures Producer—Graf Productions to Locate in San Francisco," *San Francisco Chronicle*, 12 March 1922; "Graf to Bring Big Star Cast for New Film," *San Francisco Chronicle*, 29 March 1922; "Metro to Release Picture," *San Francisco Chronicle*, 24 October 1922; Irving Ackerman (San Francisco movie exhibitor), interviews by author, 1966–67; *Film Daily Year Book, 1924*, p. 236.

23. For reactions to Graf's films, see review of *Half a Dollar Bill, World*, 15 November 1923, p. 630; review of *Half a Dollar Bill, Photoplay*, February 1924, p. 88; review of *Half A Dollar Bill, San Francisco Chronicle*, 24 December 1923; review of *Fog, World*, 14 July 1923, p. 157; review of *Fog, Photoplay*, September 1923, p. 66; review of *Fog, San Francisco Chronicle*, 30 July 1923; review of *Forgotten Law, World*, 30 December 1922, p. 875; review of *Forgotten Law, Photoplay*, January 1923, p. 118; review of *Forgotten Law, San Francisco Chronicle*, 6 November 1922; review of *Wandering Footsteps, Variety*, 16 June 1926; review of *Wandering Footsteps, Film Daily*, 15 November 1925. For information about Graf's films in production, see "Filmy Clad Beauties Cavort on Lawn," *San Francisco Chronicle*, 15 March 1923; "*The Fog* Production Made at Pacific Studios Is Among Leaders," *San Francisco Chronicle*, 28 July 1923; "Crowds Watch Realism Made into Film Play," *San Francisco Chronicle*, 10 March 1924. For Estelle Taylor's attitude toward her profession, see "Movie Star Explains Why Film Styles Change in Making Love," *San Francisco Chronicle*, 16 March 1924.

24. For more information on Graf's financial problems, see "Five Named Conspirators by Max Graf. Sensational Charges of Extortion Through Intimidation," *San Francisco Examiner*, 25 July 1924; "Producer Says Terror Forced Stock Transfer," *San Francisco Chronicle*, 25 July 1924; "Yesterday an Extra Girl—but She 'Stars' at Last," *San Francisco Examiner*, 26 July 1924; "Graf Suit Against Firm Directors Ends," *San Francisco Chronicle*, 1 October 1924; "Graf Fully Exonerated of Embezzlement Charges," *San Francisco Chronicle*, 13 May 1925; "Max Graf's Legal Troubles at End. Film Company Litigation Adjusted," *San Francisco Chronicle*, 1 February 1927.

25. For more information on the reorganized studios, see "San Mateo Studio Leased," *San Francisco Chronicle*, 18 April 1924; "San Francisco's Future as Film Center," *San Francisco Chronicle*, 1 June 1924; "The Story of the Peninsula Studios: On the Threshold of the Golden Gate," *World*, 12 July 1924, p. 118; George C. Warren, "This City Is Getting on the Movie Map," *San Francisco Chronicle*, 13 July 1924; "Continuous Operation for Pacific Studios," *San Francisco Examiner*, 15 July 1924.

26. For more information about Woods's career, see Jacobs, pp. 102, 132, 134, 172; Ramsaye, pp. 512–13, 638, 720.

27. George C. Warren, review of *Chalk Marks, San Francisco Chronicle*, 10 December 1924; C. S. Sewell, review of *Beauty and the Bad Man, World*, 4 July 1925, p. 49. For other reactions to these films, see review of *Chalk Marks, Film Daily*, 23 November 1924; review of *Beauty and the Bad Man, Photoplay*, September 1925, p. 104; review of *Let Women Alone, San Francisco Examiner*, 10 January 1925; review of

Wise Virgin, San Francisco Chronicle, 1 September 1924. For information about the Harris-Woods films in production, see "*A Wise Virgin* to be Produced in San Francisco—to be Released by Hodkinson," *San Francisco Chronicle*, 15 May 1924; "Film Cameras Will Shoot Race Fans for Movie Play," *San Francisco Chronicle*, 16 May 1924; "'Patsy' Gets Cold in 'Nightie' Scene," *San Francisco Chronicle*, 22 August 1924; "Director Gets a Thrill from Producing a Picture," *San Francisco Chronicle*, 21 December 1924; "Mabel Ballin Making Peter B. Kyne Story at Local Studio," *San Francisco Chronicle*, 1 February 1925; "What the Stars and Directors Are Doing Now," *Photoplay*, December 1924, p. 112.

28. C. S. Sewell, review of *Awful Truth, World*, 11 July 1925, p. 183. For other reactions to Ayres's films, see review of *Her Market Value, Film Progress*, February 1925; review of *Awful Truth, Film Daily*, 5 July 1925. For information about the Ayres films in production, see "Agnes Ayres to Head Cast [at] Peninsula Studios," *San Francisco Chronicle*, 17 March 1925; "Finds Art and What Public Wants Are Entirely Different," *San Francisco Chronicle*, 9 November 1924.

29. For the Ayres controversy with Woods, see "Agnes Ayres Sues for Contract Loss. Suit Filed Against Producers Distributing Corporation," *San Francisco Chronicle*, 17 February 1926; "Agnes Ayres Is Hit With a Heavy Answer—Embonpoint 'A Disfigurement' Declare Producers," *San Francisco Chronicle*, 18 February 1926.

30. Jack L. Warner to author, 11 October 1972.

31. Robert C. McElravy, review of *Money Changers, World*, 6 November 1920, p. 110.

32. Frank Capra to author, 18 March 1972; Frank Capra, *The Name Above the Title*, pp. 18–34; "Belmont Chosen for Plum Center," *San Francisco Chronicle*, 4 March 1922; "S.F. Pictures to Get Big Welcome," *San Francisco Chronicle*, 5 September 1922.

33. Edward Weitzel, review of *Heart of the North, World*, 10 September 1921, p. 208; George C. Warren, review of *Life's Greatest Question, San Francisco Chronicle*, 13 February 1922. For other reactions to Revier's films, see review of *Broadway Madonna, World*, 11 November 1922, p. 184; review of *Broadway Madonna, Photoplay*, January 1923, p. 119; review of *Broadway Madonna, Film Daily*, 19 November 1922; review of *Heart of the North, Film Daily*, 25 September 1921; review of *Life's Greatest Question, World*, 19 August 1922, p. 610; review of *Life's Greatest Question, Film Daily*, 10 September 1922. For information about the Revier films in production, see "Star Working on New Productions," *San Francisco Chronicle*, 8 May 1921; "Two Stars Lead Big Cast in Elaborate Film," *San Francisco Chronicle*, 5 February 1922; "Harry Revier Finds Ideal Locations for His Stories in Golden Gate Park," *San Francisco Chronicle*, 12 February 1922; "Film Director Completing New Movie—Prides Himself on Speed of His Directing," *San Francisco Chronicle*, 19 February 1922; "Film Ranks in High Places—Montague Studio Work," *San Francisco Chronicle*, 27 October 1922; George C. Warren, "Eight Film Companies at Work Here," *San Francisco Chronicle*, 5 November 1922.

34. George C. Warren, review of *Isobel, or The Trail's End, San Francisco Chronicle*, 3 March 1921. For another reaction to Davis's film, see review of *Isobel, or the Trail's End, World*, 4 December 1920, p. 645. For information about the Davis film in production, see "Expenses Much Lower Than at Hollywood—25% Less," *San Francisco Chronicle*, 31 August 1921; "New Company to Make Film Here," *San Francisco Chronicle*, 10 April 1922.

35. For reactions to Belasco's films, see review of *Mysterious Witness, Photoplay,* September 1923, p. 66; review of *Enemies of Children, Photoplay,* February 1924, p. 90; Robert Ferri, review of *Her Accidental Husband, World,* 24 March 1923, p. 444; review of *Her Accidental Husband, San Francisco Chronicle,* 28 May 1923. For information about the Belasco films in production, see "Two Belascos Launch Movie Play Venture Here," *San Francisco Chronicle,* 28 September 1922; "Film Staged Inside Hotel—Shooting Final Scenes of *Her Price,*" *San Francisco Examiner,* 19 October 1922; George C. Warren, "Eight Film Companies at Work Here," *San Francisco Chronicle,* 5 November 1922; "Belasco Concern Takes New York Office," *San Francisco Chronicle,* 25 January 1923.

36. Review of *Flying Dutchman, Photoplay,* October 1923, p. 76. For another reaction to the film, see Mary Kelly, review of *Flying Dutchman, World,* 4 August 1923, p. 405. For information about this Carleton film in production, see "Difficulties in *The Flying Dutchman* Met in this Port," *San Francisco Examiner,* 24 May 1922; George C. Warren, "Celebrated Screen Stars Make Headquarters in this City," *San Francisco Chronicle,* 5 February 1922.

37. For more information on Gerson's career, see *Ben Hur,* program of New York stage production, 4 December 1899, Hoblitzelle Theater Arts Library, Humanities Research Center, University of Texas, Austin; "Paul Gerson Dramatic School, San Francisco," brochure, c. 1920, Archives of the Performing Arts, San Francisco; "Gerson Company to Begin Filming Picture Comedies," *San Francisco Chronicle,* 24 February 1921; "Picture Studio Dedicated by Visiting Star," *San Francisco Chronicle,* 11 April 1921; "Movie Studio Is Opened—Permanent Home of Paul Gerson Pictures Corporation," *San Francisco Examiner,* 11 April 1921; "Film Producers in S.F. Organize," *San Francisco Chronicle,* 24 November 1922; "Paul Gerson Sees Greater Activity," *San Francisco Examiner,* 1 May 1924; George C. Warren, "Eight Companies at Work Here," *San Francisco Chronicle,* 5 November 1922.

38. Review of *Cricket on the Hearth, Variety,* 12 March 1924. For information about its cinematographer Silvano Balboni, see *The Film Index: A Bibliography,* Vol. I: *The Film as Art,* p. 176. For reactions to other Gerson films, see review of *Waterfront Wolves, Film Daily,* 16 March 1924; review of *Paying the Limit, Film Daily,* 31 August 1924; review of *Three Days to Live, Variety,* 30 April 1924; review of *Pride of the Force, Film Daily,* 18 November 1925.

39. Review of *Boaster, Film Daily,* 6 February 1927. For other reactions to Holt's films, see C. S. Sewell, review of *Ten Days, World,* 20 December 1924, p. 739; Summer Smith, review of *Too Much Youth, World,* 21 February 1925, p. 789; review of *Too Much Youth, Film Daily,* 8 March 1925; review of *Easy Going Gordon, Film Daily,* 11 October 1925. For more information on Holt's career, see "Name Changed—'Richard Holt' Now Star in Gerson Pictures," *San Francisco Chronicle,* 16 October 1924; "What the Stars Are Doing Now," *Photoplay,* December 1924, p. 112; "Richard Holt in a Scene from *Too Much Youth,*" *World,* 7 March 1925, p. 73; "Richard Holt—the Sensational 'Find'," *Film Daily Year Book,* 1925, p. 298.

40. Review of *Going the Limit, Film Daily,* 13 September 1925.

41. Hal Mohr, interview by author, 1970; W. Stephens Bush, review of *Barbary Coast, World,* 1 November 1913, p. 474. For Mohr's early work in the Bay Area and the closing of the Barbary Coast district, see, "The Studios . . . Way Back When," *American Cinematographer,* January 1969, p. 72;

"Drawing the Curtains at Midnight on the Barbary Coast," *San Francisco Examiner,* 1 October 1913; "Old Images on S.F.'s Silver Screen," *San Francisco Chronicle,* 7 June 1964.

42. Representative Hollywood productions and personalities of the day on location in the Bay Area are described in the following: for Rudolph Valentino's presence, see "Frank Norris Sea Story on Screen," *San Francisco Call and Post,* 20 February 1922; Clarice Minot, "Renato Marrazzini Remembers. . . ," *San Francisco Examiner & Chronicle* ("California Living" section), 2 April 1978; "Wallace Reid Details Plans," *San Francisco Chronicle,* 27 July 1919; De Mille Films Church in S.F. for Spectacle," *San Francisco Chronicle,* 28 July 1923; "Oklahoma Hero Rambles Here. Millions see Tom Mix on Market Street," *San Francisco Chronicle,* 4 April 1919; review of *Rough Riding Romance, Motion Picture Magazine,* January 1920, p. 119; William S. Hart, *My Life, East and West,* pp. 278, 295; "Truckee Becoming Movie Land of 'Far North' Films," *San Francisco Chronicle,* 6 February 1922; for *Evangeline,* see John Woolfenden, "When the Peninsula Went to the Movies," *Monterey Herald* (Monterey, Calif.), 23 January 1977; for *Foolish Wives,* see "Society to Appear in Movie Scenes," *San Francisco Chronicle,* 24 November 1920, and Marjorie C. Driscoll, "Movie Scenes at Del Monte," *San Francisco Chronicle,* 29 November 1920; for *Greed,* see "Von Stroheim Making Film in Heart of Busy San Francisco," *San Francisco Chronicle,* 15 April 1923, and " 'Mc Teague' Filming Here, to Make History—Both Book and Picture Tingle with the Feel of San Francisco," *San Francisco Call,* 26 May 1923.

43. For Pickford's film activity in the Bay Area, see "Film Shooting in Golden Gate Park," *San Francisco Chronicle,* 7 October 1923; "Mary Pickford Enthusiastic Over S.F. Park. Beauty of Spots Chosen for Locations Charms Star," *San Francisco Chronicle,* 8 October 1923; Mary Pickford to author, 19 February 1968.

44. "Max Graf Has Decided on Simultaneous Opening [of] Aztec, Egyptian First-Run Theaters," *San Francisco Chronicle,* 28 February 1925.

45. Review of *Finnegan's Ball, Variety,* 26 October 1927. For other reactions to the film, see "*Finnegan's Ball* Produced on Peninsula," *San Francisco Chronicle,* 9 October 1927; review of *Finnegan's Ball, San Francisco Chronicle,* 10 October 1927.

EPILOGUE

1. Frank Stauffacher, ed., *Art in Cinema: a Symposium on the Avant Garde Film.*

2. P. Adams Sitney, *Visionary Film: The American Avant-Garde, 1943–1978,* p. 51.

3. Alfred Frankenstein, "The Experimental Films at the Museum," *San Francisco Chronicle* ("This World" section), 6 October 1946.

4. For more information on the "San Francisco school" of filmmakers, see David Curtis, *Experimental Cinema,* pp. 42–61; Sheldon Renan, "The Reel San Francisco: Over and Underground," *San Francisco,* October 1967, pp. 46–49; Hal Aigner, "San Francisco's Film Underground," *San Francisco,* November 1969, p. 54; Hal Aigner, "The Viewer's Revolution," *San Francisco,* July 1970, p. 28; Arnold Passman, "The Bastard Children of Cecil B. De Mille," *Scanlan's Monthly* (New York), July 1970, pp. 2–12; Nick Kazan, "The Rejection is Mutual," *San Francisco Examiner & Chronicle* ("California Living" section), 11 July 1971.

5. Lewis Jacobs, *The Rise of the American Film: A Critical History With an Essay on Experimental Cinema in America, 1921–1947*, p. 563.

6. Background on Frank Stauffacher is drawn from Jack Stauffacher (brother of Frank Stauffacher), interviews by author, 1980.

7. Jacobs, p. 563.

8. The strong impact of the event on participants is expressed by Cameron Macauley (Director, Extension Media Center, University of California, Berkeley, who was present at the 1946 symposium), interviews by author, 1980.

9. Sitney, p. 82.

10. James Broughton, interviews by author, 1980.

11. Jordan Belson, interviews by author, 1980.

12. Thomas Albright, "Imagery on Film," *San Francisco Examiner & Chronicle* ("This World" section), 21 April 1968.

13. Robert M. Sitton and Clyde B. Smith, "Notes on Filmmaking in the Port of St. Francis," *Lifelong Learning*, University Extension, University of California, Berkeley, 30 April 1973, p. 2.

14. For more information on post-war films and television programs shot on location in the Bay Area, see Walter Blum, "Movie Mecca North," *San Francisco Examiner & Chronicle*, ("California Living" section), 14 January 1968; Morton Beebe and Bruce J. Hayes, "Tinseltown on the Bay," *San Francisco Examiner & Chronicle* ("California Living" section), 22 August 1971; Eleanor Knowles, "San Francisco on Film," *San Francisco Examiner & Chronicle* ("California Living" section), 26 May 1974; Cynthia Robins, "Cinema and San Francisco," *San Francisco*, October 1978, pp. 43–46; Joan Eesley, "Gregg Snazelle—Pioneering Television Commercials," *Bay Views* (San Rafael, Calif.), March 1981, pp. 48–51; Lynde McCormick, "What's Happening to Hollywood?" *Christian Science Monitor*, 18 February 1981.

15. Kaufman and Ritchie quoted in Aljean Harmetz, "Hollywood's Migration North," *San Francisco Examiner & Chronicle* ("Datebook" section), 15 March 1981. For more information about Philip Kaufman, see David Sterritt, "About the Director," *Christian Science Monitor*, 12 January 1979; Judy Stone, "Director of *The Wanderers* Would Like to Settle Down," *San Francisco Examiner & Chronicle* ("Datebook" section), 5 August 1979; for more information about Michael Ritchie, see Stanley Eichelbaum, "Satire from a Teenage Pageant," *San Francisco Examiner & Chronicle* ("The Arts" section), 4 August 1974; Marian Zailian, "It's an Old-Fashioned Comedy, Update '70s Style," *San Francisco Examiner & Chronicle* ("Datebook" section), 13 November 1977; Judy Stone, "Audiences Need Something Better than Sordid Stories," *San Francisco Examiner & Chronicle* ("Datebook" section), 6 May 1979.

16. For more information about Korty's films, see Walter Blum, "Through the Camera—Brightly," *San Francisco Examiner & Chronicle* ("California Living" section), 16 August 1970; Mal Karman, "Why John Korty Doesn't Have Stars in His Eyes," *San Francisco*, February 1977, pp. 55–60; Frank McLaughlin, "Meet John Korty, Filmmaker," *Media and Methods*, December 1978, pp. 31–32; Eric C. Jendersen, "The Inventor-Artist Spirit: John Korty on Film," *Twin Cities Times* (Marin County, Calif.), 26 March 1981.

17. For reactions to Lucas's films, see Joseph Kanon, "On the Strip," *Atlantic Monthly*, October 1973, p. 125; Judith Crist, "'Feel Good' Film," *Saturday Review*, 9 July 1977, p. 40; Carll Tucker, "Our Love-Hate Affair With Technology," *Saturday Review*, 10 December 1977; Lynda Miles and Michael Pye, "The Man Who Made *Star Wars*," *Atlantic Monthly*, March 1979, pp. 47–54; Gerald Clarke, "The Empire Strikes Back! And So Does George Lucas," *Time*, 19 May 1980, pp. 66–73; Lynde McCormick, "Weeks of Work Gone in a Blink of the Eye," *Christian Science Monitor*, 4 June 1980; David Osborne, "Two Who Made a Revolution," *San Francisco*, March 1982, p. 58.

18. Lucas quoted in Martin Kasindorf, Tom Nicholson, and Deborah Prager, "The Man Who Found the Ark," *Newsweek*, 15 June 1981, p. 67.

Bibliography

Adams, Ramon F. *The Old Time Cowhand*. New York: Macmillan, 1961.

Altrocchi, Julia C. *The Spectacular San Franciscans*. New York: Dutton, 1949.

Atherton, Gertrude F. *Golden Gate Country*. New York: Duel, Sloan & Pearce, 1945.

———. *My San Francisco: A Wayward Biography*. New York: Bobbs-Merrill, 1946.

Balshofer, Fred J., and Miller, Arthur C. *One Reel a Week*. Berkeley: University of California Press, 1967.

Battcock, Gregory. *The New American Cinema: A Critical Anthology*. New York: Dutton, 1967.

Beebe, Lucius M. *San Francisco's Golden Era: A Picture of San Francisco before the Fire*. Berkeley, Calif.: Howell-North, 1960.

Bloomfield, Arthur J. *The San Francisco Opera, 1923–1961*. New York: Appleton-Century-Crofts, 1961.

The Blue Book: A Comprehensive Official Souvenir View Book Illustrating the Panama-Pacific International Exposition at San Francisco, 1915. San Francisco, Calif.: R. A. Reid, 1915.

Blum, Daniel. *A Pictorial History of the American Theatre, 1900–1950*. New York: Grosset & Dunlap, 1953.

———. *A Pictorial History of the Silent Screen*. New York: Grosset & Dunlap, 1953.

Bodeen, DeWitt, and Ringgold, Gene. *The Films of Cecil B. De Mille*. New York: Citadel Press, 1969.

Bolton, Herbert E. *Outpost of Empire: The Story of the Founding of San Francisco*. New York: A. A. Knopf, 1931.

Brady, William A. *Showman*. New York: Dutton, 1937.

Bronson, William. *The Earth Shook, the Sky Burned*. Garden City, N.Y.: Doubleday, 1959.

Burke, John. *Buffalo Bill, the Noblest Whiteskin*. New York: G. P. Putnam's Sons, 1973.

Caen, Herbert E. *Baghdad by the Bay*. New York: Doubleday, Doran, 1949.

———, and Kingman, Dong. *San Francisco: City on Golden Hills*. Garden City, N.Y.: Doubleday, 1967.

Capra, Frank. *The Name above the Title*. New York: Macmillan, 1971.

Cawelti, John G. *Six-Gun Mystique*. Bowling Green, Ohio: University of Ohio Popular Press, 1970.

Cawkwell, Tim, and Smith, John M., eds. *The World Encyclopaedia of Film*. New York: Galahad Books, 1972.

Ceram, C. W. [Marek, Kurt W.]. *Archaeology of the Cinema*. New York: Harcourt, Brace & World, 1965.

Chaplin, Charles. *My Autobiography*. New York: Simon & Schuster, 1964.

Clark, George T. *Leland Stanford*. Stanford, Calif.: Stanford University Press, 1931.

Curtis, David. *Experimental Cinema*. New York: Universe Books, 1971.

Curtiss, Thomas Q. *Von Stroheim*. New York: Farrar, Straus & Giroux, 1971.

Dana, Julian. *A. P. Giannini: Giant in the West*. New York: Prentice-Hall, 1947.

Davenport, William. *The Monterey Peninsula*. Menlo Park, Calif.: Lane Publishing, 1964.

Dobie, Charles C. *San Francisco: A Pageant.* New York: Appleton-Century, 1933.

Dugger, Leonard P., and Morosco, Helen M. *Life of Oliver Morosco, the Oracle of Broadway.* Caldwell, Idaho: Caxton Printers, 1944.

Emblen, D. L. *Peter Mark Roget.* New York: Thomas Y. Crowell Co., 1970.

Everson, William K. *American Silent Film.* New York: Oxford University Press, 1978.

———. *A Pictorial History of the Western Film.* New York: Citadel Press, 1969.

Eyles, Alan. *The Western.* South Brunswick, N.J.: A. S. Barnes, 1975.

Federal Writers' Program, Northern California. *San Francisco: The Bay and Its Cities.* New York: Hastings, 1947.

Felheim, Marvin. *The Theatre of Augustin Daly.* Cambridge, Mass.: Harvard University Press, 1956.

Fell, John L. *Film and the Narrative Tradition.* Norman, Okla.: University of Oklahoma Press, 1974.

———. *A History of Films.* New York: Holt, Rinehart & Winston, 1979.

———, ed. *Films Before Griffith.* Berkeley: University of California Press, forthcoming.

Felton, Ernest L. *California's Many Climates.* Palo Alto, Calif.: Pacific Books, 1965.

Fenin, George N. and Everson, William K. *The Western: From Silents to Cinema.* New York: Orion Press, 1962.

Film Daily Yearbook 1922–1923. New York and Hollywood, Calif.: Wid's Films and Film Books, Inc.

Freedley, George, and Reeves, John A. *A History of the Theatre.* New York: Crown Publishers, 1968.

Gagey, Edmond M. *The San Francisco Stage: A History.* New York: Columbia University Press, 1950.

Genthe, Arnold. *As I Remember.* New York: Reynal & Hitchcock, 1936.

Gernsheim, Helmut. A Concise History of Photography. New York: Grosset & Dunlap, 1965.

Gifford, Denis. *Chaplin.* Garden City, N.Y.: Doubleday & Co., Inc., 1974.

Gilliam, Harold. *San Francisco Bay.* Garden City, N.Y.: Doubleday, 1957.

———. *Island in Time: The Point Reyes Peninsula.* San Francisco, Calif.: Sierra Club, 1962.

Grimsted, David. *Melodrama Unveiled: American Theater and Culture, 1800–1850.* Chicago: University of Chicago Press, 1968.

Haas, Robert B. *Muybridge: Man in Motion.* Berkeley: University of California Press, 1976.

Hampton, Benjamin B. *A History of the American Film Industry from Its Beginnings to 1931.* Introduction by Richard Griffith. New York: Dover Publications, 1970.

Hansen, Gladys. *San Francisco Almanac: Everything You Want to Know about the City.* San Rafael, Calif.: Presidio Press, 1980.

Hart, William S. *My Life: East and West.* Boston: Houghton, Mifflin, 1929.

Hawgood, James A. *America's Western Frontiers.* New York: A. A. Knopf, 1967.

Hendricks, Gordon. *Origins of the American Film.* New York: Arno Press, 1972.

Herman, Hal C., ed. *How I Broke into the Movies.* Los Angeles, Calif.: Hal C. Herman, 1930.

Horan, James D. *The Great American West: A Pictorial History from Coronado to the Last Frontier.* New York: Crown Publishers, 1959.

———. *The Authentic Wild West.* New York: Crown Publishers, 1976.

Irwin, Will. *The City That Was: A Requiem of Old San Francisco.* New York: Huebsch, 1906.

———. *Old Chinatown: A Book of Pictures by Arnold Genthe.* New York: M. Kinnerley, 1913.

———. *The House That Shadows Built.* Garden City, N.Y.: Doubleday, Doran, 1928.

Jackson, Joseph H. *My San Francisco.* New York: Crowell, 1953.

Jacobs, Lewis. *The Rise of the American Film: A Critical History.* New York: Harcourt, Brace, 1939.

———. *The Rise of the American Film: A Critical History with an Essay on Experimental Cinema in America, 1921–1947.* New York: Teachers College Press, 1968.

———, ed. *Introduction to the Art of the Movies.* New York: Noonday Press, 1960.

Jones, Idwal. *Ark of Empire: San Francisco's Montgomery Block.* New York: Doubleday, 1951.

Kahn, Edgar M. *Cable Car Days in San Francisco.* Palo Alto, Calif.: Stanford University Press, 1940.

———. *Tamalpais: Enchanted Mountain.* San Francisco, Calif.: Roxburghe Club, 1945.

Knight, Arthur. *The Liveliest Art: A Panoramic History of the Movies.* New York: Macmillan, 1957.

Kroeber, A. S. *Handbook of the Indians of California.* Berkeley: California Book Co., Ltd., 1953.

Kroeber, Theodora. *Ishi in Two Worlds.* Berkeley: University of California Press, 1961.

Lahue, Kalton C. *Bound and Gagged: The Story of the Silent Serials.* South Brunswick, N.J.: A. S. Barnes, 1968.

Lasky, Jesse L. *I Blow My Own Horn.* Garden City, N.Y.: Doubleday, 1957.

Leroy, Mervyn. *Mervyn Leroy Take One.* New York: Hawthorn Books, 1974.

Lewis, Oscar. *Big Four.* New York: A. A. Knopf, 1938.

———. *Bay Window Bohemia: An Account of the Brilliant Artistic World of Gaslit San Francisco.* Garden City, N.Y.: Doubleday, 1956.

———. *Bonanza Inn: America's First Luxury Hotel.* New York: A. A. Knopf, 1939.

———. *This Was San Francisco.* New York: David McKay, 1962.

Lindsay, Nicholas Vachel. *The Art of the Moving Picture.* New York: Macmillan, 1915.

Lloyd, Benjamin E. *Lights and Shades in San Francisco.* San Francisco, Calif.: Bancroft, 1876.

Longstreet, Stephen. *The Wider Shore: A Gala Social History of San Francisco's Sinners and Spenders, 1849–1906.* Garden City, N.Y.: Doubleday, 1968.

Loos, Anita. *A Girl Like I.* New York: Viking, 1966.

Lyons, Timothy J. *The Silent Partner: The History of the American Film Manufacturing Company, 1910–1921.* New York: Arno Press, 1974.

McCabe, John. *Charlie Chaplin.* Garden City, N.Y.: Doubleday, 1978.

McDonald, Conway. *The Films of Charlie Chaplin.* New York: Citadel Press, 1965.

MacDonnell, Kevin. *Eadweard Muybridge: The Man Who Invented the Motion Picture.* Boston: Little, Brown, 1972.

McDowell, Bart. *The American Cowboy in Life and Legend.* Washington, D.C.: National Geographic Society, 1972.

Macgowan, Kenneth. *Behind the Screen: The History and Techniques of the Motion Picture.* New York: Delacorte Press, 1965.

Manvell, Roger. *Chaplin.* Boston: Little, Brown, 1974.

Marion, Frances. *Off with Their Heads! A Serio-Comic Tale of Hollywood.* New York: Macmillan, 1972.

Moffat, Frances. *Dancing on the Brink of the World.* New York: Putnam, 1977.

Morley, Jim. *Gold Cities: Grass Valley and Nevada City.* Berkeley, Calif.: Howell-North, 1965.

Mozley, Anita V., ed. *Eadweard Muybridge: The Stanford Years, 1872–1882.* Stanford, Calif.: Stanford University Press, 1972.

———. *American Photography: Past into Present.* Seattle, Wash.: University of Washington Press, 1976.

Munden, Kenneth W., ed. *The American Film Institute Catalog: Feature Films, 1921–1930.* New York: R. R. Bowker, 1971.

Neville, Amelia R. *The Fantastic City.* Boston: Houghton Mifflin Co., 1932.

Newhall, Beaumont. *The History of Photography from 1938 to the Present Day.* New York: The Museum of Modern Art, 1949.

New York City Works Projects Administration, Writers Program. *The Film Index: A Bibliography.* Vol. I: *The Film as Art.* New York: Museum of Modern Art, H. W. Wilson Co., 1941.

Niver, Kemp T. *Motion Pictures from the Library of Congress Paper Print Collection, 1894–1912.* Berkeley, Calif.: University of California Press, 1967.

Norris, Kathleen. *My San Francisco.* New York: Doubleday, Doran, 1932.

Nye, Russell B. *The Unembarrassed Muse: The Popular Arts in America.* New York: Dial Press, 1970.

Older, Cora M. *San Francisco: Magic City.* New York: Longmans, Green, 1961.

Olmstead, Roger, and Watkins, T. H. *Here Today: San Francisco's Architectural Heritage.* San Francisco, Calif.: Chronicle Books, 1968.

———. *Mirror of the Dream.* New York: Oxford University Press, 1973.

Pickford, Mary. *Sunshine and Shadow.* Foreword by Cecil B. De Mille. Garden City, N.Y.: Doubleday, 1955.

Pollack, Peter. *The Picture History of Photography.* New York: Henry N. Abrams, Inc., 1958.

Pratt, George C. *Spellbound in Darkness: A History of the Silent Film.* Greenwich, Conn.: New York Graphic Society, 1973.

Quigley, Martin, Jr. *Magic Shadows: The Story of the Origin of Motion Pictures.* New York: Quigley Publishing Co., 1960.

Quinn, Arthur H. *A History of the American Drama from the Civil War to the Present Day.* New York: Harper, 1927.

Ramsaye, Terry. *A Million and One Nights: A History of the Motion Picture.* New York: Simon & Schuster, 1926.

Rayhill, Frank. *The World of Melodrama.* University Park, Pa.: Pennsylvania State University Press, 1967.

Renan, Sheldon. *An Introduction to the American Underground Film.* New York: Dutton, 1967.

Rocq, Margaret M. *California Local History.* Stanford, Calif.: Stanford University Press, 1970.

Rosenberg, Bernard, and Silverstein, Harry. *The Real Tinsel.* New York: Macmillan, 1970.

Schuster, Mel, comp. *Motion Picture Performers: A Bibliography of Magazine and Periodical Articles, 1900–1969.* Metuchen, N.J.: Scarecrow Press, Inc., 1971.

Sitney, P. Adams. *Visionary Film: The American Avant-Garde.* New York: Oxford University Press, 1974.

Sklar, Robert. *Movie-Made America: A Social History of American Movies.* New York: Random House, 1975.

Slide, Anthony. *Early American Cinema.* New York: A. S. Barnes, 1970.

Smith, Henry N. *Virgin Land: The American West as Symbol and Myth.* Cambridge, Mass.: Harvard University Press, 1950.

Spehr, Paul C. *The Movies Begin: Making Movies in New Jersey, 1887–1920.* Newark, N.J.: The Newark Museum, 1977.

Starr, Kevin. *Americans and the California Dream, 1850–1915.* New York: Oxford University Press, 1973.

Stauffacher, Frank, ed. *Art in Cinema: A Symposium on the Avant Garde Film.* San Francisco, Calif.: San Francisco Art in Cinema Society and San Francisco Museum of Art, 1947.

Stewart, John, comp. *Filmarama.* Vol. 1: *The Formidable Years, 1893–1919.* Metuchen, N.J.: Scarecrow Press, Inc., 1975.

Stillman, Jacob D. B. *The Horse in Motion.* Boston: J. R. Osgood, 1882.

Truitt, Evelyn M. *Who Was Who on Screen.* New York: R. R. Bowker Co., 1974.

Tuska, Jon. *The Filming of the West.* Garden City, N.Y.: Doubleday, 1976.

Tutorow, Norman E. *Leland Stanford: Man of Many Careers.* Menlo Park, Calif.: Pacific Coast Publishers, 1971.

U.S. Library of Congress. Copyright Office. *Catalogue of Copyright Entries, Cumulative Series: Motion Pictures, 1894–1912, and 1912–1939.* Washington, D.C., 1951.

U.S. Weather Bureau. *Climates of the States.* With new material by James A. Ruffner. Detroit: Gale Research Company, 1978.

Vardac, A. Nicholas. *Stage to Screen: Theatrical Method from Garrick to Griffith.* Cambridge, Mass.: Harvard University Press, 1949.

Wagonknecht, Edward. *The Movies in the Age of Innocence.* Norman, Okla.: University of Oklahoma Press, 1962.

Warner, Jack L. *My First Hundred Years in Hollywood.* New York: Random House, 1965.

Wing, Ruth, ed. *The Blue Book of the Screen.* Hollywood, Calif.: The Blue Book of the Screen, 1923.

Wister, Owen. *The Virginian: A Horseman of the Plains.* New York: Grosset & Dunlap, 1902.

Zukor, Adolph. *The Public Is Never Wrong.* New York: Putnam, 1953.

Index

References to illustrations follow other
page references and are in italics.

Abrott, Lorin, *52*
Abstract films. *See* Film as art
Actors, movie. *See* Players, Bay Area motion picture
Actors, stage: in films, 39, 55, 74, 77, 78, 80, 86, 113, 119, 124, 125. *See also* Stage shows
Adams, Claire, *123*
Adaptations, of literature for film. *See* Plots, story film
Ade, George, 49
Alameda County, 105
Alcazar Theatre (San Francisco), 14, 67, 73, 77, 124, 125
"Alkali Ike," 55
Alkali Ike's Auto, 57
Alkali Ike's Bride, 54, *53*
Altemas, Edna, *115*
Amarilly of Clothesline Alley, 132
American Graffiti, 135, 140
Anderson, Gilbert M., 15, 39–65, 67, 71–72, 90, 108, 140, 141, *56*, *61*; as "Broncho Billy," 15, 48–52, 65, 67, 90, 120, 134, 141, *40*, *47*, *48*, *49*, *50*, *61*, *62*, *63*, *64*. *See also* Essanay Film Manufacturing Company; Spoor, George K.; Westerns
Angus, Hal, 55
Animation, 27, *28*, *29*, *30*, *31*. *See also* Motion Pictures, prehistory of
Arnold, John R., 117
Art in Cinema, 135, 136–37, 138, 139
Aryan, The, 73, 131
Atherton, Gertrude, 79, 127
Augusta (Maine), 13
Authors, San Francisco Bay Area, 14, 49–50, 79, 81, 113, 120, 127
Autobiography of Miss Jane Pittman, The, 140
Awful Truth, The, 99, 121, *120*
Ayres, Agnes, 121, *120*

Ballad of Fisher's Boarding House, The, 122
Ballard, Carrol, 141
Ballin, Mabel, *119*

Banner Studio, 105. *See also* Appendix A
Bara, Theda, 89
Barbary Coast, The, 99, 128, *126*
Barnum, P. T., 43
Bart, Dan, 73
Baxter, Warner, 121, *119*, *120*
Bay Area. *See* San Francisco Bay Area
Beauty and the Bad Man, 120, *119*
Bed, The, 137
Beery, Wallace, 55, *54*
Belasco, Edward, 99, 124
Belmont, 122, *123*
Belson, Jordan, 135, 138, 140. *See also* Film as art
Bennett, Belle, 97, *87*
Berkeley (Calif.), 42
Bernhardt, Sara, 83, 85
Bernstein, Isadore, 114
Beyfuss, Alex, 70–71, 90, 91, 92, 93, 94, 97. *See also* California Motion Picture Corporation
Bierce, Ambrose, 127
Birds, The, 139
Birth of a Nation, The, 89–90, 120
Black Stallion, The, 141
Bleacher Hero, The, 121
Blind Hearts, 113
Boardman, True, 55, *49*, *61*
Boaster, The, 127
Bodega Bay, 139
Bohemian Club, 33
Bolinas (Calif.), 41
Boone, Daniel, 43
Bosworth, Hobart, 99, 113–14, *109*, *110*
Boulder Creek (Calif.), 73
Brady, William A., 91
Broadway Madonna, The, 122
"Broncho Billy." *See* Anderson, Gilbert M.
Broncho Billy and the Claim Jumper, 62

Broncho Billy and the Revenue Agent, 51
Broncho Billy and the Vigilante, 61
Broncho Billy—Guardian, 63
Broncho Billy's Adventure, 51
Broncho Billy's Bible, 51–52, *50*
Broncho Billy's Pal, 50, *47*
Broncho Billy's Redemption, 49
Broncho Billy's Surrender, 55
Broncho Billy's Teaching, 62
Broncho Billy Well Repaid, 62
Broughton, James, 135, 137, 141. *See also* Film as art
Buffalo Bill Cody, 43–44
Bullitt, 13
Burlingame, 112, 132
Burt, Frank, 112
Bushman, Francis X., *56*
Byers, Clara, *86, 87*

California, history of: as plot material for films, 67, 71–72, 77, 79, 94, 127
California, Northern: scenic attractions of, for films, 14–15, 67, 79, 127–32, 139, 140–41, *68, 96, 112, 130, 132;* scenic attractions of, for still photography, 14, 19, 72. *See also* Cinematography; Photography, still; San Francisco Bay Area; individual communities by name
California, Southern, 41, 72, 108. *See also* Hollywood
California Motion Picture Corporation, 15, 41, 67–97, 99, 108, 125, 134, *66, 69, 70, 71, 75, 76, 93;* distribution of, 90–96; dramas of, 85–94, *83, 84, 85, 86, 87, 88, 89, 90, 91, 93, 94, 95;* players and staff of, 68, 70–71, 72, 73, 74, 80, 81, 96, 97; studio of, 71–73, 91, 92, *71;* Westerns of, 67, 77, 78–83, 97, *68, 75, 79, 80, 81, 82, 84, 96. See also* Michelena, Beatriz; Middleton, George E.; Plots, story film; Appendixes A, D
Cameramen. *See* Cinematographers
Cameras, motion picture. *See* Cinematography
Cameras, still, 14, 18, 19, *21, 22. See also* Photography, still
Capra, Frank, *122*
Carew, Ora, 125
Carewe, Edwin, 131
Carleton, Lloyd, B., 125
Carleton, William T., *116*
Carmel (Calif.), 131
Carney, Augustus, 55, *53*
Carson, Kit, 43
Carson, Robert, 74, 97
Cato, Bill, 55, 62
Censorship, 107–8
Chalk Marks, 120, 140
Champion, The, 58
Chaplin, Charles, 51, 57–58, 62, *55, 56*
Characterization, 44, 48–51, 75, 80, 85–88, 89, 113. *See also* Hero, Western
Chicago (Ill.), 41
Christmas without Snow, 140
Church, Frederick, 39, 55, *54*
Cinemamatic techniques, 43–44, 48, 52, 71–72, 74, 76–77, 89–90, 113, 127, 135–41
Cinematographers, 51, 74, 105, 107, 117, 128, *52, 53, 59, 76, 98. See also* Appendixes A, C, D, E
Cinematography, 67, 73, 74, 107, 121, 128, 137, 138–39, 141, *103, 104, 130, 132. See also* California, Northern: scenic attractions of, for films; San Francisco Bay Area: scenic attractions of, for films
Cineograph Theatre (San Francisco), 100, *102*

Claire, Ina, 121
Clansmen, The, 109, 120
Clayton, Marguerite, 55, *54, 61, 62*
Clement, Roy, 55, *48, 49, 62*
Cody, Buffalo Bill, 43–44
Colorado, 13, 41
Color motion pictures, 15, 71, 107, 134. *See also* Appendix A
Comedies, motion picture, 55–58, 122, 133. *See also* Appendix A
Connery, William J., 118
Cooper, James F., 43
Coppola, Francis Ford, 140
Corbett, "Gentleman Jim," 15
Covarrubias, Nicholas, 73, 77
Cowboys, 41, 48–51, 55, *38, 59, 60. See also* Essanay Film Manufacturing Company; Hero, Western; West, the; Westerns; Appendix C
Cowpuncher's Law, The, 41
Cradle of Courage, The, 131
Crazy Quilt, 139
Cricket on the Hearth, The, 125
Crockett, Davy, 43
Crystal Springs Lake (Calif.), 113
Cupid Angling, 107, *104*
Cutting. *See* Editing
Cycles, 138

Daddy Long Legs, 132
Daly, Augustin, 75
Dance at Silver Gulch, The, 54, *50*
Dark Angel, The, 131
Darrow, Frankie, *116*
da Vinci, Leonardo, 27, *28*
Davis, George B., 124
De Mille, Cecil B., 72, 73, 90, 93, 119, 131
Deren, Maya, 137
Direction, motion picture. *See* Cinematic techniques
Directors, San Francisco Bay Area, 39, 43, 58, 71–72, 79–80, 92, 96, 105, 107, 122–23, 139–41, *69. See also* Appendixes A, C, D, E for individual names
Distribution, 41, 43, 62–63, 71, 89–94, 100–101, 107–8, 113, 116, 118–19, 141, *40. See also* Motion pictures: first public exhibition of; Nickelodeons
Dixon, Thomas, 109
Documentary films, 99, 103, 105, 107, 128, 136, 140, *126*
Dohrman, A. B. C., 118
Don't Change Your Husband, 90
Dorothy Vernon of Haddon Hall, 132
Double, acting, 55, 80
Douglass, Leon F., 15, 99, 107, 134, 141, *98, 103, 104*
Draga, Maria, *111*
Dragonslayer, 141
Dressler, Marie, 59

Eastwood, Clint, 139
Easy Going Gordon, 127
Edison Studio (New York), 40
Editing, motion picture. *See* Cinematic techniques
Educational films, 105, 107, 139
Eliason, Joseph A., 109
EMI—Elstee Studio, 141
Emlay, Earl, 74, 79
Empire Strikes Back, The, 140
Enemies of Children, 124
Essanay Film Manufacturing Company, 38–65, 71, 99, 105;

comedies of, 55–58, *55, 56, 57;* distribution of, 41, 43–45, 62–63; players and staff of, 39, 51, 52, 54–57; studio of, at Niles, *45, 46, 47, 52;* Westerns of, 13, 15, 41, 43–44, 47–55, 59, 63–65, 67, 71, 83, 134, 141, *47, 48, 49, 50, 59, 61, 62, 63, 64. See also* Anderson, Gilbert M.; Spoor, George K.; Plots, story film; West, the; Westerns; Appendixes A, C
E.T.—The Extra-Terrestrial, 141
Evangeline, 131
Exactus Photo-Film Company, 105
Exhibition. *See* Distribution; Nickelodeons

Fair, Elinor, *110*
Fairbanks, Douglas, 73, 107
Fairfax (Calif.), 41
Faust, 89, *90, 91*
Feature films, 63, 65, 67, 70, 71, 72, 74, 83, 89–90, 94, 97, 107, 113–14, 118, 127, 129, 131, 140, 141. *See also* Distribution; Appendixes A, B
Felton (Calif.), 41
Film, acetate, 105
Film as art, 135–38. *See also* "San Francisco School" of filmmakers
Filmmakers, experimental. *See* Film as art
Films, nonlinear. *See* Film as art
Finger of Justice, 107–8, *105, 106*
Finnegan's Ball, 133
Fisher, Edna, 39
Flame of Hellgate, The, 81, 94, *96*
Flying Dutchman, The, 125, *124*
Fog, The, 117
Foolish Wives, 99, 131, *130*
Forgotten Law, The, 117, *115*
Fox, William, 61, 91, 97
Fox Films, 91
Francis, Alec B., *115*
Frankenstein, Alfred, 136
Franklin Institute (Philadelphia), 31
Frederick, Pauline, 83
Frontier. *See* West, the; Westerns
Funnyman, 139

Gaiety Theatre (San Francisco), 59
George, "Texas," 55
Gerson, Paul, 100, 125, 127, 134, 140, 141, *125*
Gerson Pictures Corporation, 125–27. *See also* Appendix A
Giannini, A. P., 112
Girl on the Stairs, The, 121
Going the Limit, 13, 127, 140
Gold!, 77, *78*
Golden Gate Park, 58, 105, 121, 122, 132
Golden Gate Weekly, The, 73, 74
Goldwyn, Samuel, 72, 131, 136
Goodwins, Fred, *57*
Graf, Max, 41, 99, 113, 116–18, 121, 133, 134, 141, *114, 118*
Graf Productions, Inc., *114,* 116–18. *See also* Appendix A
Grauman, Sid, 113
Great Alone, The, 114, *111, 112*
Great Train Robbery, The, 44
Greed, 130, 131, 132
Griffith, D. W., 72, 74, 89, 93–94, 97, 120

Half a Dollar Bill, 117, *116*
Half Breed, The, 73
Hall, Ella, *124*
Hampton, Benjamin B., 14, 122

Harris, Elmer, 99, 119–20
Harris, Mildred, *117*
Hart, William S., 59, 63, 73, 131
Harte, Bret, 43, 67, 81, 83, *78*
Hatton, Raymond, *116*
Hawks, Jack, 105
Heart of Juanita, The, 81, 94, *82*
Heart of the North, The, 123
Her Accidental Husband, 99, 124
Her Market Value, 121
Hero, Western, 41, 43, 48–51, 80. *See also* West, the; Westerns
Hervey, Wilna, *123*
Heyl, Reno R., 31
Hidden Mine, The, 41
His New Job, 58
Hitchcock, Alfred, 139
Hodkinson, W. W., 94, 108–9, 112, 113, 119
Hollywood, 13, 15, 42, 72, 89, 93, 108, 139
Holt, Jack, 97, *80*
Holt, Richard, 127, *125*
Hopkins, Mark, 19
How Slippery Slim Went for the Eggs, 57
Hulette, Gladys, 125

Ince, Ralph W. *See* Appendixes A, E
Ince, Thomas H., 59, 73
Independent film production, 70, 99–100, 105, 107, 108, 112–13, 120, 121, 127, 133, 134, 139, 141. *See also* Distribution; Appendixes A, D, E
Industrial Light and Magic, 141
Infinity, 138
Ingram, Rex, 116, 129, *128*
In the Park, 58
Intolerance, 93–94
Isaacs, John D., 19
Ishi, 73–74
Isobel, or the Trail's End, 124

Jacksonville (Fla.), 13
Jasper, John, 112
Jazz Singer, The, 133
Jitney Elopement, A, 58, *56*
Johnson, Emory, 55, *49, 50, 53, 61*
Jolson, Al, 133
Jones, John W., 43
Joy, Ernest, *87*
Just Squaw, 94, *81, 84*

Kalem Company, 72
Kaufman, Philip, 139
Keanograph Studio, 105
Kenyon, Charles, 74
Kercher, Irvin, 141
Kodak, Eastman, 105
Korty, John, 139–40
Kroeber, Alfred L., 74
Kruschuke, Emil, 74
Kyne, Peter B., 49, 79, 120, 127

Laemmle, Carl, 91, 97
Landis, Cullen, *117*
Lasky, Jesse, 72, 93
Lasky Feature Play Company, 72
Last Night of the Barbary Coast, The. See Barbary Coast, The
Lawton, William, *18, 35, 36*

Leatherstocking Tales, 43, 50
Leon Douglass Natural Color Motion Picture Company, 107. *See also* Appendixes A, E
Lesser, Sol. *See* Appendixes A, E
Let Woman Alone, 121
Liberty Studio, 105
Life's Greatest Question, 123–24
Light, 138
Lighting, motion picture, 73, 112, *47. See also* Sets, motion picture; Studios, motion picture
Lily of Poverty Flat, The, 81
Lindblom, Sadie. *See* Appendixes A, E
Little Princess, The, 132
Lloyd, Benjamin E., 27
London, Jack, 14, 79, 94, 113, 127, *109*
Lonedale Operator, The, 90
Long, Walter, *111*
Los Angeles (Calif.). *See* Hollywood
Los Gatos (Calif.), 41
Lowney, Raymond, *120*
Lucas, George, 15, 41, 135, 140–41
Lucasfilm, 41, 140–41

McGuire, Paddy, *57*
McKim, Robert, *110, 123*
Mackley, Arthur, 39, 55
Magic lantern, 27, 29, *31*
Man in Him, The, 62
Marin County, 41, 73, 79, 107, 139–40, *70*
Mason, Dan, *122, 123*
Meditation, 138
Melodrama, 44, 74–77, 113. *See also* Stage shows, influence of, on films
Metro Pictures, 116, 118
Michelena, Beatriz, 15, 77–79, 91–93, 97, 108, 141, *68, 77, 79–92, 94–96*
Michelena, Fernando, 77–78
Middleton, George E., 71, 78, 80, 91, 92–96, 97, 107, 108, *69, 79*
Mignon, 83, 90, *86, 87, 88*
Miles, Herbert E., *103*
Miles Brothers, 15, 99, 100–101, 103–4. *See also* Appendix A
Miller, Patsy R., 121, *119*
Mill Valley (Calif.), 103
Minty's Triumph, 82
Mrs. Wiggs of the Cabbage Patch, 80, 88
Mix, Tom, 63, 131
M'Liss, 73, *132*
Mohr, Hal, 128
Momentum, 138
Money Changers, The, 122, *123*
Monterey (Calif.), 99
Monte Rio (Calif.), 80
Moran of the Lady Letty, 129
Morosco's Grand Opera House (San Francisco), 14
Morrison, Albert, *94*
Mother's Day, 137
Motion, studies of, 27–32. *See also* Motion pictures, prehistory of; Photography, still
Motion picture companies, San Francisco Bay Area. *See* Appendixes A, C, D, E for individual names
Motion Picture Patents Company, 62–63
Motion pictures: first public exhibition of, 13, 31, *32, 33, 34, 35, 36;* origins of, 13–15, 17–37, *20, 21, 22, 23, 24, 25, 26, 32, 33, 34, 35, 36;* prehistory of, 27, 28, 29, 30, 31. *See also*

Animation; Cinematic techniques; Cinematographers; Cinematography; Color motion pictures; Distribution; Documentary films; Educational films; Feature films; Independent film production; Lighting, motion picture; Melodrama; Nickelodeons; Projectors; Props, historic; Sets, motion picture; Short films; Studios, motion picture; Westerns
Movies Go West, The, 55
Mulhall, Jack, *115*
Museum of Modern Art (New York), 136
"Mustang Pete," 55
Muybridge, Eadweard, 15, 19, 22–25, 31–37, 134, 141, *18, 33, 36;* first exhibition of motion pictures by, 32–36
Mysterious Witness, The, 124

Nazimova, Alla, 83
Neilan, Marshall, 73
Newsreels. *See The Golden Gate Weekly*
New York (N.Y.), 13, 39, 40–41, 72, 90–93, 100, 107–8, 114, 119–20, 125
Nickelodeons, 41, 44, 51, 55, 63, 71, 74, 100, *40*
Nigh, William, 74, 79, 97, *86*
Night Out, A, 58, *55*
Niles (Calif.), 39, 41, 43, 45–46, 47, 58, *42*
Niles Canyon, 43, 132, *42, 53, 57, 133*
Nilsson, Anna Q., *116*
Norris, Kathleen, 79, 127
Northern California. *See* California, Northern
Notes on the Port of St. Francis, 136
Nuptiae, 137

Oakland (Calif.), 42
O'Brien, George, 114, *111*
Olcott, Sidney, 71–72
Orpheum Vaudeville Theatre (San Francisco), 59, 73, 100, *131*

Pacific Studio, 112, 113, 114, 118, *108, 109. See also* Appendix A
Padilla, Frank, 74, 96
Pageant of San Francisco, The, 77, 78, *76*
Palace Hotel, 124
Palo Alto (Calif.), 17, 32, 105, *20*
Panama Pacific International Exposition, 77, 107
Panorama (of San Francisco), 19, *27*
Paramount Pictures, 72, 91, 93, 94
Parsons, Louella, 55
Passion Flower, The, 81, *82*
Paterson (N.J.), 44
Paying the Limit, 125
Payne, Herbert, 70, 72, 90, 92, 97
Peacocke, Leslie T., 74
Peninsula Studio, 118–19, 120–21, 133; *108, 109. See also* Appendix A
Persistence of vision, 29. *See also* Motion pictures, prehistory of; Roget, Peter Mark
Peters, House, 81, 97, 124, *68, 80, 83, 87, 96*
Peters, Thomas Kimmwood, 99, 105, 134
Peterson, Sidney, 135, 137
Philadelphia (Pa.), 31
Photography, motion picture. *See* California, Northern: scenic attractions of, for films; Cinematography; San Francisco Bay Area: scenic attractions of, for films
Photography, still: contributions to, by Muybridge, 37; effect of, on visual arts, 25–27; stop-motion, 14, 18, 19–26, *23, 24, 25, 26, 34, 35, 36*
Phyllis of the Sierra, A, 81, *82*

Pickford, Mary, 73, 77, 78, 84–85, 89, 107, 131, *132, 133*
Pike, William, 81, 96, 97, *82, 83, 84, 85, 87, 89, 90, 91, 94*
Players, Bay Area motion picture, 39, 52, 54, 55, 57, 80, 81, 96, 97, 116–18, 121. *See also* Appendixes A, C, D, E
Pleasanton-Sunol area (Calif.), *132, 133*
Pleasure Garden, The, 137
Plots, story film: from drama, 43–44, 74–76, 83, 86–88, 119–20, 121, 125, 133; from literature, 67, 79, 81, 83, 122, 124, 125, 127; from news events, 90; original, 52, 120–21, 135–36, 137, 140–41; from popular magazines, 49–50, 54; from Western themes, 43–44, 48–55, 79, 81, 83, 94, 95, 96, 127. *See also* Authors, San Francisco Bay Area; Melodrama; Stage shows, influence of, on films; West, the
Poppy Girl's Husband, The, 131
Porter, Edwin S., 44, 103
Potel, Victor, 57, *61, 63*
Potted Psalm, The, 135, 136, 137
Powelson, Arthur, 74
Pride of the Force, The, 125
Primal Lure, The, 73, 131
Prisoner of Zenda, 129
Producers, San Francisco Bay Area, 15, 39, 43, 48, 58, 65, 68–71, 94, 99–100, 101–4, 105, 107, 113–14, 116–18, 119–20, 121, 122, 124, 125–27, 133, 134, 139–41. *See also* Appendixes A, C, D, E for individual names
Producers Distributing Corporation, 119, 134
Production. *See* Studios, motion picture
Projector, early motion picture, 31, *32*
Props, historic, 48, 73, 127, *60. See also* Studios, motion picture
Purviance, Edna, 58

Raiders of the Lost Ark, The, 140, 141
Rambeau, Marjorie, 125
Ray, Charles, 72
Ray, Man, 137
Realm of Children, The, 105
Rebecca of Sunnybrook Farm, 132, *133*
Rector, Josephine, 39, 52, 54–55, *53*
Reentry, 138
Reid, Wallace, 129, *130*
Return of the Jedi, The, 140, 141
Revier, Harry, 100, 122–23
Richter, Hans, 137
Ridgley, Cleo, *115*
Ritchie, Michael, 139
Riverrun, 139
Roach, "Spider," 55, *52*
Robbins, Jesse, 39, 41, 51, *52, 53*
Robson, Andrew, 81, 96, *82, 88, 92*
Roget, Peter Mark, 29
Roland, Ruth, 107, *104*
Romance of the Redwoods, 73
Rose of the Misty Pool, The, 81
Rough Riding Romance, 131

Sacramento (Calif.), 19
Sais, Marin, 97
Salisbury, Monroe, *111, 112*
Salomy Jane, 67, *68, 80, 96*
"Salomy Jane's Kiss," 67
Salvation Nell, 83, 86, *85*
Samadhi, 138
San Anselmo (Calif.), 41, 51
San Francisco (Calif.), 13–15, 17, 19, 27, 33, 35–37, 39, 42, 57,
58, 59, 70–71, 73, 74, 91, 94, 100, 103, 118–20, *32, 101, 126;* film production in, 13, 99, 103–5, 107, 108–11, 113–14, 117, 121–28, 129–33, 135–38, 140–41, *105, 106, 129, 130, 131, 132;* impact of 1906 earthquake and fire on film production in, 104; panoramic early photograph of, 19, *27*
San Francisco Art Association, 32–33, 135
San Francisco Bay Area: contemporary film makers of, 135–41; scenic attractions of, for films, 13–15, 41–43, 47–48, 51, 58, 67, 72–73, 99, 103, 107, 109, 111–12, 127–33, 135, 139, 140, 141, *42, 53, 70, 126, 129–33. See also* Authors, San Francisco Bay Area; California, Northern: scenic attractions of, for films; Theaters, San Francisco Bay Area
San Francisco Museum of Art, 135
"San Francisco School" of filmmakers, 136–39. *See also* Film as art
San Jose (Calif.), 41
Sankey, Bessie, 55
San Mateo (Calif.), 105, 112, 114
San Rafael (Calif.), 41, 57, 73, 107, 114
Santa Barbara (Calif.), 13–14
Santchi, Tom, 125
Sausalito, 136
Saville, Ruth, 55
Scottish Chiefs, 113
Scouts of the Plains, The, 44
Sea Lion, The, 113
Sea Wolf, The, 94, 113
Selbie, Evelyn, 55, *49, 61*
Selig Studio (Chicago), 41
Sellers, Coleman, 31
Selznick, Lewis J., 90–91, 94
Sets, motion picture: exteriors, 47, 73, 114, *75, 76, 93;* interiors, 73, 91, 112, 124, *47. See also* Lighting, motion picture; Studios, motion picture
Shadow of a Doubt, 139
Shaw, Brinkley, 39, 55–57
Short films, 41, 59, 61, 63, 71–72, 74, 121, 128, 135–38, *122, 123, 126. See also* Appendix A
Shotgun Ranchman, The, 49
Sills, Milton, 116, *114, 115*
Slapstick comedy, movie, 55–57. *See also* Comedies
"Slippery Slim," 57
Smith, Paul, 107
"Snakeville" comedies, 55
Sonoma County, *89*
Sound motion pictures, 133–34, 137–41
Spielberg, Stephen, 141
Spoor, George K., 41, 43, 45, 58, 61–62. *See also* Anderson, Gilbert M.; Essanay Film Manufacturing Company
Stage shows, influence of, on films, 44, 55, 72, 73, 77, 83–90, 119, 120, 121, 124, 125, 133. *See also* Actors, stage: in films; Melodrama; Plots, story film; Theaters, San Francisco Bay Area
Stanford, Leland, 15, 17–37, *18;* contribution of, to motion pictures, 15, 37, 134, 141; story about wager of, on running gait of a horse, 22, *20, 21, 24*
Star system, 78
Star Wars, 135, 140, 141
"States Rights" distribution, 94. *See also* Distribution
Stauffacher, Frank, 135, 136–37, 141. *See also* Film as art; "San Francisco School" of filmmakers
Stevenson, Robert L., 79
Stewart, Roy, *123*
Stillman, J. D. B., 37
Studios, motion picture, 13, 40–41, 58, 72–73, 92, 103–4, 105,

111–14, 118–19, 125, 141, *45, 46, 47, 52, 54, 70, 71, 108, 109.* *See also* California Motion Picture Corporation; Essanay Film Manufacturing Company; Motion pictures; Pacific Studios; Peninsula Studios; Appendixes A, C, D

Talkies. *See* Sound motion pictures
Tamalpais, Mount, 103, *70*
Taylor, Estelle, 118, *117*
Ten Commandments, 131
Ten Days, 127
Testing Block, The, 131
Theaters, motion picture. *See* Nickelodeons
Theaters, San Francisco Bay Area, 14, 33, 39, 42, 59, 73, 74, 77, 78, 86, 124. *See also* Actors, stage: in films; Alcazar Theatre; Stage shows, influence of, on films
Those Daring Young Film Makers by the Golden Gate, 96
Three Days to Live, 125
"Three Godfathers, The," 49, 50
THX-1138, 140
Todd, Harry, *49, 52, 61*
Too Much Youth, 127
Totheroh, Roland, 51
Tramp, The, 58, *57*
Trip Down Mt. Tamalpais, A, 103
Turpin, Ben, 39, 57, 58, *55*
Twain, Mark, 14, 79
Twentieth-Century Fox, 91
Two-Gun, Man, The, 41

Under the Gaslight, 75
United Keanograph Studio, 105. *See also* Appendix A
Universal Studios, 91
University of California Extension Media Center, 139
Unwritten Law, The, 77, 84, 90, *88, 89*

Valentino, Rudolph, *129*
Valley of the Giants, The, 129, *130*
Vertigo, 139
Vim Motion Picture Company, 105
Virginian, The, 43, 50
Vitagraph Studio (New York), 40
Von Stroheim, Eric, 99, *130, 131, 132*

Wandering Footsteps, 116, 117–18
Warner, Jack, 121

Waterfront Wolves, 125
West, the: 14, 19, 40, 43–44, 51, 72, 73, 77, 81, 97, 120, 127, 134; as an environment for films, 41, 67, 71–72, 77, 94, 97, 127, 141, *38, 60, 68, 70, 96, 112, 130;* as plot material for films, 40, 43–44, 48–55, 67, 81, 83, 120, *76, 78, 79. See* California, Northern: scenic attractions of, for films
West Orange (N.J.), 44
Western Hearts, 51
Westerns, 13, 41, 43, 44, 50–52, 54, 127, 134, *40, 47–50, 53, 59–64;* feature length, 59, 61, 67, 83, 94, 127, *68, 75, 80, 81, 82, 96. See also* Cowboys; Hero, Western
What Others Started, Sophie Finished, 57
White, Leo, *56*
White, Stewart E., 113
White Hands, 114, *110*
Whitney Brothers, 137
Who Are the DeBolts, and Where Did They Get Nineteen Kids?, 140
Why Broncho Billy Left Bear Country, 51
Why Change Your Wife?, 90
Wilbur, Crane, 107, *105*
Wild West shows, 44
Williard, Lee, 55, *47, 61, 62*
Willis, Edwin B., 74, 91, 97
Wilson, Lois, 97
Winning a Peach, 71
Wise Virgin, A, 121
Wister, Owen, 43
Woman Who Dared, The, 74, 84, 88, 91, *92, 93, 94*
Wood, Freeman, *110*
Woods, Frank E., 99, 119–20, 140, 141, *118*
Woodside (Calif.), 112
World, 138
World Film Corporation, 90–91, 114
World War I, 90
World War II, 136
Writers, San Francisco Bay Area. *See* Authors, San Francisco Bay Area

Yosemite Valley, 19

Zoetrope, 29, 31, *16, 30*
Zoetrope Studios, 140
Zoogyroscope, 32
Zukor, Adolph, 61, 91, 97